AS/A-LEVEL Chemistry

ob King

Exam Revision Notes

Philip Allan Updates
Market Place
Deddington
Oxfordshire
OX15 0SE

tel: 01869 338652
fax: 01869 337590
e-mail: sales@philipallan.co.uk
www.philipallan.co.uk

First published 1999
Revised 2002

ISBN 0 86003 429 1

Design by Juha Sorsa
Typeset by Magnet Harlequin, Oxford
Printed by Raithby, Lawrence & Co. Ltd, Leicester

Environmental information
The paper on which this title is printed is sourced from Forestry Stewardship Council approved mills using wood from managed, sustainable forests.

P00291

Contents

Unit 8 Acid–base equilibria

Unit 9 Redox reactions

Unit 10 Periodicity

Introduction

Using these revision notes

These revision notes contain all the important ideas and facts that you need to know to do well in the A-level examination. They have been designed to cover the main syllabuses and, as such, may include some information that you do not need. You should familiarise yourself with the syllabus content on which your examination is set and use these revision notes as part of your overall revision programme.

The revision notes are divided logically into units and in each unit the facts and explanations are clearly set out to help you focus on the key points. The margin notes highlight difficult areas and the common traps into which students fall. They also give helpful advice and suggestions on how to improve your answers and exam technique.

Use these revision notes to complement your own notes and the main texts. They will consolidate, condense and explain many ideas and provide an economical final revision source leading up to the examination.

The revision process

Revision should be a continuous process throughout your study. However, towards the end of the A-level course you will have to intensify your revision and focus on the examination itself. **There is no doubt that the earlier you start this preparation, the more successful you are likely to be.**

Devise a revision timetable – and stick to it

The only way to stick to a timetable is to be realistic about it – plan revision periods in small chunks, with regular breaks, and remember to allow yourself some free time. Flexibility is also important. If something crops up which means that you are unable to revise during a scheduled period, just swap some of your future free time for the current work period.

Devise ways and means of remembering information

Chemistry is a subject full of details and you must know your notes well. There is no easy way to remember information but there are some useful tricks which can assist you:

- **Use mnemonics** to help you memorise key points. For example, four main features of transition metals and their compounds are **colour**, **cat**alytic behaviour, **varying** oxidation states and **complex** formation. Try remembering 'a **coloured cat** with a **complex** wearing a collar on which there are **varying** flashing lights' to remind you.
- **Create mental pictures** to help remember information that is required in a certain sequence (like telling a story in a film).
- **Use spider diagrams** to trigger key words, particularly when summarising organic pathways. Make them as memorable as possible using colours and patterns.
- If you find reaction mechanisms difficult to remember, **see them as a row of pictorial symbols** on which written information is 'hung'. Most mechanisms consist of an arrangement of arrows in space. Try to remember the visual representation of these arrows on the page and then, once you can recall the arrangement, place the relevant information on the arrows.

- Sometimes it can be helpful when revising to **speak the words** as you read them. The association of mouth movements with certain words enables the mind to 'hear' and retrieve them more effectively.
- Use colour coding to differentiate layers of importance and help the retention of the important themes. For example, red could be for definitions, blue for reactions, etc.

Test yourself regularly

This does not have to be in a formal way, with pen and paper, but can be whilst waiting at the bus stop, in the bath or doing the washing up. Practise recalling your mnemonics and mental pictures, and doodle your spider diagrams. The more frequently you do this, the faster you will become and the more ingrained will be the information. This will help avoid the 'mind going blank' in the examination.

Practise doing past papers

You can either write or just note your answers, outlining key points in your approach to a question. Practising timed questions will speed up your writing and thinking and also give you a good 'feel' for the amount of time you have available to answer a question on the day.

Multiple-choice past papers are an excellent preparation as they cover large areas of the syllabuses and give a good impression of the examiners' objectives.

Examination technique

Examinations can terrify students, but good exam technique can overcome the stress.

- **Work out how you intend to spend the time allowed** reading the question, planning, writing, checking, etc. Do not spend any more time than allocated on a particular question. Move on, and start picking up marks on the next question. If you have time at the end of the exam, then go back to the question and put the 'icing on the cake'.
- **Target those questions that you think you may like to attempt** by scanning the paper quickly at the outset of the examination. Pick the question you feel most confident to do first, and make a start. You may well find that ideas and thoughts pop into your mind which relate to the other questions you have targeted. Jot them down on a piece of paper, and refocus on the question you are doing.
- **Read the questions very carefully.** Mistakes are often made when reading a question. Read the question several times, trying to focus on what **exactly** the examiner is trying to ask (see also the question checklist below).
- **Give yourself time to think and plan your answers.** Do not just blindly put pen to paper. You may well end up wasting more time this way with a badly structured and confused answer.
- **With long answer questions, try to plan your line of attack.** On a piece of rough paper, brain-storm all of the relevant ideas and points onto a simple spider diagram so that you can see how they interrelate.
- **With multiple-choice questions, you must take your time and think.** It is very easy to jump at answers and then realise after the examination that you misread a word.
- **In calculations, always explain what you are doing**, show your workings, give units and clearly indicate the answer. Easy marks are lost by not giving the appropriate units.
- **The number of significant figures should be quoted correctly.** If you are given data to three significant figures, quote your answer to the same degree of accuracy.

- **If you are 'stuck', try picturing in your mind the relevant page of your revision notes.** The information you are looking for may well present itself in your mind's eye.
- **What happens if you cannot do a question?** Try not to panic. Concentrate on your breathing and relax for a moment before either returning to the same question or (for a confidence boost) tackling an easier question.
- **What happens if your mind goes blank?** Again, do not panic. Try to relax and think about something mundane – what are you having for dinner, or when did you last polish your shoes? Very slowly reintroduce yourself to your surroundings and try again. Begin a chain reaction in your head by thinking of, for example, the alcohol functional group and recall everything you know about it and its transformations. This may help to trigger off enough to enable you to answer a question.

Question checklist

Sometimes it is difficult for students to focus on what exactly is being asked for in a question. The following may be a useful guide:

- **Account for** means give reasons for.
- **Analyse** means break down into the component parts.
- **Assess** means work out how important it is, and for whom.
- **Comment on** is an open-ended term, asking you to recall relevant material. The mark allocation will guide you on the length of answer that you should give. For example, 'Comment on your answer to the previous question (a calculation of lattice energy for silver bromide) bearing in mind that silver bromide has a theoretical value for the lattice energy of...'
- **Compare/contrast** means look for the similarities and differences between.
- **Consider** means take into account, weigh up the advantages/disadvantages.
- **Criticise** means give your views and discuss the evidence.
- **Define** asks for only a formal statement – often the meaning of a word or principle. For example, 'Define standard enthalpy of combustion' or 'Define rate constant'.
- **Demonstrate** means to prove with examples.
- **Describe what you would see...** This means that you state the expected observation without mentioning chemical names. For example, 'when adding a dull grey solid (zinc powder) to a blue transparent liquid (copper(II) sulphate solution), a colourless and transparent liquid (zinc sulphate solution) and a pinky-brown solid (copper metal) are formed'.
- **Differentiate** means show how the ideas, etc. differ.
- **Discuss** asks for an evaluation or an analysis of a topic. For example, 'Discuss the chemistry of lithium paying particular attention to the atypical nature of its compounds'. You must present both sides where possible, giving the pros and cons and any implications.
- **Evaluate** means discuss the arguments that others have put for and against – you may wish to add your own views.
- **Examine** means investigate, consider all the evidence.
- **Explain** implies that you should give reasons and refer to relevant theory. For example, 'Explain why heating 2-bromobutane in ethanolic potassium hydroxide results in the formation of but-2-ene as well as but-1-ene'.
- **Illustrate/interpret** means to make clear, using examples.
- **Justify** means to make out a case for a particular point of view.
- **Outline** asks for a short account of important points. For example, 'Outline the principles involved in the extraction of the metal aluminium from bauxite'.

- **Predict or deduce** implies that you are not expected to recall the answer but to arrive at it by making connections between items of information given in the question.
- **Relate** means show how one thing is connected to another, show the extent to which they are alike or different.
- **Sketch** means that a **freehand** drawing is allowed. However, you should take care to show that diagrams and graphs are labelled and the curve or straight line is neatly drawn (not plotted). For example, 'Sketch a graph to show how a distribution of molecules is affected by an increase in temperature'.
- **State** asks for a short to-the-point answer. For example, 'State Le Chatelier's principle'.
- **Suggest** is used when there is more than one correct answer. For example, 'Suggest a structure for molecule A when it is heated with aqueous sodium hydroxide solution'.
- **Summarise** means give a brief account of the main points without details or examples.
- **What do you understand by...** This implies that you should give a definition and also some comment on the significance of the term or terms. The mark allocation will guide you on how much detail to give. For example, 'What do you understand by the term transition metal?'

Rob King

UNIT 1 Writing chemical equations

At the end of this unit, you should be familiar with:

- which products form in a reaction
- symbols and formulae
- writing overall balanced chemical equations for reactions
- ionic equations

In a chemistry examination, it is essential for you to be able to write balanced chemical equations to describe the reaction being considered. Students that gain good grades, on the whole, are able to write equations for most reactions they come across, but there are a number of students who lose many marks by not knowing a few basic points.

A Which products form in a reaction?

The main emphasis here is to learn your notes, especially those that relate to the organic part of the course as there are many reactions involving the different functional groups of organic compounds. There are also many reactions in the inorganic part, especially in transition metal chemistry and the chemistry associated with Group VII of the Periodic Table. One area in which students are often weak is the reactions of acids. These reactions are summarised in Figure 1.1.

It is important to know the common reactions of acids.

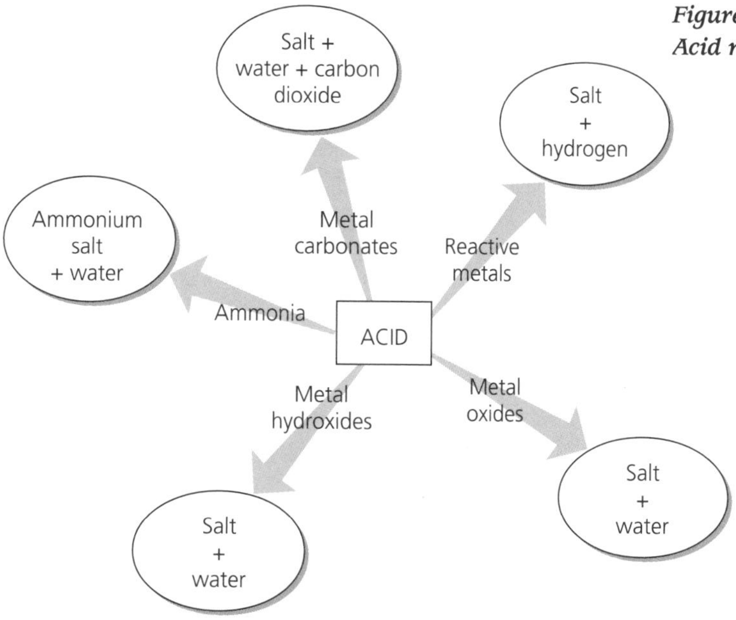

Figure 1.1* *Acid reactions

Remember:

- **sulphuric(VI) acid forms salts called sulphates**
- **nitric(V) acid forms nitrates**
- **hydrochloric acid forms chlorides**

Referring to Figure 1.1, we can see which products would form in the following reactions:

- copper(II) carbonate + hydrochloric acid → copper(II) chloride + water + carbon dioxide gas
- calcium oxide + hydrochloric acid → calcium chloride + water
- magnesium metal + nitric acid → magnesium nitrate + hydrogen gas
- potassium hydroxide solution + sulphuric acid → potassium sulphate + water

...and so on.

B Symbols and formulae

Symbols of elements and formulae of compounds and their solutions in solvents should be followed by the appropriate state symbol (in brackets). For example: solid (s), liquid (l), gas (g), in water (aq) or in another solvent, e.g. ethanol (ethanol).

1 *Elements*

Your Periodic Table includes all of the symbols of the elements. You should know all these up to, and including, krypton (Kr).

Sodium is not S or So; potassium is not P; and phosphorus is not F! These are common errors even at A-level.

1.1 Metallic elements

Always write metallic elements down as the 'symbol' with (s) to show a solid or, in the case of mercury, Hg(l). Numbers are **not** written after the symbol, e.g. Na_2, since metals do not exist as molecules under normal conditions.

Never write down Na^+ for sodium as an element; it is just Na(s) in its uncombined form.

1.2 Non-metallic elements

Many non-metallic elements exist as molecules (or groups of atoms), so remember the following:

	Hydrogen exists as H_2 molecules: $H_2(g)$
Group IV	Carbon is giant covalent as graphite or diamond, so is just C(s)
	Silicon is giant covalent: Si(s)
Group V	Nitrogen exists as $N_2(g)$, phosphorus in its white form as $P_4(s)$
Group VI	Oxygen exists as $O_2(g)$, sulphur as $S_8(s)$
Group VII	All as diatomic molecules, X_2: $F_2(g)$, $Cl_2(g)$, $Br_2(l)$, $I_2(s)$
Group VIII	All as monoatomic elements: He(g), Ne(g), Ar(g), etc.

Chlorine gas is written as Cl_2 and not 2Cl; the latter represents two isolated chlorine atoms.

2 *Compounds*

Some formulae that you should **know** are:

sulphuric(VI) acid	H_2SO_4	nitric(V) acid	HNO_3
hydrochloric acid	HCl	ammonia	NH_3
methane, ethane, etc.	CH_4, C_2H_6, etc.	sulphur dioxide	SO_2
sulphur trioxide	SO_3	sodium hydroxide	NaOH

Note that the prefixes mono- (meaning 1), di- (meaning 2), tri- (meaning 3), tetra- (meaning 4), penta- (meaning 5), etc. have, in some cases, been replaced with the oxidation number method of naming:

SO_2 is sulphur(IV) oxide, SO_3 is sulphur(VI) oxide, NO is nitrogen(II) oxide, etc.

2.1 Using ions to help

The ions in Table 1.1 can be used to work out the formulae of ionic compounds.

There are some ions and their formulae that it would be worthwhile knowing, especially those indicated with an asterisk.

Table 1.1

Formula of ion	Name of ion
CO_3^{2-}	carbonate*
SO_4^{2-}	sulphate(VI)*
NO_3^-	nitrate(V)*
NH_4^+	ammonium*
OH^-	hydroxide*
SO_3^{2-}	sulphate(IV)
NO_2^-	nitrate(III)
HCO_3^-	hydrogen carbonate
SiO_3^{2-}	silicate
ClO_3^-	chlorate(V)
PO_4^{3-}	phosphate(V)

2.2 Elements as ions

You are normally supplied with a Periodic Table in the examination, so make sure that you know how to read it.

The ions formed from elements can be worked out using the Periodic Table.

2.2a Metallic elements as ions

The oxidation state (charge) of a metal when it is part of a compound is the same as the group number in which it occurs in the Periodic Table.

For example: sodium is Na^+ (since it is found in Group I), calcium (Group II) is Ca^{2+}, aluminium (Group III) is Al^{3+}, gallium is Ga^{3+}, radium is Ra^{2+}, etc.

With transition metals, the Roman numeral in the name, after the metal of the compound, tells you the oxidation state of the metal ion. For example: copper(II) oxide contains Cu in its +2 state, iron(III) fluoride contains Fe in its +3 state, chromium(II) iodide contains Cr in its +2 state, etc. Manganese(VII) oxide contains manganese in its Mn(VII) state. The oxidation number provides the **theoretical** number of electrons that must be added to this ion in order to form an atom, i.e. 7, but the formal Mn^{7+} ion would be so highly polarising that it would induce extreme covalent character into its compounds, so ionic compounds containing the Mn^{7+} ion do not exist.

2.2b Non-metals as ions

The number of electrons required to achieve a complete outer shell will be the oxidation number in most cases (except when bonded to a more electro-negative element):

Group VIII	all zero	
Group VII	normally −1	e.g. F^- or Cl^-
Group VI	normally −2	e.g. O^{2-} or S^{2-}
Group V	normally −3	e.g. N^{3-} (nitride)

2.3 Examples of formulae

Write down the ions and then either think about how many of each you need so that the overall charge is zero or swap the charges over in their simplest ratios.

Brackets are needed when the symbol for an ion containing more than one element needs to be multiplied.

For example:

calcium hydroxide

- ions present: Ca^{2+} and OH^-
- we need two OH^- ions to balance the charge on a Ca^{2+} ion, so the formula is $Ca(OH)_2$
- or Ca^{2+} ⤨ OH^- = $Ca(OH)_2$

In copper(I) sulphide, the oxidation state of the copper is +1, so the formula is Cu_2S. The formula for copper(II) sulphide is CuS.

Other formulae:

magnesium oxide	MgO
copper(I) sulphide	Cu_2S
manganese(II) nitrate	$Mn(NO_3)_2$
iron(III) carbonate	$Fe_2(CO_3)_3$
nickel(II) carbonate	$NiCO_3$
potassium sulphate(VI)	K_2SO_4
lithium carbonate	Li_2CO_3
ammonium nitrate	NH_4NO_3
ammonium sulphate	$(NH_4)_2SO_4$

C Writing overall balanced chemical equations for reactions

Consider the following examples:

- **aluminium + iodine →**
  complete the equation: aluminium + iodine → aluminium iodide
  replace each substance with an appropriate formula and state symbols:
  $Al(s) + I_2(s) \rightarrow AlI_3(s)$
  balancing gives: $2Al(s) + 3I_2(s) \rightarrow 2AlI_3(s)$

- **potassium hydroxide + sulphuric(VI) acid →**
  potassium hydroxide + sulphuric(VI) acid → potassium sulphate(VI) + water
  $KOH(aq) + H_2SO_4(aq) \rightarrow K_2SO_4(aq) + H_2O(l)$
  balancing gives: $2KOH(aq) + H_2SO_4(aq) \rightarrow K_2SO_4(aq) + 2H_2O(l)$

- **calcium carbonate + hydrochloric acid →**
  calcium carbonate + hydrochloric acid → calcium chloride + water + carbon dioxide
  $CaCO_3(s) + HCl(aq) \rightarrow CaCl_2(aq) + H_2O(l) + CO_2(g)$
  balancing gives: $CaCO_3(s) + 2HCl(aq) \rightarrow CaCl_2(aq) + H_2O(l) + CO_2(g)$

- **manganese(IV) oxide + hydrochloric acid →**
  manganese(IV) oxide + hydrochloric acid → manganese(II) chloride + water + chlorine gas

$MnO_2(s) + HCl(aq) \rightarrow MnCl_2(aq) + H_2O(l) + Cl_2(g)$
balancing gives: $MnO_2(s) + 4HCl(aq) \rightarrow MnCl_2(aq) + 2H_2O(l) + Cl_2(g)$

D Ionic equations

Many students find ionic equations very demanding. Make sure that you practise them.

This type of equation is frequently used to ascertain exactly what is happening in a reaction. Electron half equations are another type of equation that is used to show what is happening in terms of electron transfer in a redox process.

Ionic half equations have electrons in them; ionic equations do not.

For example, in the reaction $2Al(s) + 3F_2(g) \rightarrow 2AlF_3(s)$, the two electron half equations are $Al \rightarrow Al^{3+} + 3e^-$ (an oxidation) and $F_2 + 2e^- \rightarrow 2F^-$. Do not allow yourself to be confused between normal ionic equations and electron half equations.

The rules to follow in writing out ionic equations are:

- split into constituent ions any substance that dissolves in water (aq) to form ions
- cancel any ions that appear both on the left and on the right-hand side (these ions are called spectator ions)

The equation you are left with is an ionic equation for the reaction.

1 Examples of ionic equations

Convert the following ordinary chemical equations into ionic equations:

- **$K_2SO_4(aq) + BaCl_2(aq) \rightarrow BaSO_4(aq) + 2KCl(aq)$**
  Split any substance in solution (aq) into ions:
  $2K^+(aq) + SO_4^{2-}(aq) + Ba^{2+}(aq) + 2Cl^-(aq) \rightarrow BaSO_4(s) + 2K^+(aq) + 2Cl^-(aq)$
  Cancel any spectator ions:
  $2K^+(aq) + SO_4^{2-}(aq) + Ba^{2+}(aq) + 2Cl^-(aq) \rightarrow BaSO_4(s) + 2K^+(aq) + 2Cl^-(aq)$
  Leaving:
  $SO_4^{2-}(aq) + Ba^{2+}(aq) \rightarrow BaSO_4(s)$

- **$Na_2CO_3(aq) + Ca(NO_3)_2(aq) \rightarrow 2NaNO_3(aq) + CaCO_3(s)$**
  $2Na^+(aq) + CO_3^{2-}(aq) + Ca^{2+}(aq) + 2NO_3^-(aq) \rightarrow 2Na^+(aq) + 2NO_3^-(aq) + CaCO_3(s)$
  $Ca^{2+}(aq) + CO_3^{2-}(aq) \rightarrow CaCO_3(s)$

- **$NaOH(aq) + HNO_3(aq) \rightarrow NaNO_3(aq) + H_2O(l)$**
  $Na^+(aq) + OH^-(aq) + H^+(aq) + NO_3^-(aq) \rightarrow Na^+(aq) + NO_3^-(aq) + H_2O(l)$
  $H^+(aq) + OH^-(aq) \rightarrow H_2O(l)$

Check your answer by making sure that the elements and the charge balance on each side. Sometimes the elements balance and the charge does not.

- **$AlCl_3(aq) + 4NaOH(aq) \rightarrow NaAl(OH)_4(aq) + 3NaCl(aq)$**
  $Al^{3+}(aq) + 3Cl^-(aq) + 4Na^+(aq) + 4OH^-(aq) \rightarrow Na^+(aq) + Al(OH)_4^-(aq) + 3Na^+(aq) + 3Cl^-(aq)$
  $Al^{3+}(aq) + 4OH^-(aq) \rightarrow Al(OH)_4^-(aq)$

- **$Zn(s) + HgCl_2(aq) \rightarrow ZnCl_2(aq) + Hg(l)$**
  $Zn(s) + Hg^{2+}(aq) + 2Cl^-(aq) \rightarrow Zn^{2+}(aq) + 2Cl^-(aq) + Hg(l)$
  $Zn(s) + Hg^{2+}(aq) \rightarrow Zn^{2+}(aq) + Hg(l)$

You will learn to recognise certain reactions and you should eventually be able to write down the ionic equation without having to go through the steps above.

Sometimes, ionic equations are best remembered; however, make sure that they are used in the correct chemical context.

- **Neutralisation between an acid and soluble base (alkali):**
  $H^+(aq) + OH^-(aq) \rightarrow H_2O(l)$
  also written as $H_3O^+(aq) + OH^-(aq) \rightarrow 2H_2O(l)$
- **The reaction between a soluble metal oxide and an acid:**
  $O^{2-}(aq) + 2H_3O^+(aq) \rightarrow 3H_2O(l)$
- **The reaction between a Group II metal and an acid:**
  $M(s) + 2H^+(aq) \rightarrow M^{2+}(aq) + H_2(g)$
- **The reaction between two ions resulting in a precipitate:**
  $Cu^{2+}(aq) + CO_3^{2-}(aq) \rightarrow CuCO_3(s)$
  $Pb^{2+}(aq) + 2I^-(aq) \rightarrow PbI_2(s)$

UNIT 2 Atomic structure

At the end of this unit, you should be familiar with:

- the structure of atoms
- the relative atomic mass scale
- the mass spectrometer
- electronic structure

A The structure of atoms

Atoms consist of a nucleus, comprising protons and neutrons, and electrons that move around the nucleus. Table 2.1 summarises important information regarding the relative charge and relative mass of each of the three particles from which atoms are made.

Table 2.1

Particle	Relative charge	Relative mass
Proton	+1	1
Neutron	0	1
Electron	−1	$\frac{1}{2000}$

The atoms of the elements calcium, phosphorus and argon can be represented as:

$^{40}_{20}Ca$ $^{31}_{15}P$ $^{40}_{18}Ar$

where the larger number is called the mass number and the smaller number is called the atomic number.

For atoms, the atomic number is also equal to the number of electrons as the overall charge of an atom is zero (the number of positively charged protons must be equal to the number of negatively charged electrons).

- **Mass number: the total number of protons and neutrons.**
- **Atomic number: the number of protons in the nucleus.**
  Each element has its own characteristic atomic number.

Referring to the above examples:

- a calcium atom has 20 protons, 20 electrons and 20 neutrons (40 − 20)
- a phosphorus atom has 15 protons, 15 electrons and 16 neutrons (31 − 15)
- an atom of argon has 18 protons, 18 electrons and 22 neutrons (40 − 18)

1 *The structure of ions*

Ions, i.e. particles with different numbers of protons and electrons, have an overall charge. Removing a negatively charged electron from a neutrally charged atom creates a positively charged ion and vice versa.

Ions do not have the same number of protons and electrons. An atom of sodium (11 protons and 11 electrons) reacts by losing its outer shell electron. In doing so, it now forms a positively charged ion. Remember that the atom has a zero charge. The number of positively charged protons is equal to the number of negatively charged electrons, so the overall charge is zero. However, when the sodium atom loses its outer electron, it has lost one negatively charged electron; there are now only 10 electrons and 11 protons in the nucleus, so the overall charge is + 1, that is 11 − 10. Table 2.2 lists some other ions with the numbers of protons, neutrons and electrons in each. Note that the atomic number is **always** equal to the number of protons, whether the particle is an atom or an ion.

Ions	Protons (+)	Neutrons (0)	Electrons (–)	Overall charge
$^{37}_{17}Cl^-$	17	20	18	–1
$^{35}_{17}Cl^-$	17	18	18	–1
$^{32}_{16}S^{2-}$	16	16	18	–2
$^{27}_{13}Al^{3+}$	13	14	10	+3

Table 2.2

2 *Isotopes*

The chemical properties of isotopes are identical since these depend on the outer electronic configuration of the atoms (isotopes differ in their nuclear composition only).

Isotopes are atoms of an element with the same number of protons but different numbers of neutrons, i.e. atoms with the same atomic numbers but different mass numbers.

The element carbon has three different isotopes; all of its isotopes have the atomic number 6 but different mass numbers:

$^{12}_{6}C$ $^{13}_{6}C$ $^{14}_{6}C$

Table 2.3 shows the numbers of protons, neutrons and electrons in each of these three isotopes of carbon:

Table 2.3

Isotopes	Protons	Neutrons	Electrons
^{12}C	6	6	6
^{13}C	6	7	6
^{14}C	6	8	6

B The relative atomic mass scale

^{12}C is the standard to which all other atom masses are compared.

The relative atomic mass (RAM) is the comparative mass of an atom of an element with $\frac{1}{12}$ of an atom of ^{12}C (the standard to which all other atoms are compared). On this scale, ^{12}C assumes the relative atomic mass of 12 exactly. Note that the relative atomic mass does not have any units.

$$\text{Relative atomic mass} = \frac{\text{average mass of an atom} \times 12}{\text{mass of an atom of } ^{12}\text{C}}$$

1 *Isotopic considerations*

The element chlorine has two isotopes with mass numbers of 35 and 37. How do we give chlorine a relative atomic mass, as a single number, when there is more than one isotope? All we do is calculate an average value for the relative atomic mass by multiplying the relative abundance of each isotope by the corresponding relative atomic mass.

% abundance of $^{35}_{17}Cl$ is 75.5% % abundance of $^{37}_{17}Cl$ is 24.5%

Using these figures, we obtain an average relative atomic mass for chlorine:

$$(75.5\% \text{ of } 35) + (24.5\% \text{ of } 37) = \left(\frac{75.5}{100} \times 35\right) + \left(\frac{24.5}{100} \times 37\right)$$

$= \mathbf{35.49}$ **(no units)**

Therefore, 35.49 is the average relative atomic mass of the element chlorine on the relative atomic mass scale. Note that chlorine is quoted as having a relative atomic mass of 35.5 in most copies of the Periodic Table and now you can see why – it takes into account the abundance of the isotopes ^{35}Cl and ^{37}Cl (and this is also why other elements do not have whole number RAMs).

- **Calculate the relative atomic mass for krypton, Kr, using the information in Table 2.4.**

Remember that the average RAM is the sum of each mass number multiplied by its respective percentage abundance.

Table 2.4

Isotopes	$^{78}_{36}Kr$	$^{80}_{36}Kr$	$^{82}_{36}Kr$	$^{83}_{36}Kr$	$^{84}_{36}Kr$	$^{86}_{36}Kr$
% abundance	0.35	2.3	11.6	11.5	56.9	17.4

The average value for the relative atomic mass of krypton is therefore the sum of each percentage abundance multiplied by its respective mass number, i.e.

$$\left(\frac{0.35}{100}\times 78\right)+\left(\frac{2.3}{100}\times 80\right)+\left(\frac{11.6}{100}\times 82\right)+\left(\frac{11.5}{100}\times 83\right)+\left(\frac{56.9}{100}\times 84\right)+\left(\frac{17.4}{100}\times 86\right)$$

$= \mathbf{83.93}$ **(no units)**

Note that on the relative atomic mass scale, the average value for carbon is often written as 12.011 and for hydrogen as 1.00797. These average values take account of the existence of other isotopes for these elements, that is ^{12}C, ^{13}C and ^{14}C as well as ^{1}H, ^{2}H and ^{3}H, all occurring in differing abundances.

C The mass spectrometer

Other modern spectroscopic techniques are discussed in Unit 19.

The mass spectrometer is a very powerful device that analyses a substance, whether an element or a compound, and measures the masses and the relative abundances of the components or fragmented parts. A mass spectrum is then produced that shows the mass-to-charge ratio (m/z) of each fragment (on the x-axis) and the relative abundance of each respective component (on the y-axis). A diagram of a mass spectrometer is shown in Figure 2.1.

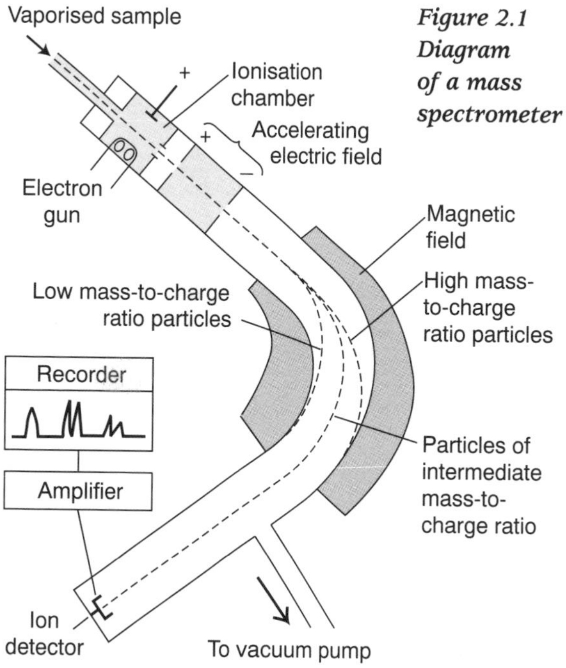

Figure 2.1 Diagram of a mass spectrometer

You must be familiar with the five major steps involved in its operation.

Step 1: vaporisation
The sample is injected into the vaporisation chamber and heated. It under-goes a phase change and will emerge from the chamber in the form of a gas.

For example:
- bromine liquid to gaseous bromine solid, $Br_2(l) \rightarrow Br_2(g)$
- solid benzoic acid to gaseous benzoic acid, $C_6H_5COOH(s) \rightarrow C_6H_5COOH(g)$

Note that ionic samples inevitably have much higher boiling points than organic molecules and this makes vaporisation very difficult.

Step 2: electron bombardment (ionisation)
By increasing the potential difference across two plates, electrons are produced from the negative cathode and move across to the positively charged anode. Sometimes, this part of the spectrometer is called an electron gun. When the gaseous molecules or atoms diffuse past the electron beam, the high energy electrons may knock off one electron, or sometimes more, from the outer shell of the moving particles; this process is called ionisation.

Electrons are never gained by the vaporised particles to form negative ions.

All of the ionisation takes place in the gas phase – watch the state symbols.

For example:
- the ionisation of a gaseous sodium atom, $Na(g) \rightarrow Na^+(g) + e^-$
- the ionisation of an ethanol molecule, $C_2H_5OH(g) \rightarrow [C_2H_5OH(g)]^{+\bullet} + e^-$

If molecules move past the electron gun, they will be ionised (as above) and then may undergo a fragmentation (a molecular split). In this process, a molecule with a positive charge (since it has lost one of its electrons) may rearrange its electron distribution and, in doing so, may break into two smaller fragments.

For example:

$$[CH_3CO_2C_2H_5(g)]^{+\bullet} \rightarrow [CH_3CO(g)]^{\bullet} + [C_2H_5O(g)]^{+}$$

m/z = 88 m/z = 45

Step 3: electrostatic acceleration
The positively charged ions are accelerated towards a negatively charged plate and as they do so their kinetic energy increases. The effect of the electrostatic acceleration is also to focus the positively charged ions into a beam prior to the next stage in the process.

Remember from your physics that 1 volt is the same as 1 Joule per coulomb of charge, so all ions are supplied with the same degree of kinetic energy. Given that kinetic energy is equal to $\frac{1}{2}mv^2$, the ions with more mass will be moving with less velocity since the kinetic energy must be the same and vice versa for ions of low mass.

Step 4: magnetic deflection
The positive ions that have been electrostatically accelerated possess different masses and the majority of them have one positive charge (although other charges are possible). The ions are now 'sorted' according to their mass and their charge using a very strong magnetic field. The deflection depends on the mass-to-charge ratio of each ion or mass/charge (m/z). **The smaller the ratio, the greater will be the deflection.**

The ions $^{16}O^+$ and $^{32}S^{2+}$ would be deflected equally since they have the same mass-to-charge ratio (both 16).

Low mass ions undergo significant deflection and **high mass ions** undergo little deflection in the magnetic field. Ions with a **high charge** undergo a larger deflection than ions with a **low charge**.

Step 5: detection

The positively charged ions have now been sorted according to their mass-to-charge ratio; they then move towards a detector. When the positively charged ions hit the detectors, they accept an electron and, in doing so, cause a current to flow. If there are two ions (of the same m/z) that arrive at the same time, then twice the electrical current flows.

From each electrical conductor in the detector, an electrical current will be produced that is proportional to the number of ions of that particular mass-to-charge ratio that arrive per second. The current produced is called an **ion current**. The various ion currents are then amplified (magnified) so that they may be measured by a computer. The computer then produces a graph of ion current (% abundance) on the y-axis against mass-to-charge ratio on the x-axis; this is the mass spectrum.

The m/z of the ion $M^{+\bullet}$ gives the relative molecular mass of the original molecule – this is important when analysing the molecule.

Figure 2.2 shows some mass spectra for (a) a monoatomic element, e.g. lead; (b) a diatomic element, e.g. bromine; and (c) an organic compound, e.g. ethanol.

In the case of organic compounds like methyl ethanoate, **fragmentations** are possible, producing fragments of different mass-to-charge ratios.

For example:

$$[CH_3CO_2CH_3(g)]^{+\bullet} \rightarrow [CH_3CO(g)]^{\bullet} + [CH_3O(g)]^{+}$$
$$m/z = 74 \qquad m/z = 43 \qquad m/z = 31$$

The mass-to-charge ratios of the fragments can often lead to their identification and hence the original molecule can be identified.

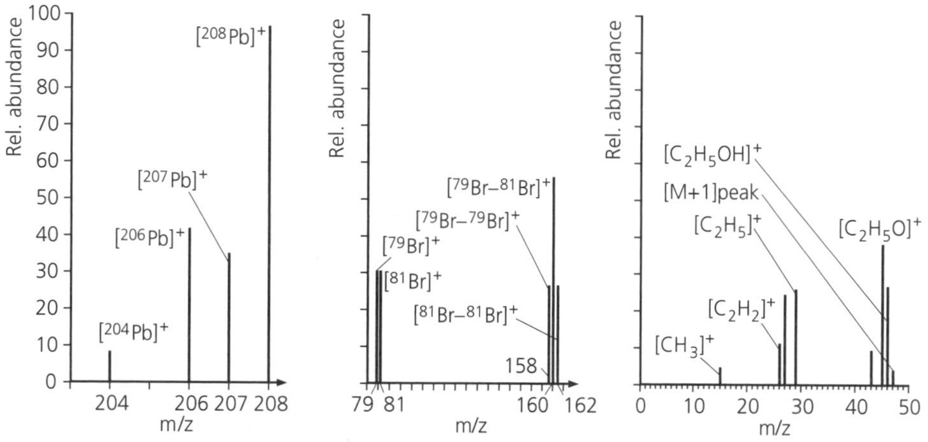

(a) Lead, Pb (b) Bromine, Br_2 (c) Ethanol, C_2H_5OH

Figure 2.2 Examples of mass spectra

The molecular ion peak (the peak of highest mass-to-charge ratio containing ^{12}C) can lead directly to the identification of the molecule. A peak at (M + 1) is usually due to the presence of one ^{13}C atom isotope in the molecule.

D Electronic structure of atoms

At GCSE-level you would have been taught the idea of the electronic configuration. This simply arranges the available number of electrons into shells (in which electrons have similar energy) around the positively charged nucleus. The shells are numbered according to their relative energies from the nucleus. The first shell is closest to the nucleus (and with the lowest energy) and has within it a maximum of two electrons. As more electron shells are added, the electrons move further away from the nucleus and gain in energy.

1 Electron shells

Ionisation enthalpies can be used to provide evidence for the electronic structure of atoms.

- **The standard first ionisation enthalpy is defined as the heat energy required to remove a mole of electrons from a mole of gaseous atoms in order to form a mole of gaseous ions all with a single positive charge at 298 K and 1 atmosphere pressure.**

Ionisation energies are measured in the gas phase.

For example:

$Li(g) \rightarrow Li^+(g) + e^-$

$Cl(g) \rightarrow Cl^+(g) + e^-$

$O(g) \rightarrow O^+(g) + e^-$

Ionisation energies are always endothermic since energy must be supplied for an electron to overcome the nuclear attraction.

It is possible to measure the ionisation enthalpy required to remove further electrons from the same element. These are called the second ionisation enthalpy (to remove the second mole of electrons) and the third ionisation enthalpy (to remove the third mole of electrons), and so on.

For example:

- the first ionisation enthalpy of aluminium
  $Al(g) \rightarrow Al^+(g) + e^-$
- the second ionisation enthalpy of boron
  $B^+(g) \rightarrow B^{2+}(g) + e^-$
- the third ionisation enthalpy of nitrogen
  $N^{2+}(g) \rightarrow N^{3+}(g) + e^-$

If we consider one element only, and plot the consecutive ionisation energies for that element, the resulting graph yields some important information about electronic structure. For example, Table 2.5 lists the consecutive ionisation energies for the element oxygen.

Table 2.5

Ionisation enthalpy/kJ mol^{-1}	Ionisation involved	
1310	$O(g) \rightarrow O^+(g) + e^-$	1st ionisation
3390	$O^+(g) \rightarrow O^{2+}(g) + e^-$	2nd ionisation
5320	$O^{2+}(g) \rightarrow O^{3+}(g) + e^-$	3rd ionisation
7450	$O^{3+}(g) \rightarrow O^{4+}(g) + e^-$	etc.
11000	$O^{4+}(g) \rightarrow O^{5+}(g) + e^-$	etc.
13300	$O^{5+}(g) \rightarrow O^{6+}(g) + e^-$	etc.
71000	$O^{6+}(g) \rightarrow O^{7+}(g) + e^-$	etc.
84100	$O^{7+}(g) \rightarrow O^{8+}(g) + e^-$	etc.

If a graph is plotted of $\log_{10}$ of the ionisation energy against the number of the electron being removed, it is clear from the graph (see Figure 2.3) that six of the eight electrons are removed a lot more easily than the two that are closest to the nucleus. Therefore, in an atom of oxygen, two electrons are in the first shell and six are in the outer shell.

It is not easy to see evidence for the sub-shells using these graphs (only the shells). The energy between sub-shells within a shell is relatively small.

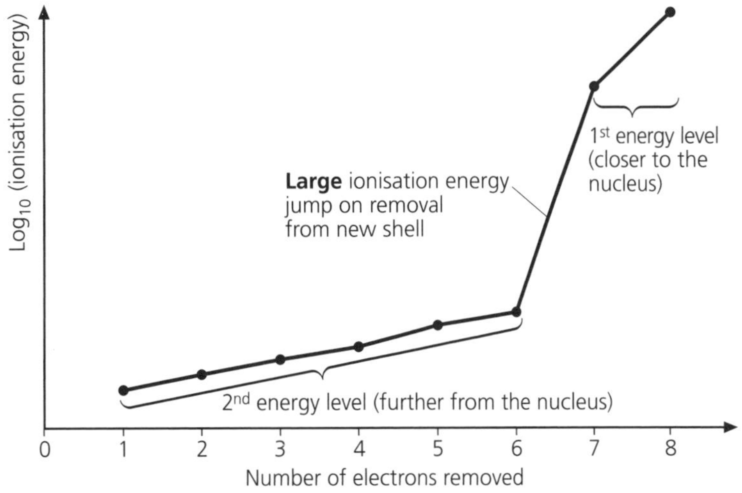

Figure 2.3 Graph of $\log_{10}$ ionisation energy vs number of the electron being removed for oxygen

It can be seen that of the eight electrons, two electrons are closer to the nucleus than the other six. There are therefore six outer electrons. We can analyse other ionisation energy plots for other elements and find that a similar pattern seems to be present.

Make sure that you use the correct words in the correct context.

Each **shell** is divided into **sub-shells** (or sub-levels) and then each sub-shell is made up of **orbitals**. An orbital is allowed to contain a maximum of two electrons.

The ionisation energies may be given in numerical form rather than as a graph. For example, the first six consecutive ionisation enthalpies for the elements X, Y and Z are shown in Table 2.6.

Look for the biggest jump. The point at which the jump starts indicates the group number. So, if the ionisation enthalpies are 502, 966, 3390, 4700, 6000, 7700, 9000, 10200, then this element is in Group II.

Table 2.6

	1st	2nd	3rd	4th	5th	6th
X	1090	2350	4610	6220	37800	47000
Y	590	1150	4940	6480	8120	10700
Z	966	1950	2730	4850	6020	12300

- **In which groups of the Periodic Table would X, Y and Z be found?**

In X, there is a large jump in ionisation enthalpies from electron number 4 to electron number 5. This indicates that electron 5 is more tightly bound by the nucleus and it is likely to be the start of a new shell of electrons closer to the nucleus. There are four electrons in the outer shell of X, so it is in Group IV of the Periodic Table.

The third electron would require too much energy, an investment of energy that would not be recovered by the lattice energy when the new ions bonded to form their lattice structure.

In Y, the largest jump is between electron 2 and electron 3. This means that there are two electrons in the outer shell of Y, so Y is in Group II. The electrons that are easier to remove are those that Y loses when it reacts to form an ion.

In Z, there are five electrons in the outer shell, so we place Z in Group V.

2 Order of filling sub-shells

If a copy of the Periodic Table is available in the examination, it can be used to determine the order of electron filling of the sub-shells within an atom, as shown in Figure 2.4.

s-block | d-block | p-block

				$1s^1$													$1s^2$
$2s^1$	$2s^2$											$2p^1$	$2p^2$	$2p^3$	$2p^4$	$2p^5$	$2p^1$
$3s^1$	$3s^2$											$3p^1$	$3p^2$	$3p^3$	$3p^4$	$3p^5$	$3p^6$
$4s^1$	$4s^2$	$3d^1$	$3d^2$	$3d^3$	$3d^5$	$3d^5$	$3d^6$	$3d^7$	$3d^8$	$3d^{10}$	$3d^{10}$	$4p^1$	$4p^2$	$4p^3$	$4p^4$	$4p^5$	$4p^6$
$5s^1$	$5s^2$	$4d^1$	$4d^2$	$4d^3$	$4d^5$	$4d^5$	$4d^6$	$4d^7$	$4d^8$	$4d^{10}$	$4d^{10}$	$5p^1$	$5p^2$	$5p^3$	$5p^4$	$5p^5$	$5p^6$
$6s^1$	$6s^2$	$5d^1$	$5d^2$	$5d^3$	$5d^5$	$5d^5$	$5d^6$	$5d^7$	$5d^8$	$5d^{10}$	$5d^{10}$	$6p^1$	$6p^2$	$6p^3$	$6p^4$	$6p^5$	$6p^6$
$7s^1$	$7s^2$																

The 4f and 5f block starts in this area.

Figure 2.4 The Periodic Table with outer electron configuration shown

Move horizontally through the 1s and then into the 2s and the 2p and so on. This is the order in which the sub-shells fill, lowest energy first.

If a Periodic Table is not available, then there is a way of recalling the order in which the sub-shells are filled. Remember the arrangement of sub-shells in Figure 2.5.

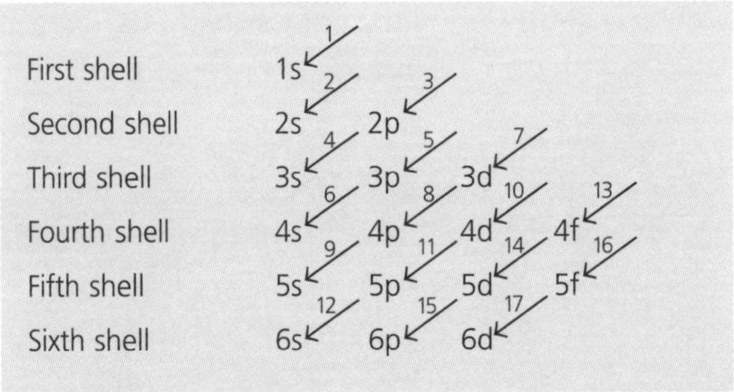

Figure 2.5 Arrangement of sub-shells

Draw diagonal lines, like those shown, and gradually move along the lines downwards (starting at number 1). The lines should cross, in order, the sub-shell that fills up next. The result should be as follows, in order of lowest energy first:

1s, 2s, 2p, 3s, 3p, 4s, 3d, 4p, 5s, 4d, 5p, 6s, 4f, 5d, 6p, etc.

The Aufbau (or building) Principle: electrons enter the lowest energy available.

Note that the Periodic Table is arranged in the order in which the sub-shells fill with electrons, that is the sub-shells from lowest energy to highest energy. So, it should be of little surprise that the order starts with the 1s since this is the orbital closer to the nucleus, and lower in energy, and then the 2s and then the 2p (although the latter two sub-shells are relatively close in energy compared with the 1s and 2s sub-shell difference in energy). After the 3s is filled with two electrons, the 3p is filled with six electrons. Then the 4s is filled before the 3d.

Table 2.7 gives examples of electronic configurations.

Table 2.7

Element	Atomic number	Electronic configuration
Sodium, Na	11	$1s^2, 2s^2, 2p^6, 3s^1$
Na^+		$1s^2, 2s^2, 2p^6$
Potassium, K	19	$1s^2, 2s^2, 2p^6, 3s^2, 3p^6, 4s^1$
K^+		$1s^2, 2s^2, 2p^6, 3s^2, 3p^6$
Sulphur, S	16	$1s^2, 2s^2, 2p^6, 3s^2, 3p^4$
S^{2-}		$1s^2, 2s^2, 2p^6, 3s^2, 3p^6$
Gallium, Ga	31	$1s^2, 2s^2, 2p^6, 3s^2, 3p^6, 4s^2, 3d^{10}, 4p^1$
Ga^{3+}		$1s^2, 2s^2, 2p^6, 3s^2, 3p^6, 3d^{10}$
Krypton, Kr	36	$1s^2, 2s^2, 2p^6, 3s^2, 3p^6, 4s^2, 3d^{10}, 4p^6$

3 Relationship between the Periodic Table and the electronic configuration

Lithium has an electronic configuration of $1s^2, 2s^1$, with its outer electron in an s-orbital, so it is in the s-block. Its outer electron is in the second shell, so lithium is in Period 2 of the Periodic Table.

- The **sub-shell** containing the outer electrons determines the **block** of the Periodic Table in which the element is placed.
- The **group number** of the element will be same as the number of electrons in the **outer shell**.

4 Orbital box diagrams

A box represents an atomic orbital. Only a maximum of two electrons are allowed in an orbital; this is the Pauli Exclusion Principle.

Since only two electrons are allowed per orbital, the orbital is sometimes represented as a box in which two electrons, represented by half arrows, are placed. So a full 1s orbital would be represented as [⇅] and a full 2p as [⇅|⇅|⇅] and a full 3d as [⇅|⇅|⇅|⇅|⇅] and so on.

The electronic configuration for the element phosphorus would be written as: $1s^2, 2s^2, 2p^6, 3s^2, 3p^3$ or, using box notation: [⇅] [⇅] [⇅|⇅|⇅] [⇅] [↿|↿|↿]
1s 2s 2p 3s 3p

5 Trends and patterns in ionisation enthalpies

Ionisation enthalpy questions are common in examinations. Make sure that you learn to explain the trends and patterns as well as the blips.

As we saw earlier, consecutive ionisation enthalpies for a particular element yield some very important information regarding the electronic structure of the atom. When plotting a graph of the first ionisation energy for the elements against atomic number (see Figure 2.6), a regular repeating pattern is produced. This is an example of **periodicity** (a pattern in properties repeating itself at regular intervals).

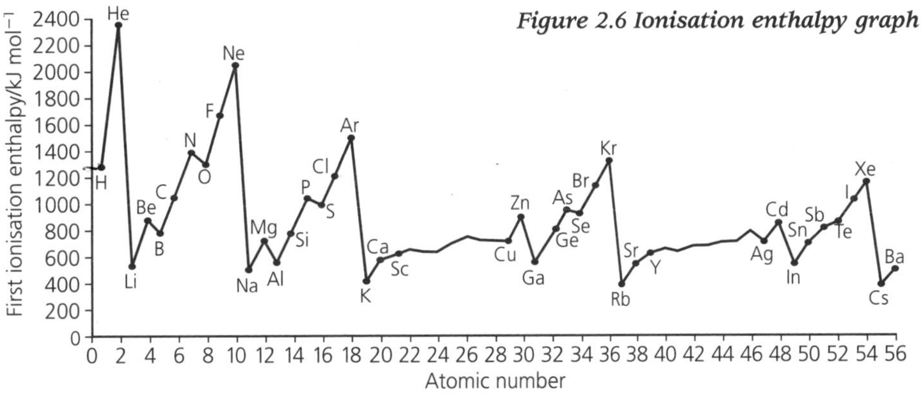

Figure 2.6 Ionisation enthalpy graph

There is some important information that you must know from this graph and you should also be able to explain the variations using your knowledge and understanding of electronic structure gained so far.

Your explanations should focus on:
- **the distance between the electron and the nucleus**
- **the nuclear charge**
- **the shielding, from the nuclear charge, provided by the inner shells on the outer electron**
- **any electron–electron repulsion taking place within an orbital**

The following explanations illustrate how these ideas may be applied to certain changes in ionisation enthalpy.

Variation down a group of the Periodic Table, e.g. lithium and sodium
Trend: a decrease
Explanation:
- despite the increased nuclear charge, the electron being removed is in a new shell progressively further from the nucleus
- the extra electron shell provides extra shielding for the removed electron from the attraction of the positively charged nucleus
- the net effect is to decrease the ionisation energy

Variation across a period from left to right
Trend: a general increase
Explanation:
- the electrons are being removed from the **same** electron shell
- the outer electron is experiencing slightly more shielding by the inner electron shells
- the nuclear charge is increasing since more protons are being added from left to right
- the electron experiences a greater attraction as the element increases in atomic number

Although the general trend is for ionisation energy to increase from left to right across a period, there are two notable small decreases.

From Group II to Group III, e.g. magnesium to aluminium or beryllium to boron
Explanation:
- despite the increased nuclear charge, the added electron is in a new p sub-shell of slightly higher energy
- this is slightly further from the nucleus
- the s^2 electrons, for the Group III element, provide some shielding
- the overall effect is for the ionisation energy to decrease

Do not forget the number of protons in the nucleus; it is not just about the electrons.

Remember, 'inter-electronic repulsion' for the Group V to VI ionisation enthalpies drops.

From Group V to Group VI, e.g. nitrogen to oxygen or phosphorus to sulphur
Explanation:
- despite the increased nuclear charge, the electron from the Group VI element is being removed from a p^4 configuration
- if there are four electrons in a p sub-shell, two of the electrons must be paired
- this inter-electron repulsion lowers the attraction between the electron and the nucleus, so the electron is easier to remove

UNIT 3 Calculations

At the end of this unit, you should be familiar with:

- the mole
- the mole and chemical equations
- calculations involving solutions
- calculations involving gases
- empirical and molecular formulae

A The mole

One mole is defined as the mass of substance (expressed in g, kg or tonnes) that contains as many elementary particles as there are atoms in exactly 12 g of the ^{12}C isotope.

The number 6×10^{23} is referred to as the **Avogadro constant**. Its value is absolutely enormous and its magnitude virtually impossible to appreciate.

We have already dealt with the relative atomic mass scale in which all elements are assigned a value for the number of times that they are more or less heavier than an atom of the ^{12}C isotope. The relative atomic mass does not have any units. We also know that the values quoted are not normally whole numbers since there are isotopes for each element.

Note that the term 'mole' is often abbreviated to just 'mol'.

The mass of 1 mole of an element or compound is its relative atomic mass (RAM) or relative formula mass (RFM) expressed in grams.

1 *Elements*

Look up the relative atomic mass (but express it in units of grams). The values for the relative atomic masses will be given to you in the examination.

See '1 mole' as measuring a certain number of particles, like the words 'dozen', 'gross' and 'millennium'.

Throughout this area of work, remember the following (or work it out logically):

$$\textbf{number of moles} = \frac{\textbf{mass taken (in grams)}}{\textbf{mass of 1 mole of that substance (in grams)}}$$

- **What is the mass of 1 mole of sulphur atoms?**
  Always work out the mass of 1 mole first.
  The relative atomic mass of elemental sulphur is 32, so the mass of 1 mole of sulphur atoms is **32 g**.
- **Calculate the mass of 0.25 moles of sulphur molecules (S_8).**
  As above, the relative atomic mass of sulphur is 32.
  If 1 mole is 32 g, then 1 mole of sulphur molecules will have a mass of (32 × 8) g, that is 256 g.
  We need 0.25 moles, so the mass will be 0.25 × 256 = **64 g**

2 *Compounds*

In order to find the mass of a mole of a compound, you need to add up the relative atomic masses of the individual elements present, taking into account the number of 'atoms' in each formula.

- **Calculate the mass of 0.12 moles of sodium dichromate ($Na_2Cr_2O_7$).**
  1 mole of $Na_2Cr_2O_7$ has a mass of: $(2 \times 23) + (2 \times 52) + (7 \times 16) = 262$ g
  0.12 moles will be have a mass of: 0.12×262 g = **31.44 g**

- **How many moles of hydrogen atoms are there in 2 g of sulphuric acid?**
  1 mole of sulphuric acid (H_2SO_4) has a mass of: $(2 \times 1) + 32 + (4 \times 16) = 98$ g
  Therefore, if 1 mole is equal to 98 g, then 2 g will be less than 1 mole (estimate it first).
  2 g will be equal to $\frac{2}{98}$ of a mole of sulphuric acid, that is 0.0204 moles.

  Think: for every sulphuric acid molecule, H_2SO_4, there are two hydrogen atoms, one sulphur atom and four oxygen atoms. So it follows that in 1 mole of sulphuric acid, there are 2 moles of hydrogen atoms (2×1 g), 1 mole of sulphur atoms (32 g) and 4 moles of oxygen atoms (4×16 g). Therefore, 0.0204 moles of sulphuric acid contains (2×0.0204) moles of hydrogen atoms, i.e. **0.0408 moles**. (It also contains 0.0204 moles of sulphur atoms and (4×0.0204) moles of oxygen atoms.)

The number of significant figures quoted in your answer should be the same as the number of significant figures quoted in the question. Do not round your answers too severely, as errors will creep in.

B The mole and chemical equations

The main types of calculation that you are expected to deal with involve:
- mass relationships between reactants and products in a reaction
- substances dissolved in water to make a solution
- volumes of gases

You must practise mole questions of this type. At A-level, you will be asked to answer questions on this area. Do not think that you can escape without practising them.

1 *Mass relationships*

1.1 Example calculations

- **Calculate the mass of carbon dioxide gas that forms when 12 g of lead(II) carbonate is heated.**

Step 1: write out the balanced symbol equation for the reaction
$PbCO_3(s) \rightarrow PbO(s) + CO_2(g)$

Step 2: calculate the number of moles of lead(II) carbonate.

$$\text{number of moles of } PbCO_3 = \frac{\text{mass used (g)}}{\text{mass of 1 mole (g)}} = \frac{12}{(207 + 12 + 48)}$$
$$= 0.0449 \text{ moles}$$

Remember that the number of moles of a pure substance is the mass of that substance in grams divided by the mass of 1 mole of that substance.

Step 3: write down the mole relationship between the lead(II) carbonate and the carbon dioxide using the equation only.
1 mole of lead oxide forms **1 mole** of carbon dioxide

Step 4: use steps 2 and 3 to state the number of moles of carbon dioxide formed. This will be equal to the number of moles of lead(II) carbonate since the molar ratio is 1 : 1.

So the number of moles of CO_2 is also 0.0449 moles (to 3 sig figs).

Step 5: calculate the mass of carbon dioxide.
mass of CO_2 = mass of 1 mole × number of moles
= (12 + 16 + 16) × 0.0449 = **1.978 g of CO_2 gas**

- **An alternative method is to state the known masses as shown.**
  $PbCO_3(s) \rightarrow PbO(s) + CO_2(g)$
  1 mole   1 mole
  Convert to grams: 267 g gives 44 g
  1 g of $PbCO_3$ gives: 1 g which gives $\frac{44}{267}$ g (dividing both sides by 267)
  Actual mass used: 12 g which gives $12 \times \frac{44}{267}$ (multiplying both sides by 12)
  Final line: 12 g gives **1.978 g of CO_2 gas**

The use of a '1g line' can help with the mathematics here.

Either of the above methods is correct. The use of the 1 g line in the final method reduces the chance of inverting the fraction $\frac{44}{267}$ to $\frac{267}{44}$, which is a common error. Look at your answer and ask yourself whether it is reasonable. If 267 g of lead(II) carbonate gives 44 g of carbon dioxide, then 12 g of lead(II) carbonate should certainly give a lot less than 267 g, not more.

Always ask yourself whether your answers are reasonable. Silly errors in examinations make a difference, not just in terms of a few marks but often in terms of a grade.

- **Calculate the mass of sodium carbonate needed to form 40 g of sodium chloride in the following reaction:**
  $Na_2CO_3(s) + 2HCl(aq) \rightarrow 2NaCl(aq) + H_2O(l) + CO_2(g)$
  40 g of sodium chloride = 40/(23 + 35.5) = 0.684 moles
  From the equation, 1 mole of sodium carbonate gives 2 moles of sodium chloride. So 0.684 moles of sodium chloride forms from 0.684/2, i.e 0.342 moles of sodium carbonate.
  0.342 moles of sodium carbonate has a mass of 0.342 × (23 + 23 + 12 + 48)
  = **36.25 g**

Questions like this may sometimes be asked in tonnes. If this is the case, use the '1 g line' method but replace the unit 'g' with 'tonne'.

C Calculations involving solutions

A **solute** dissolves in a **solvent** to form a **solution**. The usual ways in which concentration is expressed is in moles of solute per dm^3 or mol dm^{-3}, or simply M. The number of moles in a solution is calculated using the equation:

number of moles dissolved =

$$\frac{\textbf{volume of solution in cm}^3}{\textbf{1000 cm}^3} \times \textbf{concentration (in moles dm}^{-3}\textbf{)}$$

Make sure that you can manipulate this equation.

You may find it easier to work these questions out rather than remember a formula.

- **Calculate the number of moles of sulphuric(VI) acid in 15 cm^3 of a 1.5×10^{-4} mol dm^{-3} solution.**

  number of moles $= \frac{15\ cm^3}{1000\ cm^3} \times 1.5 \times 10^{-4}$ mol dm^{-3}
  $= 2.25 \times 10^{-6}$ moles of H_2SO_4

1 Solutions and equations

- **Calculate the volume of 2 mol dm^{-3} sulphuric(VI) acid required to react exactly with 50 cm^3 of 0.6 mol dm^{-3} sodium hydroxide solution.**

$2NaOH(aq) + H_2SO_4(aq) \rightarrow Na_2SO_4(aq) + 2H_2O(l)$

number of moles of sodium hydroxide $= \frac{50}{1000} \times 0.6 = 0.03$ moles

According to the equation, 0.03 moles of sodium hydroxide reacts with 0.03/2 moles of sulphuric(VI) acid (the reacting ratio according to the equation is 2 : 1 respectively).

So, 0.015 moles of sulphuric acid are required. If the starting concentration is 2 mol dm^{-3}, then, using the equation:

$$\text{number of moles dissolved} = \frac{\text{volume in cm}^3}{1000\ \text{cm}^3} \times \text{concentration (in mol dm}^{-3})$$

$$\text{gives } 0.015 \text{ moles} = \frac{\text{volume in cm}^3}{1000} \times 2\ \text{mol dm}^{-3}$$

So, on rearranging, the volume of 2 mol dm^{-3} sulphuric acid required is **7.5 cm^3.**

It is always useful to write the name of the substance to which each answer refers; it is quite easy to become confused about which substance relates to which quantity.

When doing questions involving moles, you must recognise the type of question that you are being asked to answer. Do not just blunder into it when you have not appreciated the nature of the question.

- **A 1.45 g sample of pure iron is reacted exactly with 15 cm^3 of dilute nitric(V) acid of unknown concentration. Calculate the concentration of the nitric(V) acid.**

$Fe(s) + 2HNO_3(aq) \rightarrow Fe(NO_3)_2(aq) + H_2(g)$

1.45 g of iron is 1.45/56 moles, that is 0.0259 moles.

The moles of nitric(V) acid reacting with this mass of iron will be 0.0259 × 2 (using the reacting ratios in the equation).

So, using the equation again,

$$0.0518 \text{ moles} = \frac{15\ \text{cm}^3}{1000\ \text{cm}^3} \times \text{concentration (in mol dm}^{-3})$$

Rearranging this gives the concentration of the nitric(V) acid as **3.45 mol dm^{-3}**.

D Calculations involving gases

In examinations you will normally be told the following:

1 mole of any gas at room temperature and pressure (RTP) occupies about 24 000 cm^3, *or*
1 mole of any gas under standard conditions of temperature and pressure (STP) occupies 22 400 cm^3.

Standard temperature with gases is 273 K but in most other situations it is taken as 298 K. Standard pressure in both cases is 1 atmosphere or 10^5 Nm^{-2}.

Using this data, it is possible to carry out some simple questions, for example:

- **Calculate the volume of hydrogen gas at RTP produced when 0.56 g of sodium metal reacts with water.**

$2Na(s) + 2H_2O(l) \rightarrow 2NaOH(aq) + H_2(g)$

number of moles of sodium = 0.56/23 = 0.0243 moles

number of moles of hydrogen produced will be 0.0243/2 (according to the ratios in the equation)

= 0.012 moles

Multiplying this by 24 000 cm^3 to give the volume at RTP gives **292.2 cm^3 of hydrogen gas.**

1 Equations involving gases

Equal volumes of gases contain equal numbers of particles provided the volumes are measured at the same temperature and pressure.

When we are faced with an equation such as:

$2CO(g) + O_2(g) \rightarrow 2CO_2(g)$,

we can say that 2 moles of carbon monoxide reacts with 1 mole of oxygen to give 2 moles of carbon dioxide.

Since the volume of a gas is determined, amongst other factors, by the number of molecules and **not** the gas being used, we can also say:

2 volumes of CO(g) reacts with 1 volume of $O_2(g)$ to form 2 volumes of $CO_2(g)$.

The volumes of these gases will always be in the same ratio of 2 : 1 : 2.

This statement always follows for a reaction as long as the substances being considered are gases.

When questions are set featuring reacting volumes of gases, do not assume that the gases are mixed in the exact ratio so that no reactant is left after the reaction. The challenge in these questions is normally to work out what volume of the excess gas is left over.

- **1000 cm^3 of ethane gas and 1000 cm^3 of oxygen gas are mixed and the reaction carried out at 373 K. What is the final total volume of the gaseous mixture at 373 K?**

  Assume the reaction proceeds as follows (note the state symbols):
  $2C_2H_6(g) + 7O_2(g) \rightarrow 4CO_2(g) + 6H_2O(g)$
  286 cm^3 of ethane reacts with 1000 cm^3 of oxygen gas (a 2 : 7 ratio of volumes from the equation).
  Therefore, there will be 1000 cm^3 – 286 cm^3 of ethane gas left over, i.e. 714 cm^3. (Since all of the oxygen is used up, we can associate its volume with the gas volumes of the products.)
  1000 cm^3 of oxygen gives $\frac{4}{7} \times 1000$ cm^3 of CO_2 and $\frac{6}{7} \times 1000$ cm^3 of **gaseous** water.
  The final mixture will therefore consist of 714 cm^3 of unreacted ethane, 571 cm^3 of $CO_2(g)$ and 857 cm^3 of water vapour.
  So the total final volume will be **2142 cm^3**.

2 The ideal gas equation

It is a very common mistake for students to ignore totally, or confuse, the units of the quantities fed into the equation.

The ideal gas equation takes the form:

PV = nRT

where the units are crucial for each of the quantities.

P = pressure in N m^{-2} or Pascals
V = volume in m^3
n = number of moles
R = gas constant (8.314 J K^{-1} mol^{-1})
T = temperature in K

One error likely in this type of question is in the volume conversion, e.g. from cm^3 to m^3 or dm^3 to m^3.

- **Calculate the volume of gas given that there is 0.012 moles of nitrogen at 300 °C and 200 000 N m^{-2}.**
  Check the quantities and units first.
  P = 200 000 N m^{-2}
  V = ? m^3

$n = 0.012$ moles

$R = 8.314\,J\,K^{-1}\,mol^{-1}$

$T = (300 + 273) = 573\,K$

$$V = \frac{nRT}{P} = \frac{0.012 \times 8.314 \times 573}{200\,000}$$

$= \mathbf{2.858 \times 10^{-4}\,m^3}$ **or** $\mathbf{(0.2858\,dm^3)}$

- **Calculate the temperature of a gas if there are 3 moles of hydrogen at** $\mathbf{500\,000\,N\,m^{-2}}$ **and occupying a volume of** $\mathbf{1500\,cm^3}$

  $$T = \frac{PV}{nR} = \frac{500\,000 \times 1500 \times 10^{-6}}{3 \times 8.314} \quad (10^{-6} \text{ is needed to convert from } cm^3 \text{ to } m^3)$$

  $=$ **30.07 K (–243 °C)**

Remember your volume conversions:
$\mathbf{1\,m^3 = 1000}$ **litres** $\mathbf{= 1000\,dm^3 = 10^6\,cm^3}$

Other questions involving the ideal gas equation all tend to be simple rearrangements of the original equation.

If number of moles $(n) = \dfrac{\text{mass taken (in g) (m)}}{\text{mass of 1 mole (M)}}$ or $n = m/M$

Then $PV = nRT$ becomes $PV = \dfrac{mRT}{M}$ so $M = \dfrac{mRT}{PV}$

Another simple manipulation is when density $(p) = \dfrac{\text{mass (in g) (m)}}{\text{volume (V)}}$ or $p = \dfrac{m}{V}$

Using $M = \dfrac{mRT}{PV}$ and substituting in, we produce $M = \dfrac{pRT}{P}$

It is advisable to derive these equations yourself rather than relying on memory.

- **1 g of a gas occupies** $\mathbf{5.422 \times 10^{-4}\,m^3}$ **at 300 K and** $\mathbf{100\,000\,N\,m^{-2}}$**. Calculate the relative molecular mass of the gas.**

  $m = 1$ g, $V = 5.422 \times 10^{-4}\,m^3$, $T = 300\,K$, $P = 100\,000\,Nm^{-2}$

  $$M = \frac{mRT}{PV} \quad \text{so } M = \frac{1 \times 8.314 \times 300}{100{,}000 \times 5.422 \times 10^{-4}} = 46\text{ g}$$

  The mass of 1 mole of the gas is 46 g.

  Therefore, the relative molecular mass is **46 (no units).**

- **Calculate the density of a sample of nitrogen that is at a pressure of** $\mathbf{50\,000\,N\,m^{-2}}$ **and at a temperature of –150 °C.**

  $P = 50\,000\,N\,m^{-2}$

  $T = (-150 + 273)\,K = 123\,K$

  M (for N_2) $= 28$

  $$\text{Using } M = \frac{pRT}{P},\ p = \frac{mP}{RT} = \frac{28 \times 50\,000}{8.314 \times 123} = 1369\,g\,m^{-3} \text{ or } 1.369\,kg\,m^{-3}$$

  Hence the density of nitrogen under these conditions is $\mathbf{1369\,g\,m^{-3}}$.

E Calculation of empirical and molecular formulae

The empirical formula represents the simplest possible ratio of the constituent atoms in a substance.

The molecular formula for a substance is always a whole number multiplied by the empirical formula.

The molecular formula represents the actual number of each type of atom in the molecule.

The following are worked examples of empirical formulae calculations:

- **2 g of aluminium reacts with iodine to form 30.22 g of aluminium iodide. Calculate the empirical formula of aluminium iodide.**
  Write down the actual masses for each element.
  mass of Al = 2 g mass of iodine = (30.22 – 2) g
  Convert into moles by dividing by the mass of 1 mole for each element.
  moles of Al = 2/27 = 0.074 moles moles of I = 28.22/127 = 0.222 moles
  Simplify the ratio by dividing each by the smallest number of moles.
  $\frac{0.074}{0.074} = 1$ $\frac{0.222}{0.074} = 3$
  Therefore, the formula for aluminium iodide is $\mathbf{AlI_3}$.

Remember to divide by the smallest number to convert into a simple ratio. Also, recognise possible whole number ratios 'in disguise', e.g. 1 : 1.5 is 2 : 3 and 1 : 2.5 is 2 : 5, etc.

- **A molecule contains the elements carbon, hydrogen and nitrogen only. It consists of 66.7% carbon and 7.40% hydrogen by mass. Calculate the empirical formula for this compound.**
  The percentage by mass of each element is:

carbon	nitrogen	hydrogen
66.6%	26.0%	7.4%
Convert into moles:		
66.6/12	26.0/14	7.4/1
= 5.55	= 1.86	= 7.40
Divide by the smaller number:		
5.55/1.86	1.86/1.86	7.40/1.86
= 2.98	= 1	= 3.98
To the nearest whole number:		
3	1	4

  The empirical formula is therefore $\mathbf{C_3H_4N}$.

You must not round your number too early as errors will emerge. Round at the end of the question but do quote your molar values to an appropriate number of significant figures.

- **Given that 0.34 g of the above substance, as a vapour, occupies 78 cm³ at 298 K and 100 000 N m⁻², calculate the molecular formula for the substance.**
  Using the ideal gas equation, PV = nRT
  $100\,000 \times 78/10^6 = n \times 8.314 \times 298$
  Therefore, $n = \frac{100\,000 \times 78/10^6}{8.314 \times 298} = 3.148 \times 10^{-3}$ moles
  0.34 g is equivalent to 3.148×10^{-3} moles and so 1 mole is equivalent to $0.34/3.148 \times 10^{-3}$ g, or 108 g.
  The empirical formula is C_3H_4N (RMM = 36 + 14 + 4 = 54). Since we know that the molar mass is 108 g, then twice the empirical formula would equal the molecular formula.
  So, the molecular formula is $2 \times (C_3H_4N) = \mathbf{C_6H_8N_2}$.

UNIT 4 Structure and bonding

At the end of this unit, you should be familiar with:

- bonding types
- solid structures made from ionic and covalent bonds
- deviations from ionic and from pure covalent bonding
- intermolecular forces
- shapes of molecules
- metallic structures

A Bonding

The two main types of chemical bond are **ionic** and **covalent** (the dative bond is a special type of covalent bond).

1 *Ionic bonding and giant ionic structures*

Remember that substances containing metals and non-metals are normally made up of ions.

An ionic bond is an electrostatic force of attraction between oppositely charged particles called ions. The ions then pack together to form a **giant structure**.

1.1 Elements forming ionic bonds: metal with non-metal

Metal atoms lose their outer electrons (are oxidised) to form positive ions. Metal atoms tend to possess lower ionisation energies and electron affinities than non-metals and are therefore likely to form positive ions (see Figure 4.1).

Non-metal atoms gain electrons (are reduced) to complete their outer shell since they have very negative electron affinities.

- **Metals form positive ions**
- **Non-metals form negative ions**

In ionic bonding, electrons are transferred from the metal to the non-metal to make a positive and negative ion respectively.

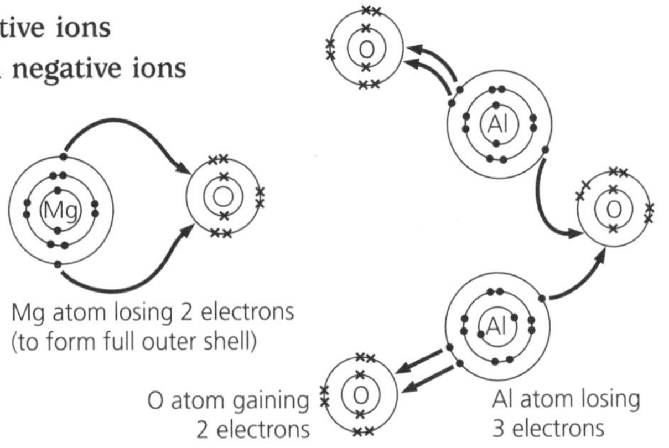

***Figure 4.1* Dot and cross diagram for the formation of MgO and Al_2O_3**

The oppositely charged ions are attracted electrostatically and form a **giant ionic structure** (see Figure 4.2).

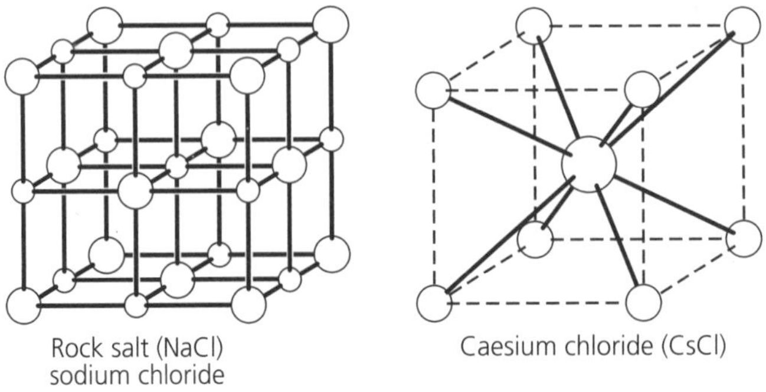

***Figure 4.2* Diagrams showing part-structures for NaCl and CsCl**

Ionic structures are good electrical conductors when molten and when in solution because ions can move and carry electrical charge. Note that it is not electrons that move but ions.

Ionic structures are poor electrical conductors when solid since **ions** cannot move and conduct (the ions are electrostatically bound into the structure).

Ionic compounds are good electrical conductors when molten and when dissolved since the **ions** can move and carry charge; as a result some decomposition will occur.

In sodium chloride, the coordination number (the number of nearest neighbours) around both Na^+ and Cl^- is 6. We call the sodium chloride structure a 6 : 6 structure.

Ionic structures have high melting points since strong electrostatic forces hold the ions together. It is difficult to overcome these forces and free the ions (see Figure 4.2).

Ionic structures dissolve in polar solvents like water since the polar ends of the water molecule can attract the ions and pull the structure apart (see Figure 4.3). They are also attracted to and stabilise the ions once in solution.

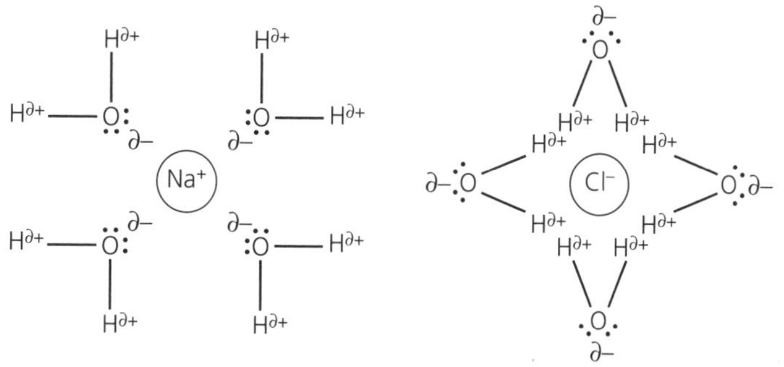

Figure 4.3 Water molecules surrounding Na^+ and Cl^- ions – a process known as hydration

2 Covalent bonding and structures consisting of covalent bonds

A covalent bond is one in which two atoms share at least one pair of electrons. Two electrons constitute a single bond, e.g. C–H, N–H, C–O. If two pairs of electrons are involved, a double bond is formed, e.g. C=C, C=O, O=O; and if there are three pairs, a triple bond is formed, e.g. C≡C and N≡N.

2.1 Elements forming covalent bonds: non-metal with non-metal

Covalent bonds are of similar strength to ionic bonds. When covalent substances melt or boil, it is the intermolecular force that is overcome and not the breaking of covalent bonds within the molecule.

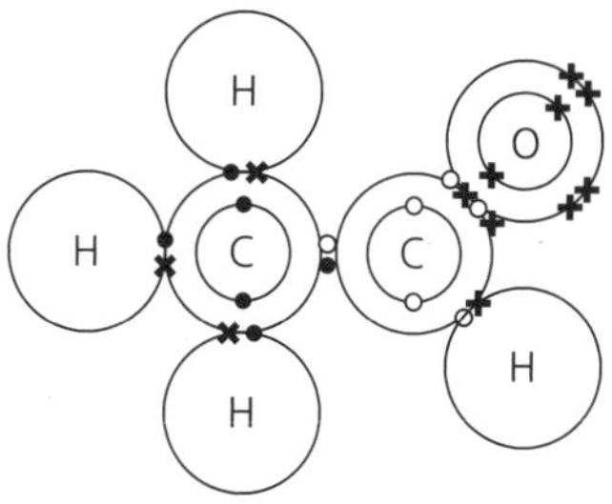

Figure 4.4 Formation of ethanal, CH_3CHO

Covalent bonds are strong bonds. These bonds hold the atoms together by using the attractive force between the bonding pairs of electrons and the positively charged nuclei.

Electron density is concentrated **between** the two nuclei and the bonding is said to be directional in that it concentrates in a certain region in space.

A group of atoms bonded together by covalent bonding is called a **molecule**.

Covalent bonds can form either simple molecular structures or giant structures.

Two kinds of structure can result depending on whether there are many separate molecules loosely packed together (simple molecular) or one giant structure (giant covalent or giant molecular) in which atoms are held together, throughout the giant structure, by strong covalent bonds.

Simple molecules do not have an overall charge, so their intermolecular forces (forces acting between molecules) are relatively weak.

Make sure that you realise the pictorial or visual differences between these structures: try to imagine the discrete nature of a simple molecular structure and the vastness of a giant molecular structure.

- **Structure summary: solid structures made from ionic and covalent bonds**

ionic bonds form	giant ionic structures
covalent bonds form	simple molecular (covalent) structures or giant molecular (covalent) structures

2.2 Simple molecular structures

A simple molecular structure contains separate molecules weakly attracted to each other to form a regular arrangement (see Figure 4.5). The weak attraction means the solid has a low melting point because only weak forces must be overcome in order to separate the molecules and cause melting.

Since the molecules are not charged, most will not attract water molecules and so are insoluble in water. Polar molecules are the exception to this general rule (see Section A.4.1).

Remember that when a substance made of molecules melts or boils, the forces between the molecules have to be overcome and not the forces holding the atoms together in the molecule.

Substances with simple molecular structures tend to be soluble in molecular solvents like hydrocarbons since there are very similar intermolecular forces acting between the molecules and in between the solvent molecules. The solution made does not conduct electricity because there are no ions formed when the substance dissolves.

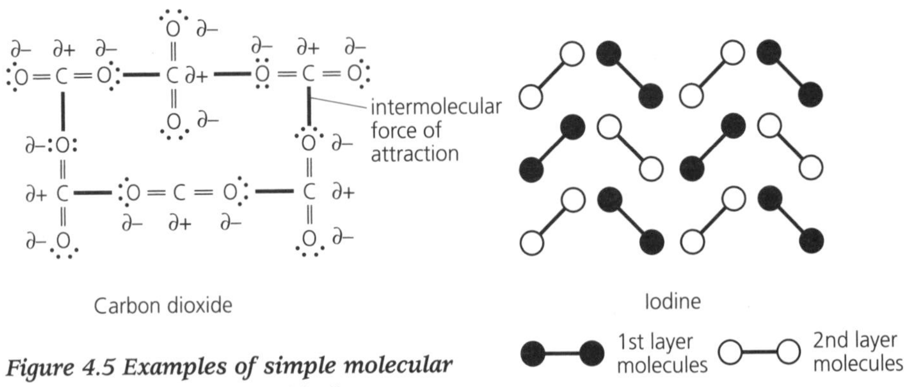

Figure 4.5 Examples of simple molecular solids, carbon dioxide and iodine

2.3 Giant covalent or macromolecular

Giant covalent structures contain millions of atoms which are all strongly covalently bonded throughout the structure.

There are no separate small molecules in this structure (contrast with the simple molecular case).

In graphite, the layers alternate as ABABABAB..., i.e. one layer is not placed directly on its neighbour but it will be above the next layer in sequence.

Since the whole structure is strongly held together, the melting point tends to be very high.

The strong bonding means that these solids do not dissolve in either water (a polar solvent) or covalent solvents.

Important examples include graphite and diamond (see Figure 4.6).

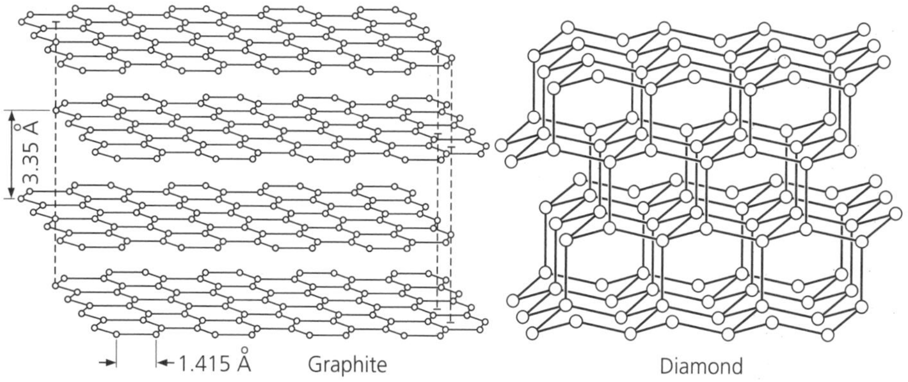

Figure 4.6 Structures of graphite and diamond

Graphite has a layered structure in which mobile **electrons** move parallel to the layers but find it more difficult moving across the layers. Van der Waals forces act between the layers and these are relatively weak; therefore these layers may slide over each other.

As a result, graphite conducts electricity fairly well (in one direction) and has a fairly good thermal conductivity in the same direction since the strong bonds and the electrons enable thermal energy to be transferred efficiently throughout the structure.

Diamond is a superb thermal conductor, yet there are no free electrons in this structure. The strong, extensive C–C bonding and the symmetry of the lattice facilitate effective thermal transmission in this case.

Diamond consists of many carbon tetrahedra covalently bonded together to form a very compact, symmetrical and rigid structure. There are no free electrons in this structure so it will not conduct electricity, but the strong bonding enables diamond to be an excellent thermal conductor.

2.4 Sigma (σ) and pi (π) bonds

Atoms that are covalently bonded together do so by overlapping their atomic orbitals to form molecular orbitals. The shared electrons forming the bond form the molecular orbital. There are two main types of molecular orbital, σ and π. The covalent bonds which result are known as σ and π bonds.

Sigma and pi bonds are molecular orbitals. They represent a region in space in which the electron has a high probability of being found.

The factor that determines the type of covalent bond is the type of the atomic orbital overlap. All single covalent bonds can be termed σ bonds and they have a 'sausage-like' shape, whereas a π bond has a shape like two pieces of a bun above and below the sausage (see Figure 4.7). A double bond is a σ and a π bond (the sausage in the bread bun); a triple bond is 1σ and 2π bonds.

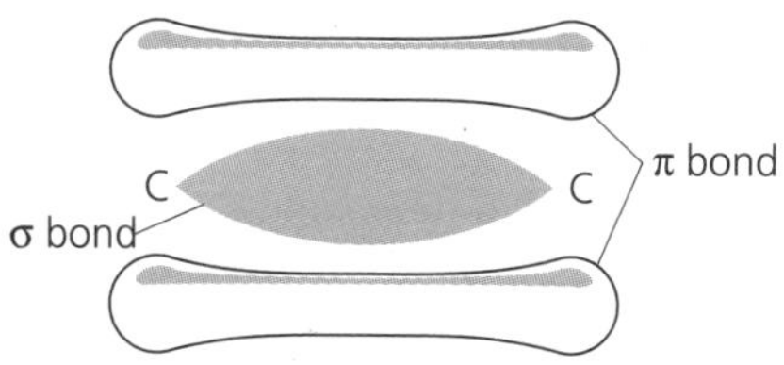

Figure 4.7 A double bond C=C

2.5 The dative bond

Covalent bonds are formed when two atoms share an even number of electrons and, in nearly all of these bonds, each of the atoms donates an equal number of electrons in order to form the bond.

A dative bond is defined as a bond formed between two atoms in which one atom donates both electrons.

A dative covalent bond is represented by the symbol →. The arrow originates from the atom donating the electron pair. The dative bond can normally be considered to be an ordinary single covalent bond, but it does possess ionic character (it is more polar).

Examples of species having dative bonds:

- the ammonium ion, NH_4^+
- the nitrate(v) ion, NO_3^-

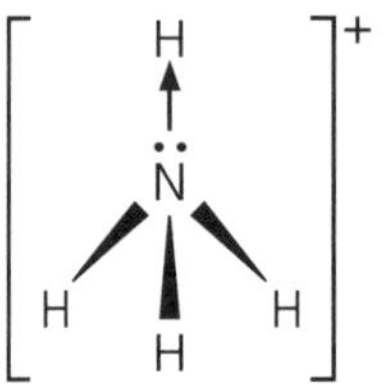

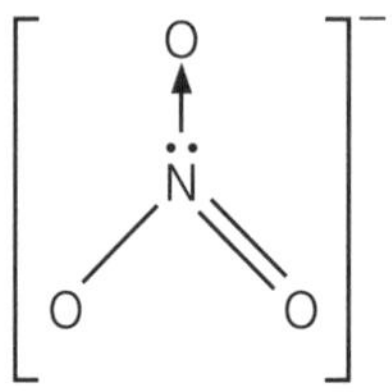

3 Deviations from pure ionic and from pure covalent bonding

Most chemical bonds are not purely ionic or covalent; bonds consist of degrees of ionic and covalent character.

Pure ionic bonds do not exist and the pure covalent bond is rare; the character of most chemical bonds fits between these two extreme bonding types.

Figure 4.8 summarises the arguments that are used to explain the deviations depending from which end the deviation occurs.

Figure 4.8

100% ionic character	**100% covalent character**
DEVIATION →→→→→→→→	←←←←←←←←←← DEVIATION
Polarising power of the positive ion on the spherical negative ion	Electronegativity differences of the atoms in the covalent bond

3.1 Polarising power

Polarising power is a measure of the ability of the **positive ion** to distort or to deform the spherical electron distribution of the negative ion. We say that the positive ion (the cation) is polarising and the negative ion (the anion) is polarisable.

The ions that tend to be very polarising normally:

- have small ionic radii
- have a high magnitude positive charge

Positive ions (cations) are polarising and distort negatively charged ions (these are polarisable); not the other way around.

- are metal ions, although the bare proton, H^+, is extremely polarising as a result of its very small radius

Examples of very polarising positive ions include H^+, Li^+, Be^{2+}, Al^{3+}.

Atoms that tend to be easily polarisable commonly:
- have a large ionic radius so that the outer electrons are further away from the control of the positively charged nucleus
- have a large negative charge
- are anions of a non-metal

Examples of easily polarisable negative ions include I^- (iodide), S^{2-} (sulphide), P^{3-}(phosphide).

The effect on an ionic bond, in which there is a significant degree of polarisation of the negative ion taking place, is to induce a greater degree of covalent character into the bond and the compounds. Since covalent substances are expected to be insoluble in water (a polar solvent) and soluble in non-polar solvents, to have lower melting points, and to be poorer electrical conductors than their ionic counterparts, it should be noted that ionic substances that have a high degree of covalent character tend to possess some of these properties. The following can be explained in terms of polarising power:
- the anomolous (strange) properties of beryllium and lithium compounds due to the high polarising power of the small metal ion
- the covalent character of aluminium oxide
- the existence of the proton as H_3O^+ in water and not as a bare proton

Try to use the word 'electronegativity' in the context of a covalent bond and not as an isolated atom. Do not say that fluorine is an electronegative element and so is reactive (electronegativity refers to the combined or compounded state of an element in a covalent bond).

3.2 Electronegativity differences

Electronegativity is defined as the ability or tendency for an atom to attract a bonded pair of electrons towards itself.

The atoms which tend to be more electronegative tend to have little shielding of their positively charged nucleus by electron shells. The most electronegative of all of the elements is fluorine, although chlorine, oxygen and nitrogen all have a great tendency to attract electrons in covalent bonds. When a more electronegative atom pulls the bonding electrons towards itself, it distorts the whole of the covalent bond so that it is 'fatter' at the end with the more electronegative atom (see Figure 4.9). This increases the electron density on the more electronegative atom and decreases the electron density on the less electronegative (or more electropositive atom). Therefore, the molecule develops a slight positive charge on the least electronegative atom and a slight negative charge, δ^-, on the more electronegative atom. This means that the covalent bond develops some charged or ionic character.

Polar bonds have unsymmetrical electron distributions due to vastly differing electronegativities of the atoms in the bond.

Covalent bonds that have a high degree of ionic character are called **polar** bonds and are said to possess a **dipole** (one end δ^+ and the other δ^-). Some molecules are said to be **polar**, like the water molecule, and this relies on the molecule having an overall **dipole moment** – this is a consequence of its three-dimensional shape as well as the presence of polar bonds (see section B). Where substances have polar bonds, they possess more ionic character than usual. This leads to higher melting points, greater solubility in polar solvents like water, and lower solubility in non-polar solvents, etc.

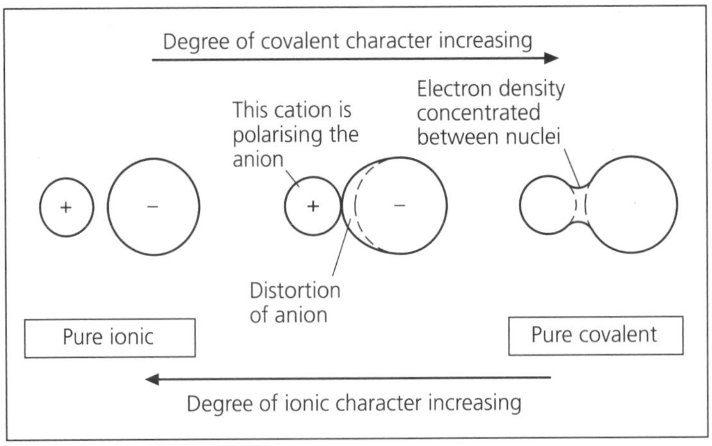

Figure 4.9
How the electron distribution changes with bond character

4 Intermolecular forces

Intermolecular forces are forces between molecules. They arise from the presence of electrons within molecules.

4.1 Dipole–dipole attractions

Polar molecules, that is molecules that have an overall dipole moment, are able to attract each other electrostatically. This force is a weak force compared to a covalent bond but it is significant in explaining higher melting and boiling points than those expected.

For example, the molecule propanone, CH_3COCH_3, has a relative molecular mass of 58 and a boiling point of 56.2 °C. Butane, C_4H_{10}, has a relative molecular mass of 58 as well but its boiling point is only −0.5 °C. The **permanent dipole** of the carbonyl C=O bond is able to attract other carbonyl groups in other propanone molecules, raising the strength of the intermolecular force (see Figure 4.10). Butane has no polar bonds (note that the C–H bond should never be considered to be polar since the electronegativity difference between carbon and hydrogen is only slight).

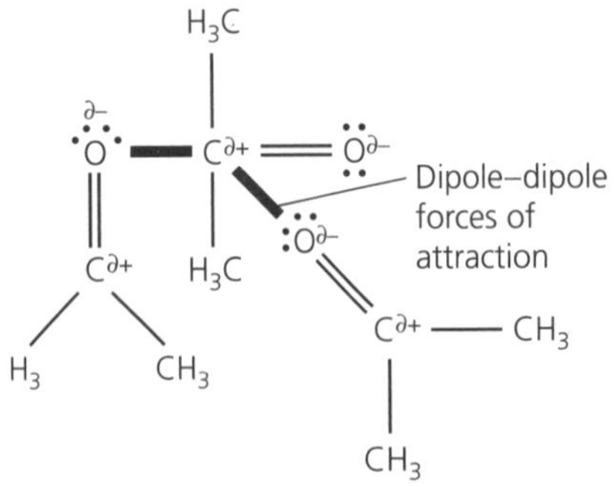

Figure 4.10 Intermolecular attraction between molecules of propanone

A covalently bonded hydrogen atom has its nucleus revealed so that lone pairs of electrons from atoms on other molecules may snuggle in very closely. This is why hydrogen bonding tends to be stronger than ordinary dipole–dipole interactions.

Other examples of bonds that possess a dipole and therefore may result in dipole–dipole interactions between molecules are: C=O in esters, C≡N in nitriles, and C–F or C–Cl bonds in halogenoalkanes or acid chlorides.

4.2 Hydrogen bonding

Hydrogen bonding is a special type of dipole–dipole attraction. The reason why it is special is due to the hydrogen atom. Hydrogen atoms only possess one electron and when this electron is shared with another atom's electron, the nucleus is no longer shielded. If the hydrogen atom is bonded to one of the electronegative few, that is F, N or O, then the proton is deshielded (it is surrounded by little electron density), leading to a slight positive charge on the hydrogen atom. This can result in significantly stronger intermolecular bonds than in the ordinary dipole–dipole case. The deshielded hydrogen atom can be attracted closely and tightly to the lone pairs of electrons of other atoms in other molecules. The intermolecular force that results is called the hydrogen bond and it is stronger than ordinary dipole–dipole interactions and is about 10 % of the strength of the ordinary covalent bond (see Figure 4.11).

Note the essential use of the lone pairs of electrons on the oxygen in forming the hydrogen bond.

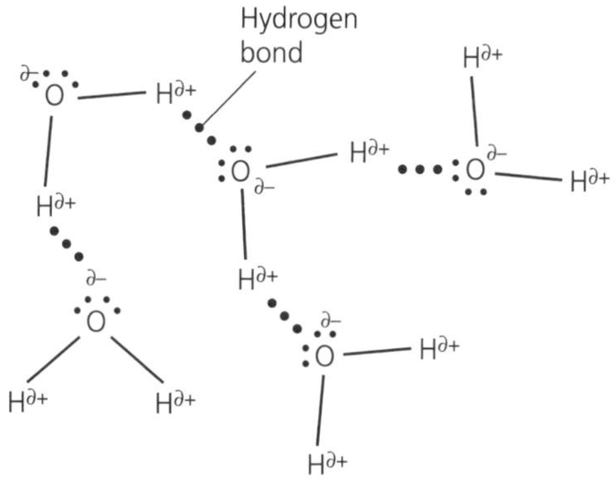

Figure 4.11 Hydrogen bonding in water

4.3 Van der Waals Forces

The van der Waals force increases if (i) there are more electrons, (ii) the polarisability of the molecules increases and (iii) side groups are removed (this increases the opportunities for 'close-contact' between adjacent molecules).

This often misunderstood intermolecular force exists between any molecules. The van der Waals force arises due to the movement of electrons in a molecule and produces a **temporary dipole moment** within a molecule that is then able to **induce** another dipole in another neighbouring molecule. The net effect is that the molecules will attract each other weakly and, as the number of electrons increases, the size of the van der Waals force also increases. The deformability or polarisability of the molecules is also important; that is, the degree to which the nucleus controls the orbiting electrons (the greater the polarisability of the molecule, the greater the van der Waals force).

The magnitude of the van der Waals force is also dependent on the shape of the molecule. Any side chains, e.g. methyl groups, jutting out from a hydro-carbon chain will prevent close contact of neighbouring molecules and therefore lower the magnitude of the van der Waals force. The increasing boiling points of the halogens, noble gases and homologous series, like the alkanes, alkenes and carboxylic acids, with increasing relative molecular mass can be explained by considering the van der Waals forces between the molecules.

It is worthwhile remembering that all species consisting of electrons will produce van der Waals forces, although these forces are often significantly less predominant than other intermolecular forces that may exist.

4.4 Ion–dipole attractions

This type of force is not really an 'intermolecular' force since it involves a molecule and an ion, but it seems appropriate to mention it here. Polar molecules like water are able to interact with ions like Na^+ or SO_4^{2-} by forming ion–dipole attractions. This force results from the ends of molecules with a permanent dipole, e.g. water, propanone or ethanoic acid, being attracted to oppositely charged ions. This explains why sodium chloride dissolves not only in water but also partially in propanone and ester solvents.

B Shapes of molecules

The three-dimensional shape of a molecule is determined by the number of bonded pairs and the number of non-bonded pairs of electrons around the central atom in the molecule – the resulting shape minimises the repulsion within the molecule.

The overall molecular shape is adopted when it minimises the energy or repulsion between the bonding and non-bonding orbitals; write this into your answers when explaining a required shape.

Number of bonded pairs around the central atom (or atom–atom links)	Number of non-bonded pairs	Name of shape with diagram and example
2	0	linear  CO_2, HCN, $BeCl_2$ $[Ag(NH_3)_2]^+$
2	2	bent 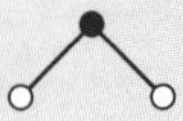 H_2O, H_2S, NO_2^- ClO_2^-
3	0	trigonal planar 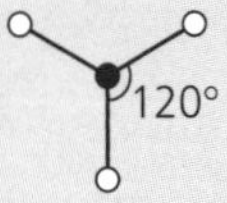 BF_3, NO_3^-, CO_3^{2-}, SO_3
3	1	pyramidal 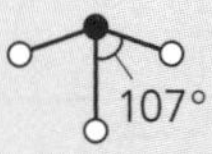 NH_3, PH_3, SO_3^{2-}, ClO_3^-
3	2	T-shape 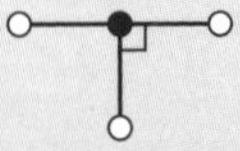 ClF_3
4	0	tetrahedral 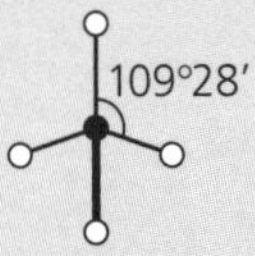 NH_4^+, CH_4, SO_4^{2-}, $CuCl_4^{2-}$
4	2	square planar 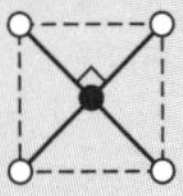 XeF_4, ICl_4^-
5	0	trigonal bipyramidal 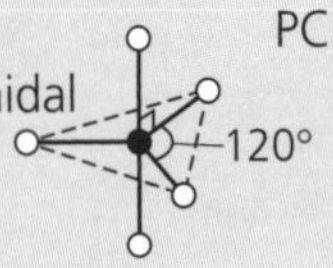 PCl_5
6	0	octahedral 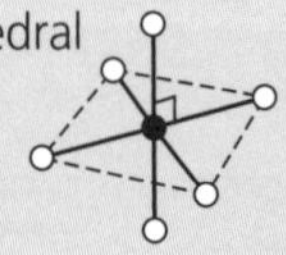 SF_6, $[M(H_2O)_6]^{2+}$ where M = metal
7	0	pentagonal bipyramidal 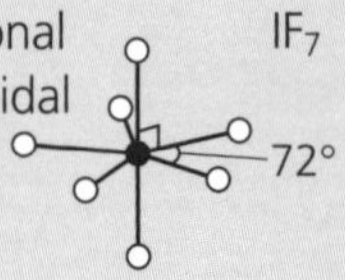 IF_7

Table 4.1

Remember the names of the shapes and at least two examples of each shape type.

Remember to quantify the number of bonded and non-bonded pairs when discussing the shape of a molecule or an ion.

There are other methods for deducing shapes of molecules, but this is a method that demonstrates a good understanding of the outer electronic structure of the central atom that is bonded (especially if you lay out your working in the way shown here).

> The VSEPR (Valence Shell Electron Pair Repulsion) theory states that the order of electron repulsion within a molecule is:
>
> **lone pair–lone pair > lone pair–bonded pair > bonded pair–bonded pair**

The likely number of bonded pairs and lone pairs (non-bonded pairs) of electrons, and the resulting shapes, are summarised in Table 4.1.

The steps that you could follow to determine the three-dimensional shapes of molecules are:

(a) write down the number of outer electrons around the **central** atom;
(b) write down the **total** number of electrons that each bonded atom is contributing towards the covalent bonds;
(c) work out how many electrons are added or removed as a result of an overall charge, e.g. +1 for a single negative charge and −1 for a single positive charge;
(d) work out how many electron pairs are present, around the central atom, in terms of bonded pairs and lone (non-bonded) pairs.

For example, what are the shapes of the following? (Answers are given following steps (a) to (d) above.)

- **the ammonium ion NH_4^+**

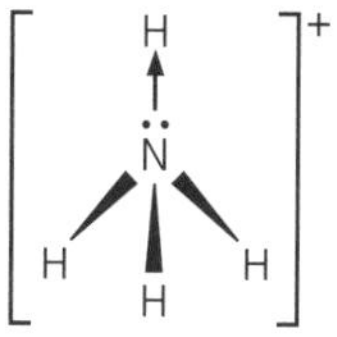

(a) 5
(b) 4 (one from each H atom)
(c) deduct one electron (for +ve charge)
(d) total number of electrons is 5 + 4 − 1 = 8
Four electron pairs, no lone pairs, so the shape is **tetrahedral**.

- **phosphorus pentachloride, PCl_5**

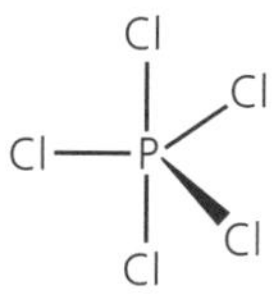

(a) 5
(b) 5
(c) 0 (no overall charge)
(d) total number of electrons is 5 + 5 + 0 = 10
Five electron pairs, no lone pairs, so the shape is **trigonal bipyramidal**.

- **the ion PCl_6^-**

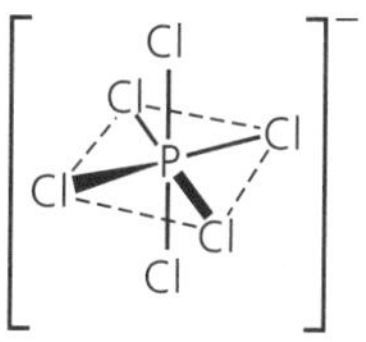

(a) 5
(b) 6
(c) add one electron
(d) total number of electrons is 5 + 6 + 1 = 12
Six electron pairs, no lone pairs, so the shape is **octahedral**.

- **the molecule IF_3**

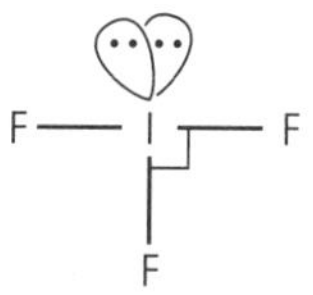

(a) 7
(b) 3
(c) 0
(d) total number of electrons is 7 + 3 + 0 = 10

Five electron pairs but only three single bonds, so two non-bonded (lone) pairs left over. The shape will be based on the trigonal bipyramid but will be distorted by the larger volume occupied by the two lone pairs of electrons. The lone pairs of electrons adopt the equatorial sites, forcing the three fluorine atoms to adopt the other three positions in the 'T' configuration of the trigonal bipyramid. The actual shape is a **T-shaped molecule**.

The minimum energy configuration is when the lone pairs of electrons are on opposite sides of the planar XeF_4 structure; contrast this with IF_3 and ICl_3 in which the lone pairs occupy the equatorial positions, forcing the bonds to form a T-shape.

- **The molecule XeF_4**

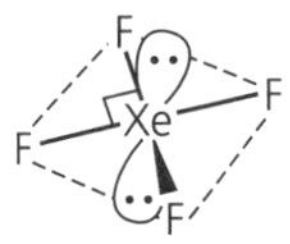

(a) 8
(b) 4
(c) 0
(d) total number of electron pairs is 12 or 6 electron pairs

The electron pairs would produce an octahedral shape, but the two lone pairs of electrons occupy sites either side of a square planar arrangement of covalent bonds. The molecule is said to be **square planar**.

C Metallic structures

A metallic structure is made up of millions of atoms of the metal packed together to form a close packed structure. The atoms are assumed to be spherical. The most efficient ways of packing spheres give a hexagonal close packed structure (hcp; layer scheme: ABABABA...) or a face centred cubic arrangement (fcc; layer scheme ABCABCABC...). The body centred arrangement (bcc) is adopted by the softer metals in which the atoms are packed less efficiently.

Metal atoms have a tendency to lose their **outer** electrons and to delocalise them within the metallic structure. Group I metals lose one electron per atom, Group II lose two, and so on. Note that the transition metals have a tendency to lose both their s electrons and their d electrons (although a d^5 is less likely to be delocalised).

Metals conduct electricity, as graphite does, due to mobile electrons. Ionic substances conduct, when molten and in solution, due to mobile ions.

Within the metallic structure, electrons are free to move or delocalise between the positive ions. This explains why metals have high melting points (electrostatic forces between ions and electrons are strong), and are excellent electrical conductors. Transition metals, that delocalise both their s and d electrons, have higher melting points, higher tensile strengths than the main block metals since they donate more electrons and the sizes of their atoms or ions formed tend to be smaller. This results in stronger metallic bonding within the metallic structure.

The strength of the metallic bond is proportional to the number of electrons delocalised divided by the radius of the atom or the ion within the structure. Metals with more delocalised electrons and smaller atoms are likely to have stronger metallic bonds. For example, the melting point trend across Period 3 is Na < Mg < Al since the number of electrons is increasing by one each time. Down Group I, the melting points decrease since atoms are larger and the same number of electrons, that is one, is delocalised in each case. Also, the melting point increases from potassium to calcium (one delocalised electron in potassium to two in calcium), but then it increases dramatically from calcium to scandium since scandium can delocalise both the $4s^2$ and the $3d^1$ electron whereas calcium can only donate its $4s^2$ electrons.

Metals consist of a close packed structure of positive ions floating in a sea of electrons.

UNIT 5 Thermodynamics

At the end of this unit, you should be familiar with:

- the concept of enthalpy change
- calculating the enthalpy change for a chemical process using Hess's Law
- the Gibb's free energy change, ΔG

A The concept of enthalpy change

Reactions in the laboratory are usually carried out at constant pressure (1 atmosphere pressure). Note that when a reaction produces a gas, it must push back the atmosphere in doing so. This is why ΔH is defined as ΔU + PΔV where ΔU is the change in heat of the system and PΔV is the work done in producing the gas.

When using the word 'stable' it is important to draw a comparison. Do not just say that an element is stable; compared with what? For example, the compound is more thermodynamically stable than the elements in an exothermic reaction.

Most chemical and physical processes occur with a change in heat content. Chemists define a quantity called the enthalpy change and its symbol is ΔH (pronounced 'delta H'). This represents the heat change at constant pressure. If we are measuring the heat change under standard conditions, that is 1 atmosphere pressure and 298 K, then the **standard enthalpy change** is being measured. Its symbol is $\Delta H^{\ominus}$. The enthalpy change is normally measured in units of kJ per mole (of reactant or product).

1 *The sign of ΔH*

- **If the reaction is exothermic, that is heat energy is transferred from the chemicals to the surroundings, then ΔH is negative.**

In this type of heat change, the energy of the products is lower than the reactants by ΔH (see Figure 5.1). The products are said to be more thermodynamically stable than the reactants.

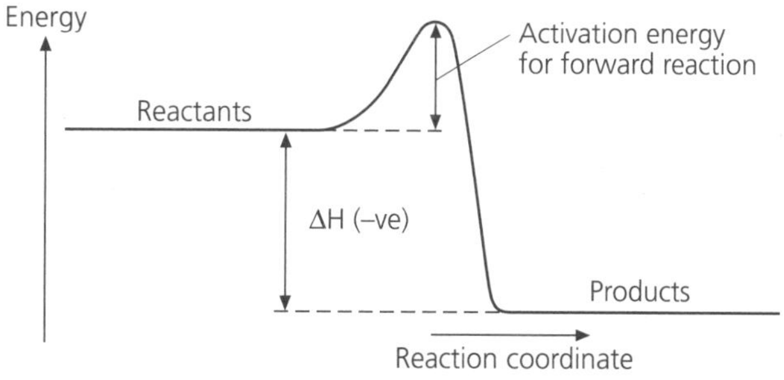

Figure 5.1 Energy profile for an exothermic reaction

- **If the reaction is endothermic, that is heat energy is transferred from the surroundings to the chemicals, then ΔH is positive.**

In this type of heat change, the energy of the products is higher than the reactants by ΔH (see Figure 5.2). The reactants are said to be more thermodynamically stable than the products.

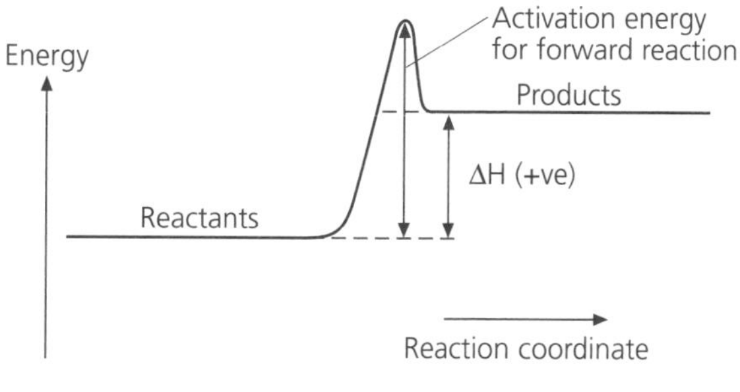

Figure 5.2 Energy profile for an endothermic reaction

When quoting a value for the enthalpy change for a reaction, it is important to realise that the value quoted refers to the equation written. If 2 moles of product are written in the equation, then the value for ΔH may be written as kJ and not necessarily as $kJ\,mol^{-1}$.

For example, the combustion of magnesium in oxygen yields magnesium oxide according to the following exothermic reaction:

$2Mg(s) + O_2(g) \rightarrow 2MgO(s) \qquad \Delta H^\ominus = -1204\,kJ$

According to this equation, when 2 moles of magnesium are burned in 1 mole of oxygen and 2 moles of magnesium oxide are formed, 1204 kJ of heat energy is released. Reference to the units of this reaction as kJ per mole or $kJ\,mol^{-1}$ must relate to the only uni-molar quantity in the equation, that is oxygen.

$\Delta H^\ominus = -1204\,kJ\,mol^{-1}\ O_2$, or $\Delta H^\ominus = -602\,kJ\,mol^{-1}$ Mg, or $\Delta H^\ominus = -602\,kJ\,mol^{-1}$ MgO

B Calculating the enthalpy change using Hess's Law

The most important law that we use to calculate the enthalpy change for a reaction is called Hess's Law.

- **Hess's Law:**
  The enthalpy change (heat change) for a reaction is independent of the path taken, whether the reaction is carried out directly or indirectly.

1 *Cycle 1: calculating $\Delta H^\ominus$ for a reaction using enthalpy of formation data*

Instead of quoting 'energy change' in your answers, use 'heat change'.

The standard enthalpy of formation, $\Delta H_f^\ominus$, is defined as the heat change when 1 mole of a substance is formed from its constituent elements in their standard states under standard conditions (298 K and 1 atm pressure).

For example:

$C(s) + 2H_2(g) + \frac{1}{2}O_2(g) \rightarrow CH_3OH(l) \qquad \Delta H_f^\ominus = -239\,kJ\,mol^{-1}$ of methanol

$6C(s) + 3H_2(g) \rightarrow C_6H_6(l) \qquad \Delta H_f^\ominus = +49\,kJ\,mol^{-1}$ of benzene

It should be noted that the standard enthalpy change of formation of an element in its standard state is **arbitrarily** taken as zero. The standard enthalpy change of formation indicates the relative thermodynamic stability of the compound formed compared to its constituent elements. The example above shows that methanol is more thermodynamically stable than its constituent elements by 239 $kJ\,mol^{-1}$, whereas benzene is less thermodynamically stable than its elements by 49 $kJ\,mol^{-1}$. It must also be understood that a reaction may have a negative enthalpy change, but it may be very slow since it has a high activation energy barrier. Reactants, in this type of reaction, are said to be kinetically stable (since they do not want to move anywhere!), although they are thermodynamically less stable than the products.

The reaction, for which we want to find $\Delta H^\ominus$, is written as:

$$\text{reactants} \xrightarrow{\Delta H^\ominus} \text{products}$$

Signs may cause a problem here. Remember that 'a minus–minus is a plus and a plus–minus is a minus'.

Using a cycle, in which the reactants and the products are broken into their respective constituent elements, the following relationship can be obtained:

$\Delta H^\ominus = \Sigma\Delta H_f^\ominus(\text{products}) - \Sigma\Delta H_f^\ominus(\text{reactants})$

Or the standard enthalpy change in a reaction is the difference between the sum of the enthalpies of formation of the products minus the sum of the enthalpies of formation of the reactants.

- **Calculate the standard enthalpy change for the following reaction given the standard enthalpy change of formation data.**
  $N_2H_4(l) + 2H_2O_2(l) \rightarrow N_2(g) + 4H_2O(l)$
  $\Delta H_f^\ominus$ data: $N_2H_4(l) = +50.4\ \text{kJ mol}^{-1}$, $H_2O_2(l) = -188\ \text{kJ mol}^{-1}$,
  $H_2O(l) = -286\ \text{kJ mol}^{-1}$
  Using $\Delta H^\ominus = \Sigma\Delta H_f^\ominus(\text{products}) - \Sigma\Delta H_f^\ominus(\text{reactants})$
  $\Delta H^\ominus = \{0 + (4 \times -286)\} - \{50.4 + (2 \times -188)\}$
  $= -1144 - (-325.6)$
  $= \mathbf{-818.4\ kJ\ mol^{-1}}$

So the reaction is **exothermic** (ΔH is negative) and the energy profile for this reaction is shown in Figure 5.3.

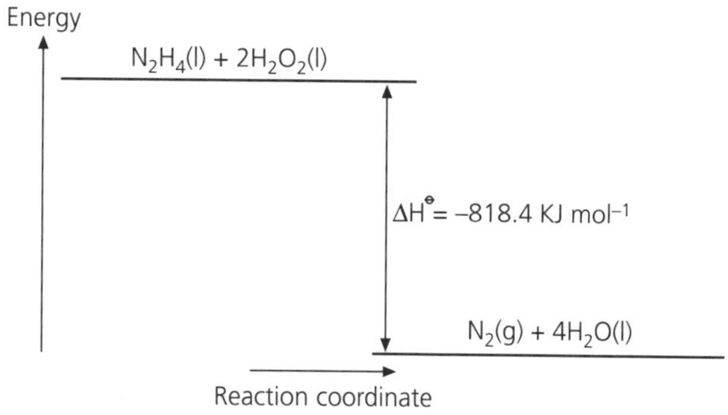

Figure 5.3 Energy profile for the reaction involving $N_2H_4(l)$ and $H_2O_2(l)$

2 Cycle 2: calculating an enthalpy change from combustion data

If a substance is partially combusted, carbon monoxide is produced, and this lowers the magnitude of the exothermic process.

The direction of the arrows in an energy cycle is very important. Make sure they are labelled correctly and that the correct sign is used for the enthalpy change for the process being considered.

The standard enthalpy of combustion, $\Delta H_c^\ominus$, is defined as the heat change that takes place when 1 mole of a substance is burned completely in oxygen under standard conditions.

For example, the equations for the standard enthalpy of combustion for methane and butan-1-ol are:

$CH_4(g) + 2O_2(g) \rightarrow CO_2(g) + 2H_2O(l)$; $\Delta H^\ominus = -890.4\ \text{kJ mol}^{-1}$
$C_4H_9OH(l) + 6O_2(g) \rightarrow 4CO_2(g) + 5H_2O(l)$; $\Delta H^\ominus = -2673.0\ \text{kJ mol}^{-1}$

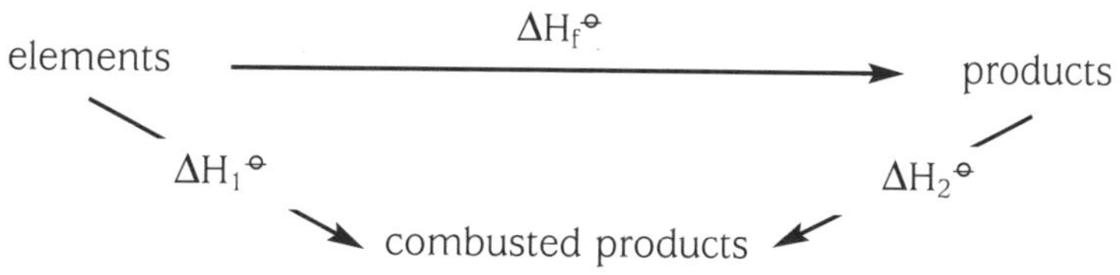

Using the cycle, it can be seen that $\Delta H_f^\ominus = \Delta H_1^\ominus - \Delta H_2^\ominus$

- Calculate the enthalpy change for the reaction below (the standard enthalpy change of formation for ethanol) using the enthalpy of combustion data provided.

 ΔH_c^\ominus data: $C(s) = -393.5\,\text{kJ}\,\text{mol}^{-1}$, $H_2(g) = -285.9\,\text{kJ}\,\text{mol}^{-1}$,
 $C_2H_5OH(l) = -1371\,\text{kJ}\,\text{mol}^{-1}$

$$2C(s) + 3H_2(g) + \tfrac{1}{2}O_2(g) \xrightarrow{\Delta H_f^\ominus} C_2H_5OH(l)$$

$$3O_2(g)\quad \Delta H_1^\ominus \searrow \qquad \swarrow \Delta H_2^\ominus\quad 3O_2(g)$$

$$2CO_2(g) + 3H_2O(l)$$

$$\Delta H_f^\ominus = \Delta H_1^\ominus - \Delta H_2^\ominus$$
$$= (2 \times -393.5) + (3 \times -285.9) - (-1371) = \mathbf{-273.7\,\text{kJ}\,\text{mol}^{-1}}$$

- Calculate the enthalpy change for the reaction below ($\Delta H^\ominus*$) using the enthalpy of combustion data given.

 ΔH_c^\ominus data: $C_4H_6(g) = -2542\,\text{kJ}\,\text{mol}^{-1}$, $H_2(g) = -285.9\,\text{kJ}\,\text{mol}^{-1}$,
 $C_4H_{10}(g) = -2877\,\text{kJ}\,\text{mol}^{-1}$

$$C_4H_6(g) + 2H_2(g) \xrightarrow{\Delta H^\ominus*} C_4H_{10}(g)$$

$$\tfrac{13}{2}O_2(g)\quad \Delta H_1^\ominus \searrow \qquad \swarrow \Delta H_2^\ominus\quad \tfrac{13}{2}O_2(g)$$

$$4CO_2(g) + 5H_2O(l)$$

$$\Delta H^\ominus* = (-2542) + (-285.9 \times 2) - (-2877) = \mathbf{-236.8\,\text{kJ}\,\text{mol}^{-1}}$$

3 Cycle 3: enthalpy changes from atomisation and bond enthalpy data

The standard enthalpy change of atomisation for a substance is the heat energy required to form 1 mole of atoms in the gas phase under standard conditions (298 K and 1 atm pressure).

For example, the standard changes of atomisation for the elements fluorine, nitrogen and carbon are:

$\tfrac{1}{2}F_2(g) \rightarrow F(g)$ $\Delta H^\ominus_{at} = +79.1\,\text{kJ}\,\text{mol}^{-1}$

$\tfrac{1}{2}N_2(g) \rightarrow N(g)$ $\Delta H^\ominus_{at} = +473\,\text{kJ}\,\text{mol}^{-1}$ (this high positive value reflects the strength of the N≡N triple bond)

$C(s) \rightarrow C(g)$ $\Delta H^\ominus_{at} = +715\,\text{kJ}\,\text{mol}^{-1}$ (this high positive value reflects on the strong giant covalently bonded structure of the graphite)

The average bond dissociation energy is the heat energy required to break 1 mole of specified bonds under standard conditions of temperature and pressure (298 K and 1 atm pressure).

- Calculate a value for the N–H bond energy in ammonia using the following reaction:

This relatively low value is explained by the weakness of the F–F covalent bond which is attributed to the lone pair–lone pair repulsions between neighbouring fluorine atoms within a molecule.

Remember that 'average' bond energy is an average for that bond in different compounds, e.g. a C-O bond in an alcohol, ester, ether, etc. It will

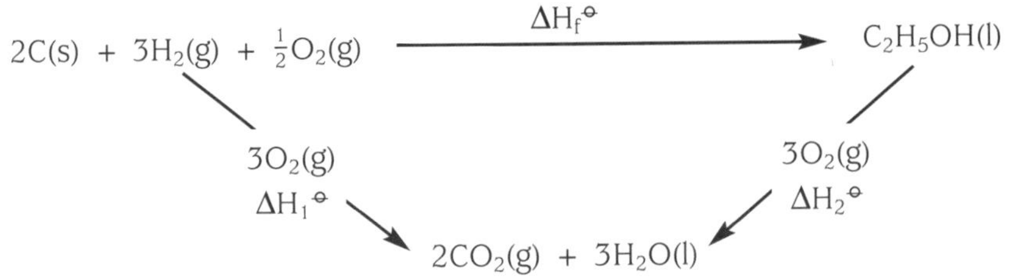

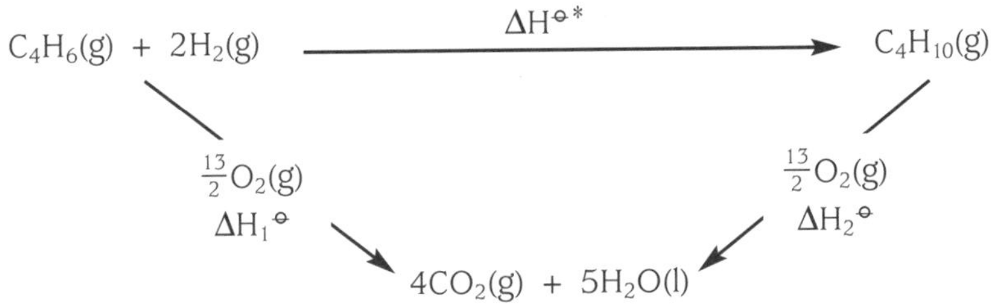

not necessarily be equal to that of the bond in the specific compound that you are considering. This may explain any discrepancies between calculated and data book values.

$N_2(g) + 3H_2(g) \rightarrow 2NH_3(g)$

Use the following information:

$\Delta H^{\ominus}_{at}$ data: $\frac{1}{2}N_2(g) = +473\ \text{kJ mol}^{-1}$, $\frac{1}{2}H_2(g) = +218\ \text{kJ mol}^{-1}$

and $\Delta H_f^{\ominus}$ for ammonia is $-46.2\ \text{kJ mol}^{-1}$

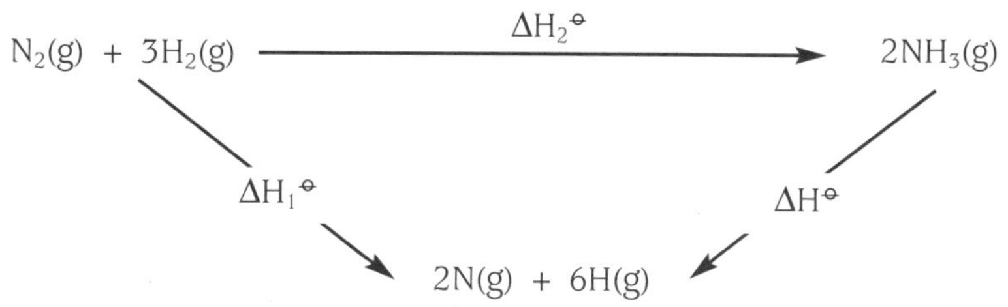

$\Delta H^{\ominus} = -\Delta H_2^{\ominus} + \Delta H_1^{\ominus} = -(-46.2 \times 2) + (473 \times 2) + (218 \times 6) = +2346.4\ \text{kJ}$

Since six N–H bonds are broken in the process represented by ΔH, the average bond dissociation enthalpy of the N–H bond is given by:

$(+2346.4/6) = \mathbf{+391.1\ kJ\ mol^{-1}}$

(data book value for the average bond dissociation enthalpy for (N–H) is $+388\ \text{kJ mol}^{-1}$)

Bond dissociation enthalpies have relevance only in reactions taking place in the gas phase.

3.1 Using bond dissociation enthalpies to calculate $\Delta H^{\ominus}$ for a reaction

- **Calculate $\Delta H^{\ominus}$ for the following reaction using average bond dissociation enthalpies.**

  $H{-}N{=}CH{-}CH{=}N{-}H(g) + 2H_2(g) \rightarrow H_2N{-}CH_2{-}CH_2{-}NH_2(g)$

  All of the following data are given in kJ mol^{-1}:

  E(N–H) = +388, E(N=C) = +613, E(H–H) = + 436, E(C–H) = +412, E(C–N) = +305

  In this reaction, it is not necessary to break **all** of the bonds in the reactants and reform **all** of the bonds in the product molecules since only a few are actually involved in the reaction. In the process, 2 × [H–H] bonds and 2 × [C=N] bonds are broken and 2 × [N–H], 2 × [C–H] and 2 × [C–N] bonds are formed.

  So, $\Delta H^{\ominus}$ for the reaction is:

  $2 \times E(N{=}C) + 2 \times E(H{-}H) - \{2 \times E(N{-}H) + 2 \times E(C{-}H) + 2 \times E(C{-}N)\} = \mathbf{-112\ kJ}$

4 Cycle 4: the Born–Haber cycle

The definition of lattice energy may differ from book to book. It is normally defined for gaseous ions → solid but can be quoted the other way round – in which case it has the opposite sign. As long as you get the sign correct, then the rest of the calculation should be unaffected.

The Born–Haber cycle is another application of Hess's Law and it involves a method by which the lattice enthalpy for an ionic material is calculated.

The standard lattice enthalpy is the heat energy released when 1 mole of an ionic lattice is formed from its constituent ions in the gas phase under standard conditions (298 K and 1 atm pressure).

For example, the lattice enthalpies for sodium chloride and calcium fluoride are:

$Na^+(g) + Cl^-(g) \rightarrow NaCl(s) \qquad \Delta H^{\ominus}_{latt} = -771\ \text{kJ mol}^{-1}$

$Ca^{2+}(g) + 2F^-(g) \rightarrow CaF_2(s) \qquad \Delta H^{\ominus}_{latt} = -2602\ \text{kJ mol}^{-1}$

- **Draw a Born–Haber cycle for calcium fluoride and use it to calculate the lattice enthalpy for calcium fluoride.**

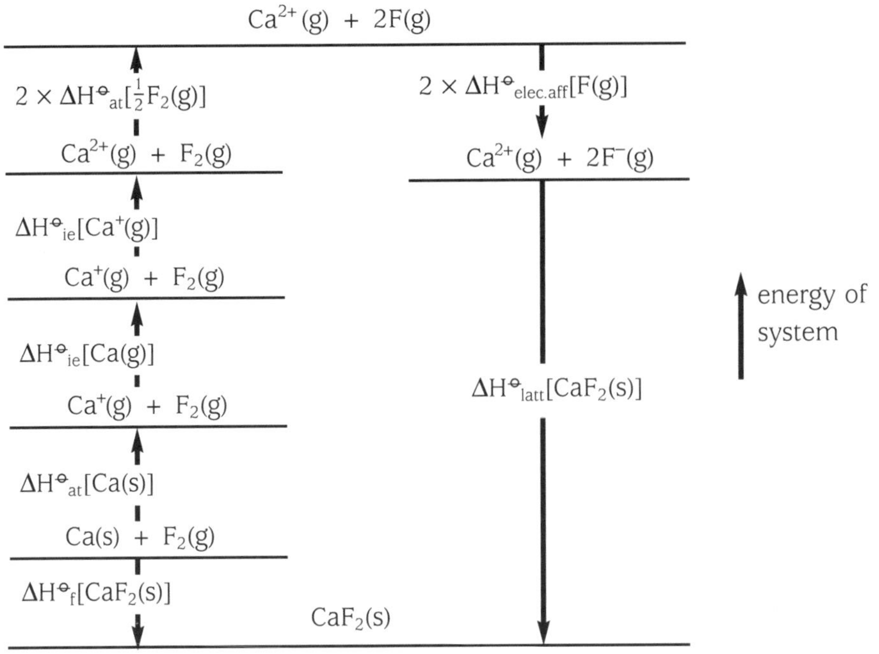

You must label the diagram fully before you carry out the calculation.

Relevant standard enthalpy data (in kJ mol^{-1}):

$\Delta H^{\ominus}_{f}[CaF_2(s)] = -1214$

$\Delta H^{\ominus}_{at}[Ca(s)] = +193$

$\Delta H^{\ominus}_{ie}[Ca(g)] = +590$

$\Delta H^{\ominus}_{ie}[Ca^{+}(g)] = +1150$

$\Delta H^{\ominus}_{at}[\frac{1}{2}F_2(g)] = +79.1$

$\Delta H^{\ominus}_{elec.aff}[F(g)] = -348$

The standard electron affinity ($\Delta H^{\ominus}_{elec.aff}$) is the heat change when 1 mole of electrons is added to 1 mole of gaseous atoms at 298 K and 1 atm pressure ($10^5 Nm^{-2}$).

Using the cycle:

$$\Delta H^{\ominus}_{latt}[CaF_2(s)] = -2 \times \Delta H_{elec.aff}[F(g)] - 2 \times \Delta H_{at}[\tfrac{1}{2}F_2(g)] - \Delta H_{ie}[Ca^{+}(g)] - \Delta H_{ie}[Ca(g)] - \Delta H_{at}[Ca(s)] + \Delta H_{f}[CaF_2(s)]$$

$$\Delta H^{\ominus}_{latt}[CaF_2(s)] = -(2 \times -348) - (2 \times 79.1) - (590) - (1150) - (193) + (-1214)$$

$$= \mathbf{-2609.2\ kJ\ mol^{-1}}$$

4.1 Uses of the lattice enthalpy

Lattice enthalpy is related to the product of the charges on the ions divided by the sum of their radii or $\Delta H_{latt} = (Z_aZ_b)/(r_a + r_b)$. This expression can be used when comparing different solids and their respective lattice energies.

For example, sodium chloride has a value for ΔH_{latt} of -771 kJ mol^{-1}, whereas magnesium oxide has a value of -3889 kJ mol^{-1}. Since the product of the charges on the ions in sodium chloride is $(+1 \times -1)$, whereas in magnesium oxide it is $(+2 \times -2)$, the lattice energy should be about four times as great for MgO than for NaCl. Any further discrepancies are due to differing ionic radii.

Using the expression for ΔH_{latt} mentioned above, it is possible to calculate a **theoretical** value for the lattice enthalpy for an ionic solid – this assumes that the solid is 100% ionic in character. When we compare this value with the one obtained using a Born–Haber cycle (in which the values are obtained **experimentally**), we can see how accurately the equation describes the actual pure ionic situation. If there is a significant difference between the 100% ionic model and the experimental Born–Haber cycle value, then we can assume that there must be some covalent character present in the substance (the 100% ionic model is not an exact fit). This is attributed to the polarising power of the small and highly charged positive ion distorting the spherical electron distribution of the negative ion, thereby inducing some covalent character.

More covalent character within an ionic bond strengthens the bond slightly, thus lowering the energy of the system and producing a slightly more exothermic lattice energy. When this solid is heated, it would be more energetically favourable to sublime to form molecules rather than form gaseous ions. This is why more covalent character lowers melting and boiling points.

The lattice enthalpy on its own does not determine how thermodynamically stable a substance will be; this is determined by the enthalpy of formation. Therefore, if the lattice energy is known together with all of the other data except the enthalpy of formation, the enthalpy of formation can be calculated. This method can be used to explain the existence and non-existence of some compounds, e.g. MgCl, $MgCl_2$ and $MgCl_3$.

4.2 Common mistakes made in using Born–Haber cycles

- The change represented by $Ca(g) \rightarrow Ca^{2+}(g) + 2e^-$ is given by the sum of the first and second ionisation enthalpy and **not** by the second ionisation enthalpy alone.
- Enthalpy of atomisations are defined according to the number of moles of atoms **formed** rather than the initial number of moles. For example, the change $N_2(g) \rightarrow 2N(g)$ is twice the atomisation of nitrogen and **not** once.
- The change $O(g) + 2e^- \rightarrow O^{2-}(g)$ is given by the first electron affinity added to the second electron affinity for oxygen and not just the second value.
- Make sure you realise that when you are considering the heat change in which the arrow is pointing, there is no need to change the sign. If you are considering the change in the opposite direction, then you must reverse the sign.

5 Cycle 5: the relationship between enthalpy of solution, ΔH_{sol}, lattice enthalpy, ΔH_{latt}, and hydration enthalpy, ΔH_{hyd}

This is one energy cycle that students frequently forget. Whenever you are asked to discuss dissolving an ionic solid in a solvent, like water, make sure you discuss it in terms of lattice enthalpy and hydration enthalpy.

The standard enthalpy of hydration is the heat change that occurs when 1 mole of gaseous ions is completely hydrated in water to infinite dilution, under standard conditions of temperature and pressure (298K and 1atm pressure).

The standard enthalpy of solution is the heat change that occurs when 1 mole of a substance is completely dissolved in water under standard conditions of temperature and pressure (298 K and 1 atm pressure).

Another cycle is constructed in which the process of dissolving is broken down into two main steps: separation of the ions in the ionic solid followed by hydrating the ions. Consider the substance sodium chloride, NaCl(s), and its solubility in water:

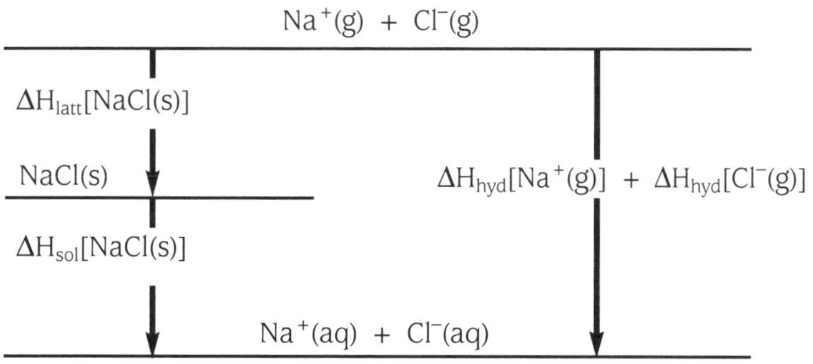

It can be seen from this that:

$\Delta H_{sol}[NaCl(s)] = \Delta H_{hyd}[Na^+(g)] + \Delta H_{hyd}[Cl^-(g)] - \Delta H_{latt}[NaCl(s)]$

If the magnitude of the hydration enthalpy is greater than the magnitude of the lattice enthalpy, then the substance will have a negative value for the enthalpy of solution and vice versa.

For sodium chloride (using the above relationship):

$\Delta H_{sol}[NaCl(s)] = +(-406) + (-364) - (-771) = \mathbf{+1\ kJ\ mol^{-1}}$

It must also be remembered that the enthalpy change alone is not the correct determinant in assessing whether a reaction takes place. The Gibb's free energy change needs to be calculated as this is the quantity that determines reaction feasibility or spontaneity.

C The Gibb's free energy change, ΔG

You will have to check with your syllabus to see whether you need to know about Gibb's free energy.

The Second Law of Thermodynamics states that for a process to be spontaneous, the total **entropy** change must be greater than or equal to zero, that is $\Delta S_{total} \geqslant 0$.

It follows that the total entropy change, $\Delta S_{system} + \Delta S_{surroundings} \geqslant 0$. Since $\Delta S_{surroundings} = -\Delta H/T$, then $\Delta S_{system} - \Delta H/T \geqslant 0$. By rearranging this we produce: $\Delta H - T\Delta S_{system} \leqslant 0$, and the magnitude by which the expression is less than zero is called the Gibb's free energy change, ΔG.

The total amount of energy available in a chemical change is not all available for doing useful work; some is needed to make sure that the total entropy change is greater than zero. Any energy left over is therefore 'free' to do useful work (Gibb's free energy).

Therefore:
$\mathbf{\Delta G = \Delta H - T\Delta S_{system}}$
ΔG must be less than zero for a process to be spontaneous.

The following points should be noted about the entropy and Gibb's free energy terms:

- **Entropy refers to the number of ways of distributing energy amongst a specified number of particles.** It therefore follows that the entropy of gases, liquids and solids are in the order: gas > liquid > solid. Entropy can be visualised as the disorder of the particles present, although this visualisation alone has limitations.
- **Entropy comes in two parts:** entropy of the system (the reaction or the region in space on which you are concentrating) and the surroundings (everything else other than the point of concern, that is the rest of the universe).
- **It is the total entropy change that determines reaction spontaneity** and not just the entropy of either the system or the surroundings.
- **The entropy change of the surroundings is given by –ΔH/T** where ΔH is the enthalpy change for the reaction in J or kJ and T is measured in Kelvin.
- **In a process, not all of the heat energy produced by the reaction is available for doing useful work**, e.g. lifting a weight on a pulley system or providing power to drive an engine. Of the total amount of available energy (ΔH), a

proportion of this will be used to make sure that the total entropy change **must** be greater than zero. The rest is then used for doing work, that is free energy. A good way of visualising free energy and its relationship with entropy change of the system and the temperature is by using the diagram below:

ΔH	
ΔG	$T\Delta S_{system}$

ΔG tells us what is possible when the reaction has come to equilibrium. It does not indicate anything about how fast the reaction will take place.

ΔH is therefore made up of two parts: a ΔG term and a TΔS term. Using the equation $\Delta G = \Delta H - T\Delta S_{system}$, the following can be analysed in terms of the sign and magnitude of ΔH and ΔS.

- **Why do some endothermic reactions work (why are they feasible)?**
  ΔH is positive. As long as ΔS is positive enough (as TΔS) to be larger than ΔH, then ΔG will be negative and therefore the reaction will be spontaneous.
- **Why does ice melt above 273 K?**
  ΔH is positive (intermolecular bonds are being broken) and ΔS_{system} is positive (entropy increases on going from a solid to a liquid). If the temperature is too low, $T\Delta S_{system}$ will be smaller than ΔH and therefore ice will not melt (at temperatures below 273 K). Above 273 K, $T\Delta S_{system}$ is larger than ΔH and therefore ΔG is negative and the ice melts.
- **Why do ammonium salts dissolve in water despite the reactions being endothermic?**
  ΔH is positive and ΔS_{system} is positive since the ions are being separated from the ordered lattice, resulting in an increase in disorder. For this process, ΔH must be smaller than $T\Delta S_{system}$, making ΔG negative and the reaction spontaneous.
- **Why does water vapour not produce liquid water above 373 K?**
  ΔH is negative since new bonds, in the form of hydrogen bonds, are forming between the molecules. ΔS_{system} is negative since gaseous molecules are forming a more ordered liquid state. The overall effect is that ΔG is positive for the process $H_2O(g) \rightarrow H_2O(l)$ above 373 K.
- **Why do solids become more soluble in water as temperature increases but gases become less soluble?**
  When solids dissolve in water, ΔS_{system} is positive and ΔH may be either positive or negative. Using $\Delta G = \Delta H - T\Delta S_{system}$, it can be seen that if $T\Delta S_{system}$ is more positive (on increasing temperature) than ΔH, then $\Delta H - T\Delta S_{system}$ will give rise to a more negative ΔG, so the process of dissolving becomes less spontaneous.

  When gases dissolve in water, ΔS_{system} is negative and ΔH is normally slightly negative. As temperature increases, $T\Delta S_{system}$ becomes more negative, so then $\Delta H - (T\Delta S_{system})$ becomes more positive, and the process becomes less spontaneous.

UNIT 6 Kinetics

At the end of this unit, you should be familiar with:

- the fundamentals of kinetics
- following the rate of a chemical reaction
- factors affecting the rate of a chemical reaction

A What is kinetics?

You should have covered a lot of this preliminary work at GCSE-level in classwork and maybe as a project.

Kinetics is the study of reaction rate.

For a reaction to proceed, various factors need to be satisfied. These factors are summarised by the **collision theory** and, briefly, for a reaction to occur, particles must:

- collide
- collide with sufficient kinetic energy
- collide with a favourable orientation

B Following the rate of a chemical reaction

In order to study the rate of a reaction, it is useful to consider techniques that enable the concentration of a reactant or a product to be monitored during the course of a reaction. The method that is used to track the concentration of a reactant or a product depends on the chemical or physical properties of the substance being considered.

Reactions must be 'quenched' before they are analysed; otherwise the reaction will continue and concentrations will change.

- **Volumetric methods**
  A sample is removed from the reaction vessel and quenched by dramatic cooling in, for example, an ice-salt bath or using a reagent to neutralise one of the reactants and thereby stopping the reaction proceeding further prior to titration. A titration is then carried out to determine the actual amount of active substance removed from the reaction at that time. The process would then be repeated at different times during the course of the reaction.

- **Production of a gas**
  If a gas is formed, its volume may be measured with time using either a graduated gas syringe or, if the gas is insoluble in water, it can be collected by displacement of water from a measuring cylinder filled with water. The concentration of reactant at time t is proportional to: (the final volume of gas) – (the volume of gas measured at time, t), i.e. $V_\infty - V_t$.

- **Colorimetric methods**
  A reactant or product may be coloured, in which case there will be a change in the colour seen in the reaction. A colorimeter may be used to measure the absorption of visible light taking place due to the presence of a coloured substance. Reactions involving iodine are often followed in this way. For

example, in the reaction between hydrogen peroxide solution and acidified iodide ions, iodine is formed: $H_2O_2(aq) + 2H^+(aq) + 2I^-(aq) \rightarrow 2H_2O(l) + I_2$.

- **Pressure changes**
  If, as a reaction proceeds, different volumes of gases are produced from those of the reactants, the pressure will change in the reaction. The reaction vessel is connected to a pressure sensor, e.g. a mercury barometer or an electrical pressure sensor, and the pressure monitored with time. The thermal decomposition of gaseous ethanal can be monitored using this method since the pressure increases with increasing time (two volumes of gaseous product to one of reactant): $CH_3CHO(g) \rightarrow CH_4(g) + CO(g)$.
- **Conductivity**
  In the reaction between the tertiary halogenoalkane 2-chloro-2-methylpropane and hydroxide ions, the electrical conductivity of the solution changes as the faster moving hydroxide ion is replaced by the slower moving chloride ions. We may therefore follow the rate by monitoring how the electrical conductivity decreases with time during the course of the reaction.

C Factors affecting the rate of reaction

1 Concentration

Concentration and its effect on reaction rate must be understood at A-level.

The rate of reaction is defined as the rate of change of concentration with time. It is measured in mol dm^{-3} s^{-1}.

For the reaction A + B + ... → X + Y + ..., the rate of reaction is equal to the rate at which the concentration of A or B are decreasing or the concentration at which the product concentrations are increasing – expressed mathematically:

$$\text{Rate (mol dm}^{-3}\text{ s}^{-1}) = \frac{-d[A]}{dt} = \frac{-d[B]}{dt} = \frac{d[X]}{dt} = \frac{d[Y]}{dt}$$

Note that d[conc]/dt represents the **instantaneous rate** of reaction at a certain time and not the **average rate** of reaction between two times. There is a big difference in asking the following two questions:

- what is the rate of reaction **at** 2 seconds? This is instantaneous rate.
- what is the rate of reaction **over** the first 2 seconds of the reaction? This is average rate.

There is a big difference between average rate and instantaneous rate.

1.1 Instantaneous rate

A graph must be produced of, say, the concentration of the reactant A with time (see Figure 6.1). A tangent is then drawn to the graph when t = 2 seconds and the gradient of the tangent drawn. Since the concentration of A is decreasing, as it is a reactant, the gradient of the line will be negative. The value of this gradient expressed in mol dm^{-3} s^{-1} is the rate of reaction at that point in time. This process may be repeated at any time to find out the corresponding instantaneous rate.

The gradient of a tangent drawn to a graph of concentration against time is equal to the rate at that time.

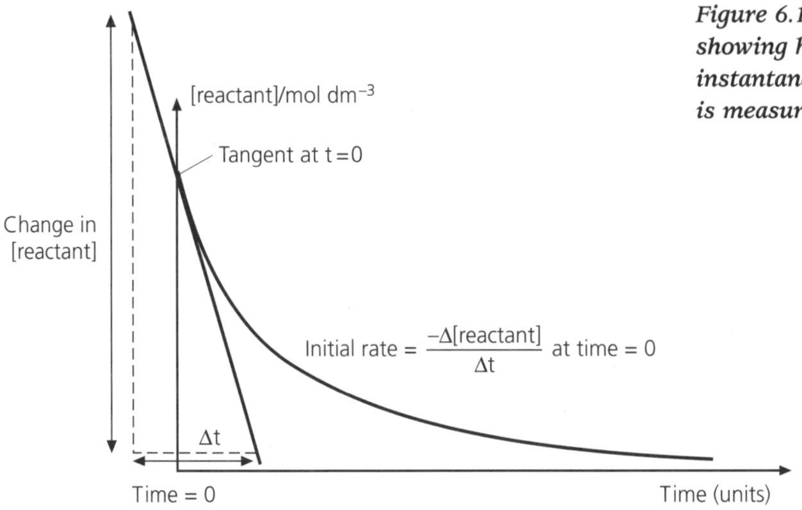

Figure 6.1 Graph showing how the instantaneous rate is measured

1.2 Average rate

To determine the average rate of reaction, we measure by how much the concentration of the reactant has decreased and divide this by the time taken for the change:

$$\textbf{average rate (in mol dm}^{-3}\textbf{s}^{-1}\textbf{)} = \frac{\textbf{change in concentration (in mol dm}^{-3}\textbf{)}}{\textbf{time taken (normally in seconds)}}$$

This result will be the average rate of reaction which will have units of mol dm^{-3}s^{-1}.

1.3 How does concentration affect the rate of a chemical reaction?

The rate equation summarises mathematically the effect of the concentration of the reactants on reaction rate:

for the general reaction: $A + B + ... \rightarrow X + Y + ...$
the rate equation is: **rate (in mol dm^{-3}s^{-1}) = $k[A]^a [B]^b ...$**

The following points about the rate equation must be noted:

- the rate of reaction is always measured in mol dm^{-3}s^{-1}
- the powers to which each concentration is raised are called **orders**. The order with respect to A is a, the order with respect to B is b, etc.

For the reaction:
$$CH_3COCH_3(aq) + I_2(aq) \xrightarrow{H^+(aq)cat} CH_3COCH_2I(aq) + HI(aq)$$

the rate equation is
rate = $k[CH_3COCH_3(aq)]^1 [I_2(aq)]^0 [H^+(aq)]^1$
(although it is not necessary to include the power '1' for first order processes).

The rate of reaction is said to be:
first order with respect to $[CH_3COCH_3(aq)]$; **first order** with respect to $[H^+(aq)]$; and **zero order** with respect to $[I_2(aq)]$.

The overall order of the reaction is simply the sum of all the individual orders.

If the rate equation is rate = $k[CH_3COCH_3(aq)]\ [I_2(aq)]^0\ [H^+(aq)]$, the overall order is 1 + 0 + 1 = 2 or second order overall.

The symbol, k, is the **rate constant** and it is constant with time and varying concentration, although it does increase with increasing temperature.

The units of the rate constant vary according to the overall order of the reaction.

The units of the rate constant vary according to the order of the reaction:

- **zero order reaction overall:**
  rate = $k[A]^0$ or rate = k, so the rate constant has units of $mol\,dm^{-3}s^{-1}$
- **first order reaction overall:**
  rate = $k[A]^1$, so units for k = units for rate/units for [A]
  = $mol\,dm^{-3}s^{-1}/mol\,dm^{-3} = s^{-1}$
- **second order overall:**
  rate = $k[A]^2$, so units for k = units for rate/units for $[A]^2$, so units for k will be $mol^{-1}dm^3s^{-1}$

1.4 Determining the order of reaction with respect to a reactant

The rate equation must be determined experimentally and it cannot be deduced by looking at the balanced equation for the reaction (the stoichiometric equation).

When one of the reactants is in excess, its concentration does not change considerably during the reaction despite the rate changing; this reactant therefore displays zero order kinetics when in excess.

Experimentally, to measure the order with respect to a reactant, it is important that concentrations of the other reactants are in a large excess (so that the observed rate is due to the changes of reagent not in excess). If the other reactant concentrations are not in excess, then the order measured for the reactant being investigated is **not** an individual order but an **overall** order. Once all of the individual orders are deduced, the overall rate equation will then be known.

A graph is plotted of the concentration of each reactant against time; the shape of the graph can be used to determine the order of the reaction with respect to that reactant.

1.5 Concentration versus time graphs

The shapes of these graphs are important. Make sure that you remember and recognise them.

Zero order reactions (Figure 6.2):

- rate = $k[A]^0$
- equation of line is $[A] = [A_0] - kt$
- the gradient of this line is equal to k

The equation of this straight line fits the general form y = mx + c where k is the gradient and A_0 is the initial concentration.

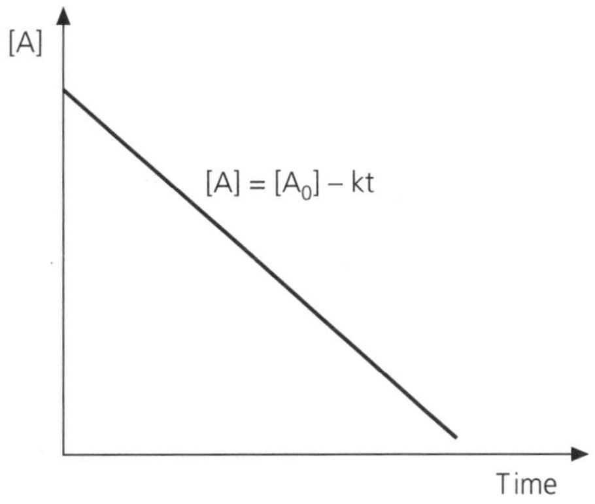

Figure 6.2

It is important to know that the half life is independent of the concentration of reactants.

First order reactions (Figure 6.3):

- rate = k $[A]^1$
- constant half life, $t_{1/2}$
- the equation of this curve is $[A] = [A_0]e^{-kt}$
- if a graph of ln[A] against time, t, is plotted, a straight line of gradient, k, results
- the rate constant is also equal to $\ln 2/t_{1/2}$ for this first order process

Figure 6.3

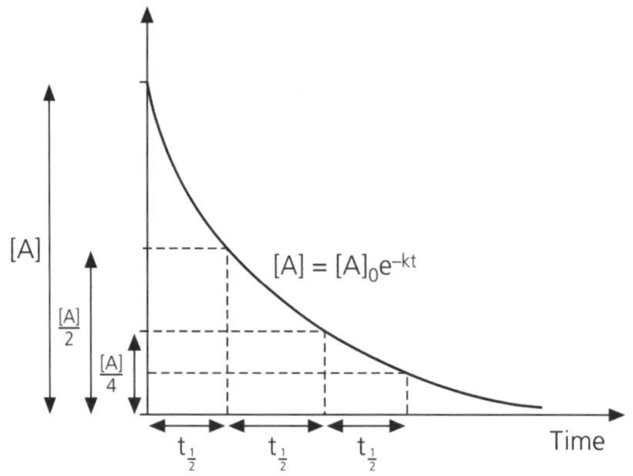

Second order reactions (Figure 6.4):

- rate = k $[A]^2$
- increasing half life

Figure 6.4

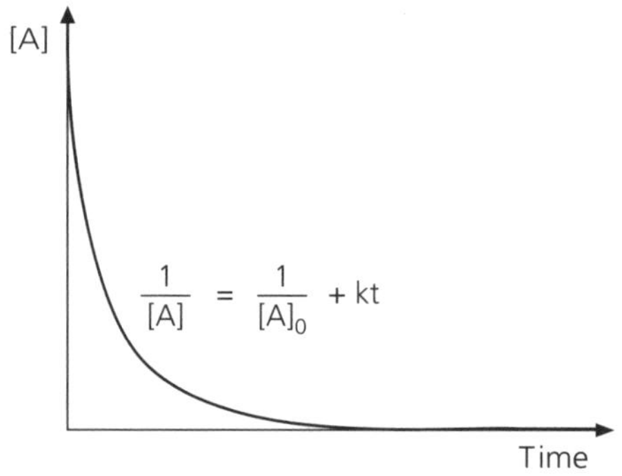

1.6 Rate versus concentration graphs

If a graph of the concentration against time is plotted, draw tangents to the graph at certain times and measure the gradient at these points. The gradients are equal to the rate at that time. Plot another graph of the rate on the y-axis against concentration on the x-axis.

Zero order reactions (Figure 6.5):

- rate = $k[A]^0$

Figure 6.5

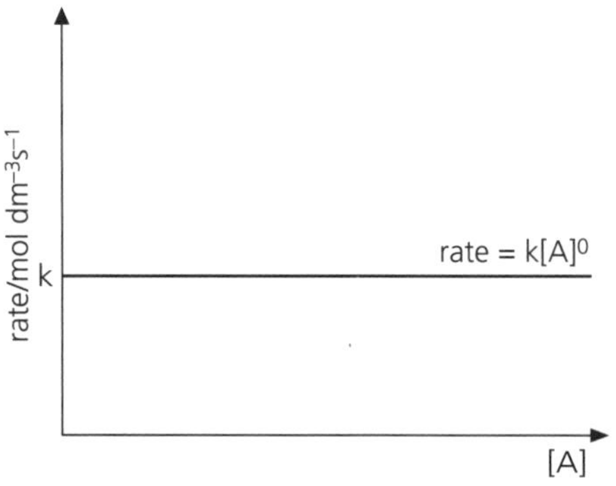

First order reactions (Figure 6.6):

- rate = $k[A]^1$

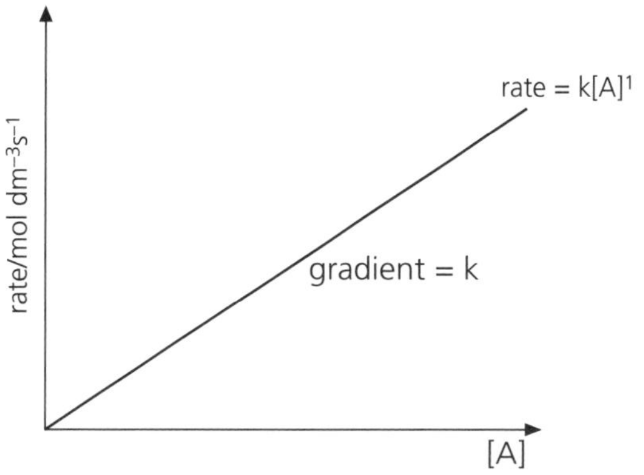

Figure 6.6

Second order reactions (Figure 6.7):

- rate = $k[A]^2$

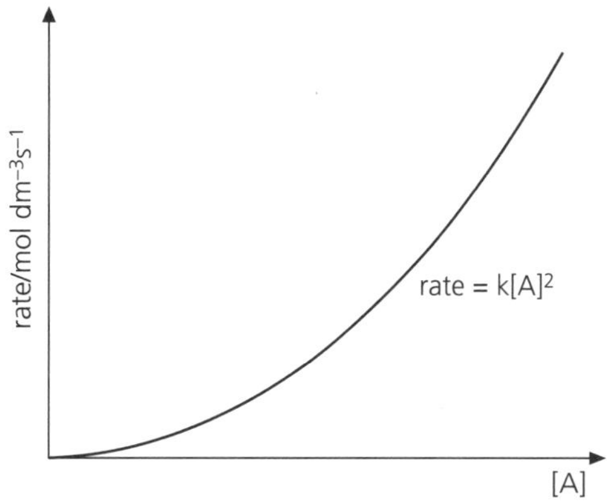

Figure 6.7

Using these graphs, the following points apply:

- **for a zero order reaction, if the concentration of a reactant is multiplied by x, the rate will be unaffected**
- **for a first order reaction, if the concentration of a reactant is multiplied by x, the rate is also multiplied by x**
- **for a second order reaction, if the concentration of a reactant is multiplied by x, the rate is multiplied by x^2**

Practise these types of questions – they are very common.

1.7 Deducing rate equations using initial rates

During a chemical reaction, it is sometimes difficult to know exactly what the concentration is of a particular reactant in order to calculate the rate. For this reason we take initial rates since we know what the concentrations are at the beginning of the reaction. The initial rates are calculated from a graph of the concentration of a reactant against time and a tangent drawn to the graph at time, t = 0. The gradient of this line is equal to the rate at the very start of the reaction.

If the initial rates are known, and the corresponding initial concentrations, the rate equation may be determined.

- **In a reaction between A, B and C, the rates in Table 6.1 were obtained using the initial concentrations shown.**

Experiment	Initial concentrations /mol dm^{-3}			Initial rate /mol dm^{-3} s^{-1}
	[A]	[B]	[C]	
1	0.05	0.03	0.12	1.2×10^{-4}
2	0.20	0.06	0.24	3.84×10^{-3}
3	0.05	0.03	0.24	2.4×10^{-4}
4	0.20	0.03	0.12	1.92×10^{-3}

Table 6.1

In order to determine the orders with respect to the reactants, we need to compare pairs of experiments and deduce the changing concentrations and their effects on the rate.

Comparing experiments 1 and 3: [A] and [B] remain the same but [C] doubles. This doubles the rate, so the order with respect to [C] must be 1.

Comparing experiments 1 and 4: [A] is multiplied by 4 and [B] and [C] stay constant. This multiplies the rate by a factor of 16. The order with respect to [A] must therefore be 2.

Comparing experiments 3 and 2: [A] is multiplied by 4 and [B] multiplied by 2; the [C] stays constant. The rate is increased by a factor of 16. We know that the order with respect to [A] is 2, so multiplying the concentration of [A] by 4 should multiply the rate by 16. But the rate **has** increased by a factor of 16 by comparing experiments 2 and 3. Therefore the change in [B] has no effect on the rate. So, the order with respect to [B] must be 0.

The overall rate equation is therefore: rate = $k[A]^2 [B]^0 [C]^1$. The reaction is third order overall.

The value for the rate constant is calculated using figures from any of the above experiments (1, 2, 3 or 4). Using experiment 1, rate = $k[A]^2 [B]^0 [C]^1$, $1.2 \times 10^{-4} = k(0.05)^2 (0.03)^0 (0.12)^1$. This gives, by rearranging, k as 0.4 and the units will be mol dm^{-3}s^{-1}/(mol dm^{-3})^3, i.e. mol^{-2} dm^6 s^{-1}.

Calculating rate constants from rate equations comes up frequently in examinations.

1.8 The rate-determining step

Many chemical reactions take place in a series of discrete stages or steps. The mechanism for the reaction indicates exactly the species involved in each stage of the reaction. The rate equation yields some important information regarding the reaction mechanism. All orders that are non-zero in the rate equation imply that changing the concentration of those reactants will alter the reaction rate.

The speed of traffic travelling along a road is often determined by the speed of the slowest moving vehicle (the rate-determining step).

The slowest step in the reaction mechanism is the rate-determining step and it controls the overall rate of the process.

Since the concentrations of reactants represented in the rate equation affect the rate, these reactants must also be involved in the rate-determining step.

The reactants in the rate equation are also the reactants participating in the rate-determining (slowest) step of the reaction. Those not involved in the rate equation (any zero-ordered reagents) take place in faster steps.

Consider the reaction between the tertiary halogenoalkane 2-chloro-2-methyl-propane and the attack by hydroxide ions:

2-chloro-2-methylpropane + $:OH^-(aq) \rightarrow$ 2-methylpropan-2-ol + $:Cl^-(aq)$

$$H_3C-\underset{\underset{CH_3}{|}}{\overset{\overset{Cl}{|}}{C}}-CH_3 + :OH^-(aq) \longrightarrow H_3C-\underset{\underset{CH_3}{|}}{\overset{\overset{OH}{|}}{C}}-CH_3 + :Cl^-(aq)$$

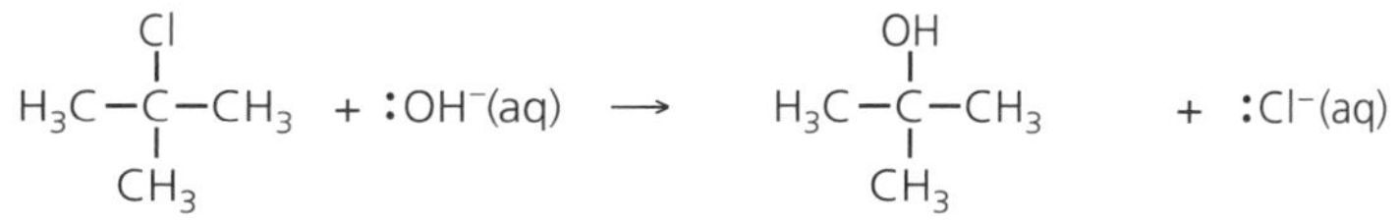

It is found that the rate equation for this reaction is:

rate = [2-chloro-2-methylpropane]1 [OH$^-$(aq)]0

This means that, in this example of a nucleophilic substitution process, a molecule of 2-chloro-2-methylpropane is involved in the rate-determining step but the hydroxide ion is not (since it is zero order, it must be involved in a fast step).

In an organic mechanism, the position of the arrows is very important. The arrows represent the path or movement of a pair of electrons.

The mechanism for this reaction is shown in Figure 6.8.

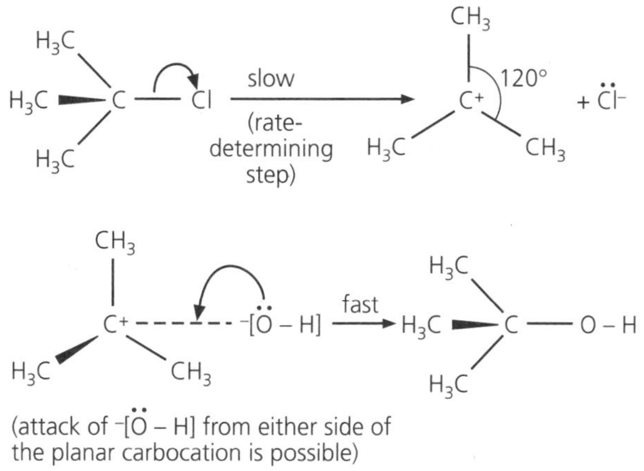

Figure 6.8 Mechanism for the reaction between 2-chloro-2-methylpropane and hydroxide ions

(attack of $^-[\overset{..}{\underset{..}{O}} - H]$ from either side of the planar carbocation is possible)

This mechanism is known as an **S$_N$1** process since it is a **s**ubstitution and involves attack by a **n**ucleophile (the OH$^-$ ion) and there is **1** molecule or species involved in the rate-determining step. There are also S$_N$2 processes and these can take place between primary or secondary halogenoalkanes and nucleophiles.

2 *Temperature*

In all reactions, as temperature is increased, the rate will also increase.

Temperature affects the rate of a reaction by increasing the proportion of molecules over the activation energy much more than the collision frequency.

The rate increases with increasing temperature because:
- the proportion of particles having an energy greater than the **activation energy** barrier increases and therefore the number of successful collisions every second increases
- the collision frequency increases with increasing temperature since there will be a greater number of collisions per second at a higher temperature than a lower one (although not all of these collisions will be successful)

However, the collision frequency only increases slightly with increasing temperature, whereas the proportion of particles with enough kinetic energy to react increases dramatically (see Figure 6.9).

The area bound by the graph and the x-axis is equal to the number of molecules present.

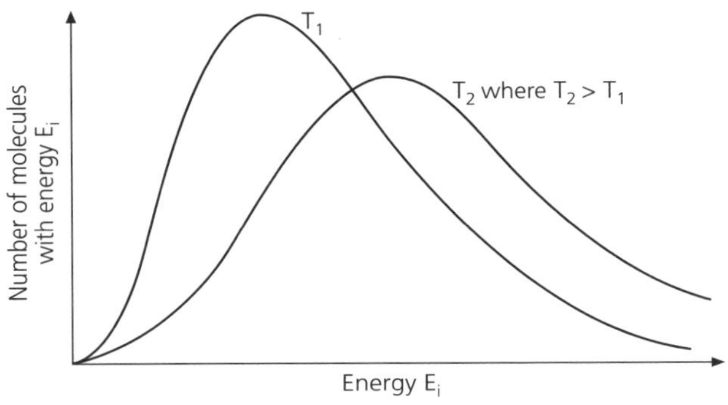

Figure 6.9 Graph of Maxwell–Boltzmann distribution at two different temperatures

The proportion of particles possessing an energy greater than the minimum energy requirement, E_{act}, is proportional to $e^{-(E_{act}/RT)}$. If this factor is multiplied by the total number of collisions (or the concentration of the particles present), then the result is the number of collisions per unit volume, every second, that results in a reaction. This is summarised in the Arrhenius equation:

The rate constant always increases with increasing temperature. However, the higher the activation energy for a process, the more likely it will be affected by an increase in temperature.

$$\mathbf{k = Ae^{-\left(\frac{E_{act}}{RT}\right)}}$$

where k is the rate constant, A is the pre-exponential factor, E_{act} is the activation energy, R is the gas constant ($8.314\,J\,K^{-1}\,mol^{-1}$) and T is the temperature in Kelvin.

The value of the activation energy for a reaction can be deduced from plotting a graph of the natural log of the rate constant on the y-axis against 1/temperature (in K^{-1}) on the x-axis. The gradient will be equal to $-E_{act}/R$.

3 The effect of pressure on gas phase reactions

This is analogous to concentrations of reagents in solutions. It is true that increasing the partial pressure of a gas may increase the rate of a reaction since there are simply a greater number of reactant molecules in a given volume. This increases the number of successful collisions per second (even though the proportion of successful collisions will be the same) as there are more particles in a given volume with the necessary activation energy to react.

4 Catalysis

There are two main types of catalysis, depending on the physical states of the reactants and the catalyst being used.

A catalyst is a chemical substance that increases the rate of a chemical reaction by providing an alternative route for the reaction to proceed with a lower activation energy (see Figure 6.10).

The catalyst, at the end of the reaction, is chemically unchanged (although it may have changed physically).

A catalyst works by increasing both the rates of the forward and the reverse processes equally. The equilibrium composition (see Unit 7), with and without the use of the catalyst, will be identical.

A catalyst does not affect the value for ΔH for a reaction; it will provide a pathway with a higher value for the rate constant (with a lower activation energy); see the Arrhenius equation.

Examples of heterogeneous and homogeneous catalysis are included in Unit 13, Transition metals.

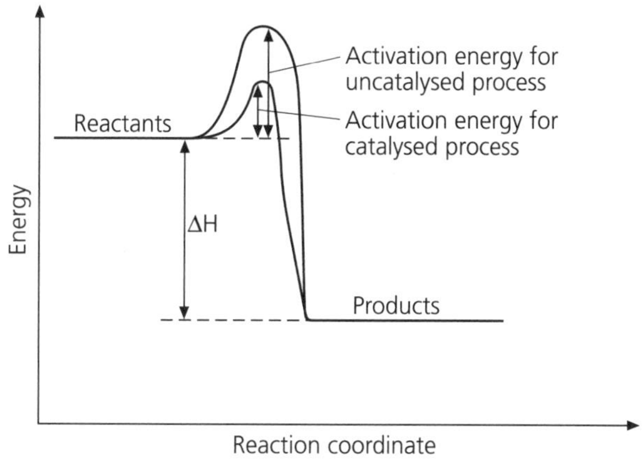

Figure 6.10 Graph showing activation energy lowering due to addition of a catalyst

4.1 Homogeneous catalysis

In homogeneous catalysis, the reactants and the catalyst are in the same physical state.

For example:

- $S_2O_8^{2-}(aq) + 2I^-(aq) \rightarrow 2SO_4^{2-}(aq) + I_2(aq)$ using solutions of iron(II) or iron(III) ions to catalyse the reaction
- $CH_3COCH_3(aq) + I_2(aq) \rightarrow CH_3COCH_2I(aq) + HI(aq)$ using $H_3O^+(aq)$ ions to catalyse the reaction
- $Fe^{3+}(aq) + V^{3+}(aq) \rightarrow Fe^{2+}(aq) + V^{4+}(aq)$ using $Cu^{2+}(aq)$ as the catalyst

The rate equation for this last process is rate = $k[Fe^{3+}(aq)]^1\,[V^{3+}(aq)]^1$, but when copper(II) ions are added, the rate equation becomes rate = $k[V^{3+}(aq)]^1\,[Cu^{2+}(aq)]^1\,[Fe^{3+}(aq)]^0$. The copper(II) ions catalyse the reaction by providing a different reaction pathway with a different reaction mechanism. In the uncatalysed reaction, iron(III) ions and vanadium(III) ions were involved in the rate-determining step but, having added copper(II) ions, vanadium(III) and copper(II) ions appear in the rate-determining step. Iron(III) ions must now be involved in a fast step in the process.

A typical reaction mechanism that explains these results may be:

Step 1 $Cu^{2+}(aq) + V^{3+}(aq) \xrightarrow{\text{slow}} Cu^+(aq) + V^{4+}(aq)$; Cu(II) → Cu(I)
Step 2 $Cu^+(aq) + Fe^{3+}(aq) \xrightarrow{\text{fast}} Cu^{2+}(aq) + Fe^{2+}(aq)$; Cu(I) → Cu(II)

In homogeneous catalysis, the catalyst (normally a transition metal) changes its oxidation state from a higher to a lower and then back up to a higher state (or vice versa). The ability of transition metals to change their oxidation state in this way makes them very efficient catalysts.

In the case of the reaction $S_2O_8^{2-}(aq) + 2I^-(aq) \rightarrow 2SO_4^{2-}(aq) + I_2(aq)$ using $Fe^{2+}(aq)$ or $Fe^{3+}(aq)$ ions to catalyse the reaction, electrode potentials are often useful in predicting what may happen in each stage during the reaction (as it would with the V(III)–Fe(III) reaction above).

$Fe^{3+}(aq) + e^- \rightleftharpoons Fe^{2+}(aq)$ $E^\ominus = +0.77\,V$
$I_2(aq) + 2e^- \rightleftharpoons 2I^-(aq)$ $E^\ominus = +0.54\,V$
$S_2O_8^{2-}(aq) + 2e^- \rightleftharpoons 2SO_4^{2-}(aq)$ $E^\ominus = +2.01\,V$

The reaction $S_2O_8^{2-}(aq) + 2I^-(aq) \rightleftharpoons 2SO_4^{2-}(aq) + I_2(aq)$ is normally slow since two negative ions need to interact to form the transition state. If iron(II) ions are added, the following processes take place more quickly because oppositely charged ions interact at each stage.

Step 1:

$S_2O_8^{2-}(aq) + 2e^- \rightleftharpoons 2SO_4^{2-}(aq)$ $E^\ominus = +2.01\,V$

$Fe^{2+}(aq) \rightleftharpoons Fe^{3+}(aq) + e^-$ $E^\ominus = -0.77\,V$

Adding gives: $2Fe^{2+}(aq) + S_2O_8^{2-}(aq) \rightleftharpoons 2SO_4^{2-}(aq) + 2Fe^{3+}(aq)$
where $E^\ominus = +2.01 + (-0.77) = +1.24\,V$

Step 2:

$Fe^{3+}(aq) + e^- \rightleftharpoons Fe^{2+}(aq)$ $E^\ominus = +0.77\,V$

$2I^-(aq) \rightleftharpoons I_2(aq) + 2e^-$ $E^\ominus = -0.54\,V$

Adding gives: $2Fe^{3+}(aq) + 2I^-(aq) \rightleftharpoons 2Fe^{2+}(aq) + I_2(aq)$
where $E^\ominus = +0.77 + (-0.54) = +0.23\,V$

Electrode potentials can be useful for explaining the mechanism for homogeneous redox processes.

Note how iron(III) may also be used as a catalyst in this process, although the pairs of reactions involved are the opposite to those above.

4.2 Heterogeneous catalysis

In heterogeneous catalysis, the reactants and the catalyst are in different physical states.

The following industrial processes are all examples using heterogenous catalysts to increase the rate at which equilibrium is reached:

- $N_2(g) + 3H_2(g) \rightleftharpoons 2NH_3(g)$ using iron metal as the catalyst
- $4NH_3(g) + 5O_2(g) \rightleftharpoons 4NO(g) + 6H_2O(l)$ using platinum (and rhodium) as the catalyst
- $2SO_2(g) + O_2(g) \rightleftharpoons 2SO_3(g)$ using solid vanadium(V) oxide

Heterogeneous processes involving gases and solid catalysts involve chemical processes taking place on the surface of a metal.

The catalyst used in this process acts by providing a surface on which the reactant molecules may form sufficiently strong bonds to enable weakening of the atom–atom bonds within the reactant molecule(s). The effect of this process is to create reactive atoms or radicals on the surface of the catalyst that may then react with other reactive species to form new products.

The process occurs in four main stages described below and shown in Figure 6.11.

The concentration of reactive atoms on the metal surface is high. This causes a rapid reaction.

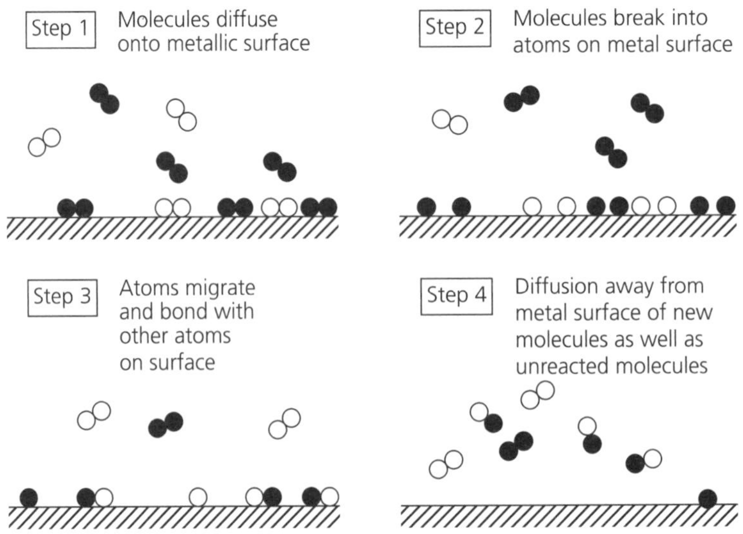
Step 1
Molecules diffuse onto metallic surface
Step 2
Molecules break into atoms on metal surface
Step 3
Atoms migrate and bond with other atoms on surface
Step 4
Diffusion away from metal surface of new molecules as well as unreacted molecules

***Figure 6.11* Four stages in a heterogeneous catalytic process on the surface of a metal**

Metallic silver bonds too weakly with many molecules (reactants and products), whereas tungsten bonds too strongly; neither of these two metals acts as an efficient catalyst. An intermediate adsorption strength is required for metals to be efficient catalysts in many cases.

Step 1
Adsorption of the reactant molecules onto the surface of the catalyst.

Step 2
The reaction occurs on the surface of the catalyst. The catalyst absorbs the reactant molecules onto its surface and this process weakens the bonds holding the atoms together, increasing the tendency for molecules to break apart.

Step 3
Atoms migrate over the surface of the metal and, as they do so, they 'bump' into other atoms and bond to form new fragments and then complete molecules.

Step 4
Desorption of the reactants or products from the surface. The rate of this desorption depends on the strength of the bonds between the reactant or product molecules and the surface of the metal: the stronger the bonds, the lower the rate of desorption.

UNIT 7 Chemical equilibria

At the end of this unit, you should be familiar with:

- reversible reactions
- factors affecting chemical equilibria
- the Equilibrium Law
- the quantification of the effect of temperature on the equilibrium constant

A Reversible reactions

The variation of the concentration with time is determined by the order with respect to each reactant. However, the important issue here is that the concentrations of reactants fall and those of the products increase to a limiting value.

A reaction will not attain equilibrium if matter is allowed to escape into the surroundings or matter enters the reaction. We say that a reaction may only attain equilibrium if it is closed.

Even though the reaction does not appear to be changing when at equilibrium, the forward and reverse processes are still continuing but at the same rate. Various radioactive isotopes can be used to 'trace' substances in the reaction and thereby determine whether product and reactants are still being interconverted when dynamic equilibrium is attained.

Many reactions are called reversible reactions since they may proceed from reactants to products or from products to reactants. If we study the general reversible reaction A + B $\rightleftarrows$ C + D and we measure the concentration of one of the reactants and one of the products versus time, a graph similar to that shown in Figure 7.1 may be produced.

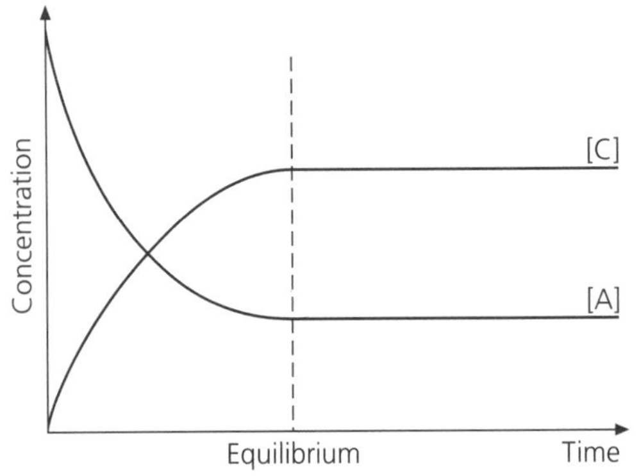

Figure 7.1 Graph of concentration of A and C versus time starting with reactants (the left-hand side of the equation: A + B → C + D)

- Since this reaction is reversible, when C and D are produced from A and B, they may react to form A and B again using the reverse reaction.
- After a certain time, the concentrations of all reactants and products remain constant.
- The concentration of the reactants never falls to zero.

It also follows that if the **rates** of the forward reaction and the reverse reaction are plotted against time, the graph in Figure 7.2 may be obtained.

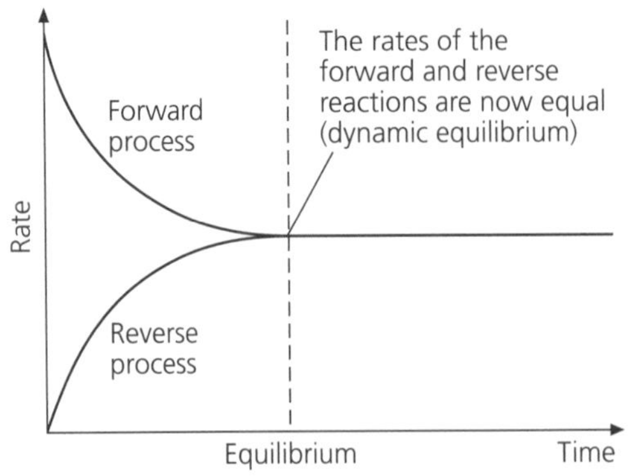

Figure 7.2 Graph of rate against time for the reverse and forward directions starting with reactants (the left-hand side of the equation: A + B → C + D)

Dynamic equilibrium is the state in a reversible reaction in which the forward and reverse reactions are occurring at the same rate.

When the reaction has achieved a state of dynamic equilibrium, we also say that the reaction has come to chemical equilibrium.

B Factors affecting chemical equilibrium

There are other ways of stating this principle, although some can be very elaborate and difficult to remember.

Le Chatelier's principle is used to predict the effect of changing conditions on a reaction when at equilibrium.

- **Le Chatelier's principle:**
  When a change is imposed on an equilibrium system, the system reacts in such a way as to oppose the change.

Since the forward reaction is exothermic, an increase in temperature will favour the reverse endothermic process. When pressure is increased, the side of the equation with the fewer molecules will be favoured. This lowers the pressure.

Once a reaction has attained a state of equilibrium, there are ways of affecting the relative amount of reactants and products in a reaction. If the reaction tends to produce, as a result of some external change, a greater number of moles of product and less reactant, the reaction's equilibrium position has moved or shifted to the right-hand side. Similarly, if, as a result of changing external conditions, the reactions shift to produce a greater number of moles of reactant and less product, the reaction's equilibrium position has moved or shifted to the left-hand side. A summary of the effect of changing the various external conditions is given in Table 7.1, using the Haber process for the production of ammonia, $N_2(g) + 3H_2(g) \rightleftharpoons 2NH_3(g)$, as an example. For this reaction, $\Delta H^{\ominus} = -46.2\,kJ/mol$.

Table 7.1

<table>
<tr><th>Changing factor</th><th>Effect on the equilibrium position</th><th>Effect on rate of forward and reverse reaction</th></tr>
<tr><td>Adding a greater number of moles of:
(a) nitrogen
(b) ammonia at constant volume</td><td>(a) more ammonia produced (left to right)
(b) more nitrogen and hydrogen produced (right to left)</td><td>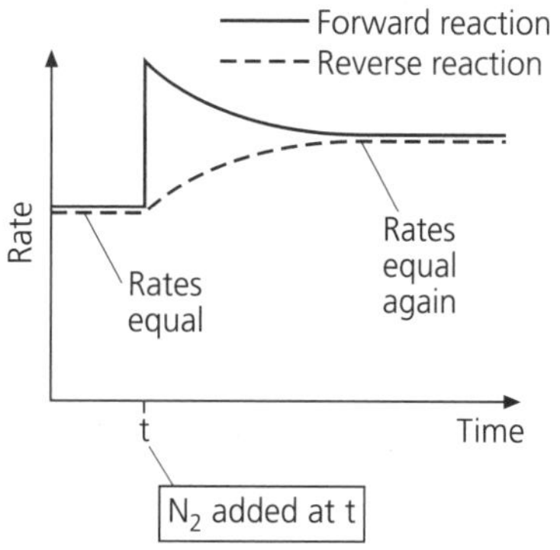

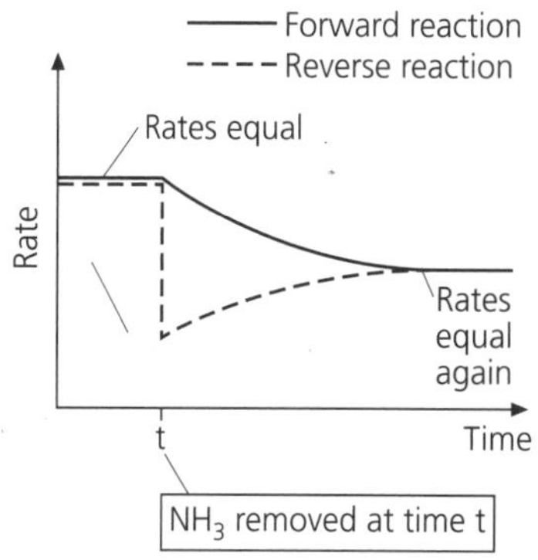
</td></tr>
<tr><td>Temperature changes:
(a) increasing
(b) decreasing</td><td>(a) less ammonia forms (right to left)
(b) more ammonia forms (left to right)</td><td>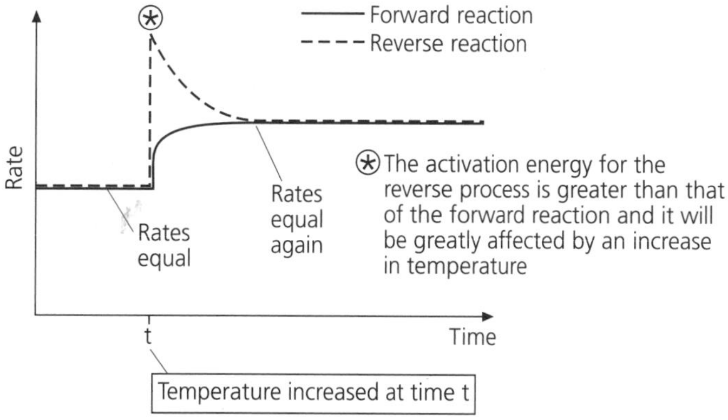
</td></tr>
</table>

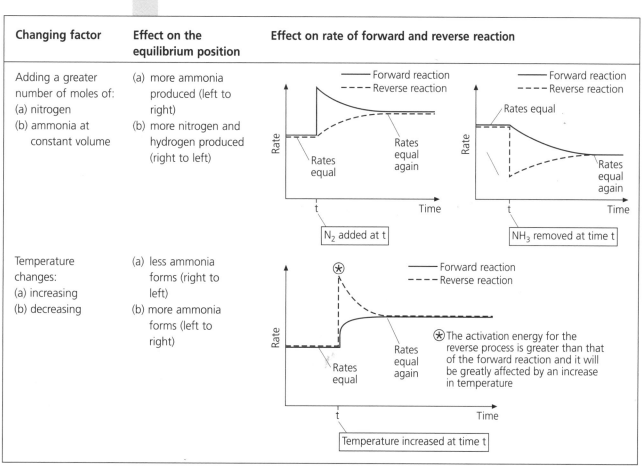

Pressure changes (at constant temperature): (a) increasing (b) decreasing	(a) more ammonia forms (left to right) (b) less ammonia forms (right to left)	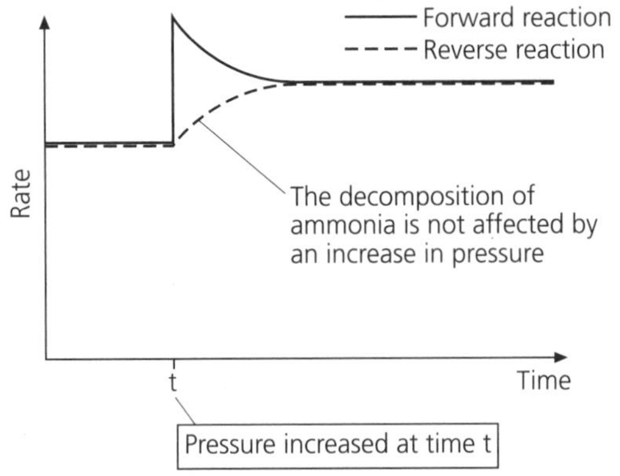
Catalysts	No effect, but the **rate** at which the same equilibrium mixture is produced increases to the same extent	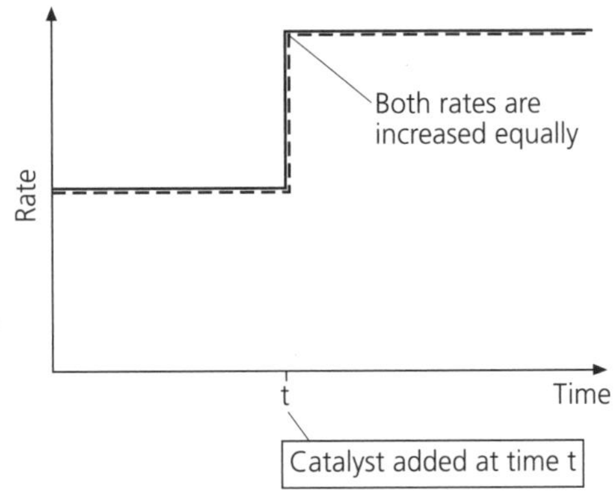

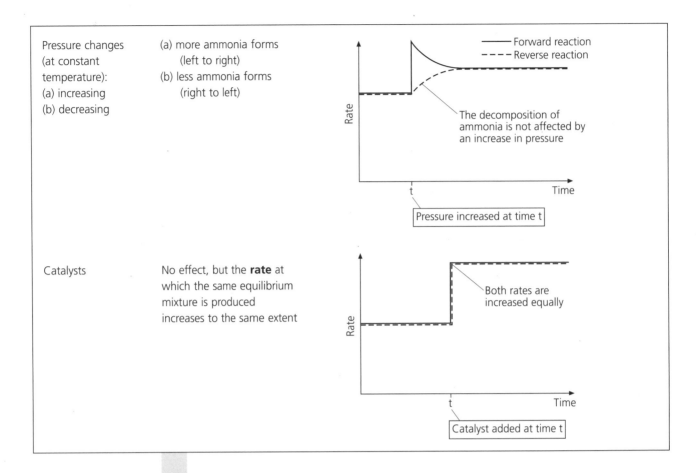

C The Equilibrium Law

For all reactions that form equilibrium mixtures, there is a relationship between the concentrations of the reactants and the products measured at equilibrium. This is stated in the Equilibrium Law.

For the general reaction: aA + bB + ... $\rightleftharpoons$ cC + dD + ...

The equilibrium constant, $K_c = \dfrac{[C]^c \times [D]^d \times ...}{[A]^a \times [B]^b \times ...}$

These brackets must be drawn as square brackets and not curved brackets.

- The square brackets represent **concentrations** of substances and not just numbers of moles. Therefore, the volume in which the substances exist needs to be known in order to calculate the concentration. The substances may be either dissolved in solutions, liquids dissolved in other liquids or gases mixed with other gases.
- Concentration is normally measured in mol/dm^3 or mol dm^{-3}.
- K_c is not affected by changes in concentration, pressure, surface area or the presence of a catalyst; only changes in temperature affect K_c.
- The equilibrium law is only true if concentrations are measured at equilibrium.
- Substances that are in huge excess at the beginning of the reaction will not change their concentration significantly during the course of the reaction and so their concentration is assumed to be constant. This concentration is normally absorbed into the value of K_c. An important example of a substance **never** to be included is water when it is being used as a solvent. However,

when it is a reactant, as in the hydrolysis of an ester, e.g. ethyl ethanoate, it should be included.

- Pure solids and liquids, whose concentrations do not change in the course of the reaction, are omitted from the expression for K_c.
- For equilibria involving gases, the equilibrium constant, K_p, is defined. Here the concentrations of reactants are given as the partial pressures (see section C.3).
- The larger the value for K_c, the greater is the proportion of products compared to reactants at equilibrium. If K_c is small, reactants predominate; if K_c is large, products predominate in the equilibrium mixture.

Table 7.2 summarises the effect of changing external conditions on the equilibrium constant, $K_{c(p)}$, and the equilibrium position.

Factor being changed	Effect on equilibrium constant K_c or K_p and the equilibrium position	
Temperature	Forward reaction **Exothermic:**	**Increasing** temperature **decreases** $K_{c(p)}$: product → reactant shift **Decreasing** temperature **increases** $K_{c(p)}$: reactant → product shift
	Forward reaction **Endothermic:**	**Increasing** temperature **increases** $K_{c(p)}$: reactant → product shift **Decreasing** temperature **decreases** $K_{c(p)}$: product → reactant shift
Concentration Pressure Surface area Catalyst presence	$K_{c(p)}$ remains constant on changing these factors, although the **rate** at which equilibrium is attained is affected	

Table 7.2

To make calculations easier in deducing the units for K_c, let 'c' represent the units of $mol\,dm^{-3}$.

Power rules: $c^A \times c^B = c^{(A+B)}$, $\frac{c^A}{c^B} = c^{(A-B)}$, $(c^A)^B = c^{(A \times B)}$. Remember your GCSE mathematics.

Water in this process is in large excess; its concentration is 'absorbed' into the constant side of the equation.

1 Example reactions and equilibrium constant, K_c, expressions

1.1 Homogeneous equilibria (reactants and products in the same physical state)

- **The industrial manufacture of ammonia, NH_3**

$N_2(g) + 3H_2(g) \rightleftharpoons 2NH_3(g)$

nitrogen gas + hydrogen gas ⇌ ammonia gas

$$K_c = \frac{[NH_3(g)]^2}{[N_2(g)][H_2(g)]^3} \quad \text{units: } \frac{c^2}{c \times c^3} = \frac{1}{c^2} = c^{-2} = (mol\,dm^{-3})^{-2} = mol^{-2}\,dm^6$$

- **The dissociation of the weak acid, methanoic acid, HCOOH**

$HCOOH(aq) + H_2O(l) \rightleftharpoons HCOO^-(aq) + H_3O^+(aq)$

methanoic acid + water ⇌ methanoate ions + hydroxonium ion

$$K_c = \frac{[HCOO^-(aq)][H_3O^+(aq)]}{[HCOOH(aq)]} \quad \text{units: } \frac{c \times c}{c} = c = mol\,dm^{-3}$$

Remember the rule: do not include solids, pure liquids and solvents in the expression for K_c.

Solid lead and lead(IV) oxide involved in this reaction are pure solids: their concentration therefore remains constant.

1.2 Heterogeneous equilibria (reactants and products in different physical states)

- **The dissolving of the sparingly soluble salt lead(II) sulphate, $PbSO_4(s)$, in water**

  $PbSO_4(s) + H_2O(l) \rightleftharpoons Pb^{2+}(aq) + SO_4^{2-}(aq)$

  lead(II) sulphate + water $\rightleftharpoons$ lead(II) ions + sulphate ions

  $K_c = [Pb^{2+}(aq)][SO_4^{2-}(aq)]$ units: $c \times c = c^2$ or $(mol\,dm^{-3})^2$, that is $mol^2\,dm^{-6}$

- **The reaction between water vapour and heated lead**

  $Pb(s) + 2H_2O(g) \rightleftharpoons PbO_2(s) + 2H_2(g)$

  lead + gaseous water $\rightleftharpoons$ lead(IV)oxide + hydrogen

  $$K_c = \frac{[H_2(g)]^2}{[H_2O(g)]^2} \qquad \text{units} = \frac{c^2}{c^2} = 1\text{, that is units cancel; no units}$$

2 *Calculations involving the equilibrium constant, K_c*

Remember to convert equilibrium quantities into concentrations in $mol\,dm^{-3}$ before substituting values into the expression for K_c.

2.1 Calculating K_c from equilibrium concentrations

- **Calculate K_c for the reaction:**

  $N_2O_4(g) \rightleftharpoons 2NO_2(g)$ given that the equilibrium concentrations of $N_2O_4(g)$ and $NO_2(g)$ are $1.2\,mol\,dm^{-3}$ and $0.25\,mol\,dm^{-3}$ respectively.

  $$K_c = \frac{[NO_2(g)]^2}{[N_2O_4(g)]} = \frac{(0.25)^2}{1.2} = \mathbf{0.0521 \text{ and the units are } mol\,dm^{-3}}$$

- **Calculate the value for K_c for the reaction:**

  $N_2(g) + 3H_2(g) \rightleftharpoons 2NH_3(g)$ given that the total volume of the container is $5\,dm^3$ and the number of moles of nitrogen, hydrogen and ammonia measured at equilibrium are 0.012, 0.036 and 0.34 respectively.

  The concentrations are: $[NH_3(g)] = 0.34/5\,mol\,dm^{-3}$, $[N_2(g)] = 0.012/5\,mol\,dm^{-3}$ and $[H_2(g)] = 0.036/5\,mol\,dm^{-3}$.

  $$K_c = \frac{[NH_2(g)]^2}{[N_2(g)][H_2(g)]^3} \text{ gives } \frac{(0.34/5)^2}{(0.012/5) \times (0.036/5)^3} = \frac{4.624 \times 10^{-3}}{8.958 \times 10^{-10}}$$

  $$= \mathbf{5.16 \times 10^6\ mol^{-2}\,dm^6}$$

2.2 Deducing whether a reaction is at equilibrium or not

Consider the reaction $2SO_2(g) + O_2(g) \rightleftharpoons 2SO_3(g)$.

K_c is equal to $10\,mol^{-1}dm^3$ at a certain temperature. The following concentrations were found in a mixture: $[SO_2(g)] = 2\,mol\,dm^{-3}$, $[O_2(g)] = 3\,mol\,dm^{-3}$ and $[SO_3(g)] = 5\,mol\,dm^{-3}$.

- **Is the reaction at equilibrium or not? If not, what change is predicted to occur to the reaction in order to attain a state of equilibrium?**

  $$K_c = \frac{[SO_3(g)]^2}{[SO_2(g)]^2[O_2(g)]} \text{ gives } \frac{(5)^2}{(2)^2 \times 3} = 2.08\,mol\,dm^{-3}$$

This is obviously not equal to $10moldm^{-3}$, which is the recognised equilibrium constant, so the reaction is not at equilibrium yet. In order to attain equilibrium, the reaction must produce more moles of SO_3 and remove some of the SO_2

and O_2 moles. Therefore, the reaction will move from the left to the right-hand side until the value of $10 mol^{-1} dm^3$ is produced. The reaction is then at equilibrium.

2.3 Calculating K_c given the number of moles of one of the substances at equilibrium

In the reaction $N_2O_2(g) \rightleftharpoons 2NO(g)$, 1 mole of $N_2O_2(g)$ was allowed to react and at equilibrium it was found that 0.15 moles of $N_2O_2(g)$ remained.

- **Calculate K_c given the total volume of the container is $10\,dm^3$**

Write down the reaction:	$N_2O_2(g) \quad \rightleftharpoons$	$2NO(g)$
Write down what you know about the starting moles:	1	0
Moles at equilibrium:	$1 - x$	$2x$
But the number of moles of N_2O_2 is 0.15, so:	$1 - x = 0.15$	$x = 0.85$ moles
Therefore at equilibrium:	0.15 moles	2×0.85 moles
What about the concentrations?	0.15/10	1.70/10

Substituting into the expression for K_c gives

$$K_c = \frac{[NO(g)]^2}{[N_2O_2(g)]} \text{ gives } \frac{(0.17)^2}{0.015} = \mathbf{1.927\ mol\ dm^{-3}}$$

Remember to lay your calculation out clearly so the examiner can award you appropriately even if you do not get the correct answer.

2.4 Calculating equilibrium concentrations using K_c when no equilibrium concentrations are known

- **$CH_3COOH(l) + CH_3CH_2OH(l) \rightleftharpoons CH_3CO_2C_2H_5(l) + H_2O(l)$**

Given that the value for K_c for this reaction is 4 (no units), **calculate the number of moles** of each substance measured at equilibrium when 3 moles of ethanol and 3 moles of ethanoic acid are mixed and then allowed to come to equilibrium.

Writing underneath each formula in the reaction:

	$CH_3COOH(l)$ +	$CH_3CH_2OH(l) \rightleftharpoons$	$CH_3CO_2C_2H_5(l)$ +	$H_2O(l)$
Starting moles:	3	3	0	0
Moles at equilibrium:	$3 - x$	$3 - x$	x	x
Let total volume be equal to V. Concentration:	$(3 - x)/V$	$(3 - x)/V$	x/V	x/V

It must be realised that it is equilibrium concentration that must be entered into the expression for K_c and not number of moles alone. Show this step in calculations even if you can see that the total volumes will eventually cancel.

$$K_c = \frac{[CH_3CO_2C_2H_5(l)][H_2O(l)]}{[CH_3COOH(l)][CH_3CH_2OH(l)]} = \frac{x/V \times x/V}{(3 - x)/V \times (3 - x)/V}$$

the Vs cancel here leaving: $x^2/(3 - x)^2 = 4$.

At this stage, take the square root of both sides and consider the positive root only in this case (the negative root, i.e. $x = -2$, gives negative starting amounts when substituted back into the original expression).

$x/(3 - x) = 2$, therefore $x = 2(3 - x) = 6 - 2x$.
Rearranging gives: $3x = 6$, therefore $x = 2$.
Substituting back into the original terms for x.

	$CH_3COOH(l)$ +	$CH_3CH_2OH(l)$ ⇌	$CH_3CO_2C_2H_5(l)$ +	$H_2O(l)$
Starting moles:	3	3	0	0
Moles at equilibrium:	3 – x	3 – x	x	x
but x = 2:	3 – 2	3 – 2	2	2
or:	1	1	2	2

K_c is unaffected when the concentrations are changed as long as the concentrations in the expression for K_c are measured at equilibrium.

So, at equilibrium, there are 2 moles each of ethyl ethanoate and water and 1 mole each of ethanol and ethanoic acid. Notice how K_c is still 4.

- **A helpful mathematical hint:**

	aA	+	bB	⇌	cC	+	dD
In the general reaction:	aA	+	bB	⇌	cC	+	dD
Starting moles:	X		Y		0		0
Moles at equilibrium:	X – ax		Y – bx		0 + cx		0 + dx

That is: **the number of moles at equilibrium = starting number of moles – (the stoichiometric number in the chemical equation multiplied by x) or, in symbolic form, X – ax or Y – bx and so on.**

For example, in the reaction between two molecules of aluminium chloride, $AlCl_3(g)$, forming the dimer, $Al_2Cl_6(g)$ (starting with, say, 0.25 moles of $AlCl_3$):

Write the balanced equation:	$2AlCl_3(g)$	⇌	$Al_2Cl_6(g)$
Starting moles:	0.25		0
Moles at equilibrium:	0.25 – 2x		x

Then the equilibrium amounts are related to a value we are given and x and then K_c calculated.

The point here is not to fall at the first hurdle.

Most students find these calculations very difficult, so do practise them.

3 *The equilibrium constant, K_p*

It is more convenient with gases to measure their partial pressures rather than their concentration.

The partial pressure, p, of a gas = $\frac{\text{number of moles of gas}}{\text{total number of moles}}$ × total pressure

or $p_a = x_a P_{total}$

where

p_a is the partial pressure of the gas

x_a is the mole fraction of the gas

P_{total} is the total pressure

3.1 Writing expressions for K_p

The method of writing these expressions is the same as for the K_c expressions except that you must not use square brackets – curved brackets are used for partial pressures.
For K_c: square brackets.
For K_p: curved brackets.

For the reaction $N_2(g) + 3H_2(g) \rightleftharpoons 2NH_3(g)$,

$$K_p = \frac{p^2(NH_3(g))}{p(N_2(g)) \times p^3(H_2(g))}$$

Units will be $(atm)^2/(atm \times atm^3) = atm^{-2}$

All partial pressures being measured at equilibrium.

3.2 Calculations involving K_p

- **Calculate the value of K_p for the reaction given that the number of moles at equilibrium of $N_2(g)$ = 1.2, $H_2(g)$ = 0.4 and $NH_3(g)$ = 2.3 and the total pressure is 6 atmospheres.**
  Calculate the partial pressures for each component.

Total number of moles = 1.2 + 0.4 + 2.3 = 3.9 moles

	$pH_2(g)$	$pN_2(g)$	$pNH_3(g)$
Mole fractions:	0.4/3.9	1.2/3.9	2.3/3.9
Partial pressures:	(0.4/3.9) × 6	(1.2/3.9) × 6	(2.3/3.9) × 6
	0.615 atm	1.846 atm	3.538 atm

Substituting into the expression for K_p:

$$K_p = \frac{p^2(NH_3(g))}{p(N_2(g)) \times p^3(H_2(g))} = \frac{(3.538)^2}{1.846 \times (0.615)^3} = \mathbf{29.151\ atm^{-2}}$$

- **Calculate the value for K_p from the following information: 1 mole of hydrogen and 3 moles of nitrogen are mixed and allowed to come to equilibrium at 250 atmospheres. It is found, on analysing the reaction mixture, that 0.33 moles of hydrogen remain.**

Write the balanced equation:	$N_2(g)$	+	$3H_2(g)$	$\rightleftharpoons$	$2NH_3(g)$
Starting moles:	1		3		0
Moles left at equilibrium:	1 – x		3 – 3x		2x

But the number of moles of hydrogen remaining is 0.33 and we know that the number of moles of nitrogen must be a third of this figure (they are mixed originally in the ratio 3 : 1 respectively).

Therefore, there must be 0.11 moles of nitrogen. Using the expression above, it can be seen that for nitrogen, the number of moles at equilibrium is 1 – x but 1 – x is equal to 0.11.

Therefore, if 1 – x = 0.11, x = 1 – 0.11 = 0.89 moles. The number of moles of ammonia, 2x, is equal to 2 × 0.89 = 1.78 moles.

Total number of moles = 0.11 + 0.33 + 1.78 = 2.22 moles

	N_2	H_2	NH_3
Calculate the mole fractions:	0.11/2.22	0.33/2.22	1.78/2.22
Convert to partial pressures:	250 × (0.11/2.22)	(0.33/2.22) × 250	(1.78/2.22) × 250
	12.387 atm	37.162 atm	200.450 atm

Substituting into the expression for K_p gives:

$$K_p = \frac{p^2NH_3(g)}{p(N_2(g)) \times p^3(H_2(g))} = \frac{(200.450)^2}{12.387 \times (37.162)^3} = \mathbf{0.0632\ atm^{-2}}$$

Alternatively, if the number of moles of hydrogen is 0.33 mol, then 3 – 3x = 0.33 and so x = 0.89 moles. Substituting into the other equilibrium amounts for nitrogen and ammonia gives their respective values as 0.11 moles and 1.78 moles. Then the procedure is the same as in the rest of this worked example.

Many students confuse K_c and K_p calculations. Although the start of each calculation is similar, K_p calculations must include the total number of moles present, the mole fractions and the partial pressures.

D The quantification of the effect of temperature on the equilibrium constant

On relating the two equations for $\Delta G^{\ominus}$, that is:

$\Delta G^{\ominus} = \Delta H^{\ominus} - T\Delta S^{\ominus}$ and $\Delta G^{\ominus} = -RT\ln K$, we produce:

$\Delta H^{\ominus} - T\Delta S^{\ominus} = -RT\ln K$ where K could be either K_c or K_p.

Therefore, making lnK the subject gives:

$\ln K = \Delta S^{\ominus}/R - \Delta H^{\ominus}/RT$.

So, if a graph is plotted of lnK on the y-axis versus 1/T (where the temperature is measured in Kelvin), a straight line is obtained of gradient $-\Delta H^{\ominus}/R$ and the intercept on the y-axis is $\Delta S^{\ominus}/R$. Figure 7.3 shows the type of straight line relationship expected for (a) an exothermic reaction and (b) an endothermic reaction.

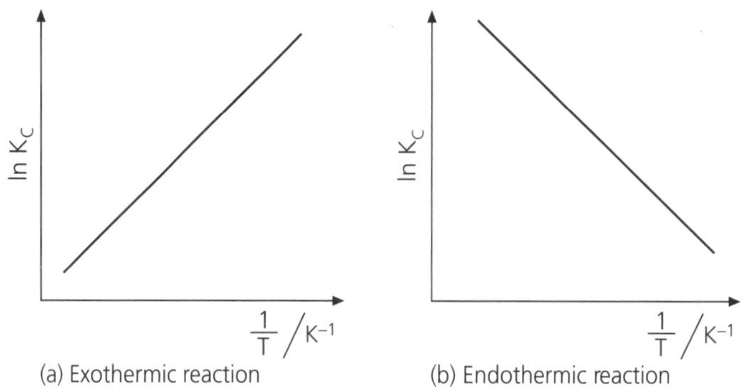

Figure 7.3
Graphs to show the relationship between the reciprocal of temperature and ln K_c for exothermic and endothermic reactions

- The **sign** of the gradient in each case is determined by the sign of the enthalpy change (it will be positive for exothermic reactions and negative for endothermic reactions) since the gradient of the line is equal to $-\Delta H^{\ominus}/R$.
- For exothermic reactions, it can be seen that on increasing temperature, 1/T decreases and lnK becomes smaller. In other words, an increase in temperature reduces the equilibrium constant. This means that there is a greater proportion of reactants and less product in the equilibrium mixture as the temperature increases (Le Chatelier's principle also predicts this – see section B). The opposite is true for the effect of temperature on endothermic reactions. The influence of temperature on the value for K_p for two reactions is shown in Table 7.3.

Table 7.3

(a) An exothermic reaction: $N_2(g) + 3H_2(g) \rightleftharpoons 2NH_3(g)$

T/K	K_p/atm^{-2}	
400	1.0×10^{2}	
500	1.6×10^{-1}	K_p gets smaller with increasing temperature
600	3.1×10^{-3}	
700	6.3×10^{-5}	

(b) An endothermic reaction: $N_2O_4(g) \rightleftharpoons 2NO_2(g)$

T/K	K_p/atm	
275	2.2×10^{-2}	
350	4.5	K_p gets larger with increasing temperature
500	1.5×10^{3}	

For an exothermic process, increasing the temperature results in a shift from the products to the reactants and so K_c or K_p decreases (the opposite is true for an endothermic process).

You should be able to plot a graph of the natural log or (ln) of the equilibrium constant (lnK) versus the reciprocal of temperature (1/T) and use it to determine the value for $\Delta H^{\ominus}$ or $\Delta S^{\ominus}$.

UNIT 8 Acid–base equilibria

At the end of this unit, you should be familiar with:

- the Brønsted–Lowry definitions of acids and bases
- strong acids and bases
- the quantities pH, pOH and pK_w
- the ionic product of water, K_w
- the acid dissociation constant, K_a
- the base dissociation constant, K_b
- salt hydrolysis
- pH titration curves
- indicators
- buffers

A The Brønsted–Lowry definitions of acids and bases

A Brønsted–Lowry acid is a proton donor in solution whereas a Brønsted–Lowry base is a proton acceptor.

1 *Conjugate acid–base processes*

Conjugate acid–base pairs differ by possession of a proton, e.g. NH_3 (base) and NH_4^+(conjugate acid) or CH_3COOH (acid) and CH_3COO^- (conjugate base).

When an acid donates a proton to a base, the acid then becomes its own corresponding conjugate base. Also, when a base accepts a proton, it transforms into the corresponding conjugate acid. Note that a conjugate acid is related to its base only by a proton transfer and, of course, this is the same for the conjugate base and its acid.

For example, ammonia (NH_3) is a base (since it can accept a proton) to form the conjugate acid; the ammonium ion (NH_4^+). Likewise, methanoic acid, HCOOH, donates a proton to form its conjugate base, the methanoate ion, $HCOO^-$.

2 *Examples of acid–base reactions*

It must be indicated which are the pairs of the substances being considered; it is a common mistake for students to omit the pairing of an acid with its conjugate base and vice versa. Use the number '1' or '2' to pair up the respective species, e.g. acid '1' goes to conjugate base '1', etc.

Underneath each substance is indicated the relevant acid–base pairs.

$CH_3COOH(aq)$	+	$HNO_3(aq)$	$\rightleftharpoons$	$CH_3COOH_2^+(aq)$	+	$NO_3^-(aq)$
base 1		acid 2		conjugate acid 1		conjugate base 2
$H_2SO_4(aq)$	+	$H_2O(l)$	$\rightleftharpoons$	$HSO_4^-(aq)$	+	$H_3O^+(aq)$
acid 1		base 2		conjugate base 1		conjugate acid 2
$CH_3NH_2(aq)$	+	$H_2O(aq)$	$\rightleftharpoons$	$CH_3NH_3^+(aq)$	+	$OH^-(aq)$
base 1		acid 2		conjugate acid 1		conjugate base 2

Water can either behave as a base (proton acceptor), to form the hydroxonium ion H_3O^+, or as an acid, by donating a proton, to form OH^-. Water is said to be **amphoteric**, since it can either donate or accept a proton, and therefore possesses both acid and base properties. The hydrogen sulphate ion, $HSO_4^-(aq)$, can do the same.

B Strong and weak acids and bases

- **A strong acid or base dissociates completely in solution.**

Hydrochloric acid, HCl(aq), is viewed as undergoing complete dissociation in solution. In other words, **all** of the molecular hydrogen chloride, HCl, once dissolved in water dissociates completely according to the equation:

$HCl(aq) + H_2O(l) \rightarrow H_3O^+(aq) + Cl^-(aq)$

Hydrochloric acid is called a monobasic acid since **1 mole** of the acid reacts with **1 mole** of base:

$H_3O^+(aq) + OH^-(aq) \rightarrow 2H_2O(l)$

Sulphuric(VI) acid is a dibasic acid since **1 mole** of acid reacts with **2 moles** of base, e.g.

$H_2SO_4 + 2NaOH \rightarrow Na_2SO_4 + 2H_2O$

Hydrochloric acid, HCl(aq), nitric(V) acid, $HNO_3(aq)$, and sulphuric(VI) acid, $H_2SO_4(aq)$, are common strong acids.

It is also useful to consider weak acids and bases in terms of the strengths of their respective conjugate bases and acids. Generally, it is true to say that a strong acid gives rise to a weak conjugate base whereas a weak acid gives rise to a strong conjugate base.

Strong bases like sodium hydroxide dissolve completely in water and are fully ionised or completely dissociated to form hydroxide ions, $OH^-(aq)$. Strong bases usually involve the oxides or hydroxides of metals, in particular those metal oxides and hydroxides found in Group I of the Periodic Table. Ammonia gas, NH_3, when in solution also exhibits basic properties, but it is a weak base.

- **A soluble base is called an alkali.**
- **Weak acids and bases involve partial dissociation in solution.**

Weak acids and bases interact with water molecules to form equilibrium mixtures.

In these equilibria, the equilibrium position lies on the left-hand side, that is reactants are favoured over products.

The weak base ammonia:

$NH_3(aq) + H_2O(l) \rightleftharpoons NH_4^+(aq) + OH^-(aq)$

or with the weak acid ethanoic acid:

$CH_3COOH(aq) + H_2O(aq) \rightleftharpoons CH_3COO^-(aq) + H_3O^+(aq).$

Note that these two solutions (a weak acid and base) contain primarily molecules of NH_3 or CH_3COOH. Very slight reaction may occur with water according to the above equations. Therefore, strong acids and bases conduct electricity more effectively than weak acids and bases since the former contain a greater concentration of ions whereas the latter consist mainly of neutral molecules that cannot carry the electrical charge.

Examples of **weak** acids are:
ethanoic acid, CH_3COOH
phosphoric(V) acid, H_3PO_4
ethanedioic acid, $(COOH)_2$
methanoic acid, HCOOH
and carbonic acid, H_2CO_3.

Examples of **weak bases** include:
ammonia and other amines.

C The quantities pH and pOH

You should familiarise yourself with the '$\log_{10}$' and 'antilog_{10}' or '10^x' function on the calculator that you will use in the examination. Calculators often vary in the sequencing in which the information is typed.

- **pH is defined mathematically as $pH = -\log_{10} [H_3O^+(aq)]$**

by rearrangement: $[H_3O^+(aq)] = \text{antilog}_{10}(-pH)$

The relationship between the concentration of hydrogen ion and pH is shown in Table 8.1.

Table 8.1

$[H_3O^+(aq)]/mol\,dm^{-3}$	10^{-14}	10^{-12}	10^{-10}	10^{-8}	10^{-6}	10^{-4}	10^{-2}	10^{0}
pH	14	12	10	8	6	4	2	0

It is also useful to define a term that corresponds to the hydroxide ion concentration. This is called pOH and it is defined in a similar mathematical fashion:

- **$pOH = -\log_{10} [OH^-(aq)]$**

D The ionic product of water, K_w

Pure water is a very poor electrical conductor, indicating that very few mobile ions are present. However, it is important to realise that there are measurable, minute quantities of both hydrogen ions and hydroxide ions present. Water dissociates as follows:

$H_2O(l) \rightleftharpoons H^+(aq) + OH^-(aq)$

or as:

$2H_2O(l) \rightleftharpoons H_3O^+(aq) + OH^-(aq)$

We can write an expression for K_c for this process, making sure that it is realised that water, in the molecular form, is in massive excess so its concentration will not change significantly. All of the constant terms are then moved onto the left-hand side of the equation giving an overall constant called K_w ('w' is for water).

- **$K_w = [H_3O^+(aq)]\,[OH^-(aq)]$** or **$K_w = [H^+(aq)]\,[OH^-(aq)]$**

K_w has units of $mol^2\,dm^{-6}$ and K_w is called the ionic product of water.

It is also true that: **$pK_w = -\log_{10}(K_w)$**

The value for K_w depends, as with all equilibrium constants, on temperature, and at 298 K its value is 10^{-14} $mol^2\,dm^{-6}$. As the temperature increases, so does K_w. This indicates that the dissociation of water is an endothermic process. As temperature increases, so does $[H_3O^+(aq)]$ and $[OH^-(aq)]$, so the products, K_w, must also increase in magnitude.

We may also derive the following important relationships:

- **pH + pOH = pK_w and since K_w = 10^{-14} $mol^2 dm^{-6}$ (at 298 K), pK_w = 14**
- **pH + pOH = 14**
- **$[H_3O^+(aq)]$ = $[OH^-(aq)]$ = 10^{-7} mol dm^{-3} in pure water at 298 K**
- **a solution in which $[H_3O^+(aq)]$ is equal to $[OH^-(aq)]$ is termed neutral**

The term 'neutral' does not mean a solution of pH7; it only means that the concentrations of hydrogen ions and hydroxide ions are equal.

It must be realised that pH + pOH only equals 14 at 298 K. As the temperature is increased, so too does K_w, so pK_w will decrease. At 373 K, K_w = 5.13×10^{-13} $mol^2 dm^{-6}$; this gives pK_w as 12.29 so pH + pOH = 12.29 at 373 K. This means that the concentrations of both the hydrogen ions and the hydroxide ions are $\sqrt{(5.13 \times 10^{-13})} = 7.16 \times 10^{-7}$M. The pH of water at 373 K is therefore $-\log_{10}(7.16 \times 10^{-7}) = 6.14$ (the pOH is also equal to 6.14) at 373 K.

1 *Calculating the pH of solutions containing strong acids or bases*

Calculate the pH of the following solutions:

- **0.1 mol dm^{-3} sulphuric(VI) acid, $H_2SO_4(aq)$**
  pH = $-\log_{10}[H_3O^+(aq)]$
  = $-\log_{10}(0.1 \times 2)$ = **0.699**

- **1.2×10^{-3} mol dm^{-3} sodium hydroxide solution, NaOH(aq)**
  pOH = $-\log_{10}[OH^-(aq)]$
  = $-\log_{10}(1.2 \times 10^{-3})$ = 2.921
  so, 2.921 + pH = 14, therefore pH = **11.079**

Calculate the concentrations of the hydrogen ion and the hydroxide ion in the following solutions:

- **hydrochloric acid, HCl(aq) of pH = 1**
  pH = $-\log_{10}[H_3O^+(aq)]$
  1 = $-\log_{10}[H_3O^+(aq)]$
  −1 = $\log_{10}[H_3O^+(aq)]$
  therefore, $\text{antilog}_{10}(-1)$ = 0.1
  so, $[H_3O^+(aq)]$ = **0.1 mol dm^{-3}**
  pOH = 14 − 1 = 13
  $[OH^-(aq)]$ = $\text{antilog}_{10}(-13)$ = **10^{-13} mol dm^{-3}**

- **0.23 mol dm^{-3} calcium hydroxide solution, $Ca(OH)_2(aq)$**
  $[OH^-(aq)]$ = **2 × 0.23** = **0.46 mol dm^{-3}**
  This figure gives pOH as 0.337
  so, pH = 14 − 0.337 = 13.663
  therefore, $[H_3O^+(aq)]$ = $\text{antilog}_{10}(-13.663)$
  = **2.173×10^{-14} mol dm^{-3}**

Calculate the pH of a solution formed when 25 cm^3 of 0.1 mol dm^{-3} hydrochloric acid is added to 24.7 cm^3 of 0.1 mol dm^{-3} sodium hydroxide solution.

- Moles of hydrogen ions in the HCl = 25/1000 × 0.1 = 0.0025 moles.
  Moles of hydroxide ions in the NaOH = 24.7/1000 × 0.1 = 0.00247 moles.

Since H^+ ion and OH^- ion react in a 1 : 1 ratio, the excess hydrogen ions in moles will be 0.0025 – 0.00247 = 3×10^{-5} moles.
This number of moles is present in (25 + 24.7) cm^3 of solution.
In moles per dm^3, the concentration is $3 \times 10^{-5} \times 1000/49.7$ = 6.04×10^{-4} mol dm^{-3}.
The pH will then be pH = $-\log_{10} (6.04 \times 10^{-4})$ = **3.22**

pH calculations of the type involving acids reacting with bases in a 1 : 1 ratio, e.g. HCl and NaOH, as well as in a 1 : 2 ratio, e.g. H_2SO_4 and NaOH, are fairly common.

To avoid problems in calculating the reagent in excess as well as the amount in excess, work in terms of number of moles of H^+ for the acid and OH^- for the base.

- **For example:**
  If 20 cm^3 of 0.1 mol dm^{-3} H_2SO_4 reacts with 40.1 cm^3 of 0.1 mol dm^{-3} NaOH and you are asked to calculate the pH of the resulting solution, then calculate the number of moles of H^+ and OH^- first:
  moles H^+ ions = $20/1000 \times 0.1 \times \underline{2}$ (from the H_2SO_4) = 0.004 moles
  and moles of OH^- ions = $40.1/1000 \times 0.1$ = 0.00401 moles
  then the excess is OH^- at 0.00401 – 0.004 = 1×10^{-5} moles in 60.1 cm^3
  (H^+ react with OH^- in a simple 1 : 1 ratio)
  the $[OH^-(aq)]$ = $1000/60.1 \times 1 \times 10^{-5}$ = 1.66×10^{-4} mol dm^{-3}
  this gives pOH as 3.78 and **pH as 10.22**.

1.1 Mathematical advice

Given the hydrogen ion concentration, many students would be able to calculate the corresponding pH by using pH = $-\log_{10}[H_3O^+(aq)]$. If, however, students are asked to calculate the hydrogen ion concentration for a given pH, more problems are often encountered.

Remember, if pH = $-\log_{10}[H_3O^+(aq)]$, then $[H_3O^+(aq)]$ = antilog$_{10}$ (–pH).

The unfamiliarity regarding how this is typed into the calculator causes some problems.

Practise the interconversion: pH → $[H_3O^+(aq)]$; many students are let down by lack of practice and use their calculators incorrectly.

Most calculators will be manipulated in the following way.

- Given the pH = 6.72, what is the value for $[H_3O^+(aq)]$?
  $[H_3O^+(aq)]$ = [10^x] [6] [.] [7] [2] [+/–] [=]
  The display should read 1.905^{-07} which is $1.905 \times \mathbf{10^{-7}}$ mol dm^{-3} (**not** 1.905^{-7}).

E The weak acid dissociation constant, K_a

An acid with the general formula, HA, will dissociate in water according to the equilibrium:

$HA(aq) + H_2O(l) \rightleftharpoons A^-(aq) + H_3O^+(aq)$

An equilibrium constant expression, involving K_a, may be written:

$$K_a = \frac{[A^-(aq)]\,[H_3O^+(aq)]}{[HA(aq)]}$$

K_a has units of mol dm^{-3} in this particular dissociation.

Taking logarithms to the base 10 and multiplying by -1 gives:

$pK_a = -\log_{10}(K_a)$ or, making K_a the subject, **$K_a = \text{antilog}_{10}(-pK_a)$**

Note the similarity of the mathematical forms of the equations $pH = -\log_{10}[H_3O^+(aq)]$ and $pK_a = -\log_{10}(K_a)$. The prefix 'p' normally infers the mathematical function '$-\log_{10}$...'

In **stronger acids**, more dissociation occurs so that the concentration of $H_3O^+(aq)$ and $A^-(aq)$ will be higher. This makes **K_a larger** and **pK_a smaller**, and vice versa for weaker acids.

1 *Calculating the pH for solutions of weak acids*

Given the starting concentration of an acid and the pK_a or K_a value, it is possible to calculate the pH of the resulting solution.

- **Calculate the pH of a solution of butanoic acid, $CH_3(CH_2)_2COOH$, of concentration 0.2 mol dm^{-3} (pK_a for butanoic acid is 4.82).**

Write the relevant equilibrium reaction:

	$CH_3(CH_2)_2COOH(aq)$	+ $H_2O(l)$ ⇌	$CH_3(CH_2)_2COO^-(aq)$	+ $H_3O^+(aq)$
Starting moles:	0.2	excess	0	0
Moles at equilibrium:	0.2 − x	excess	x	x
Concentration at equilibrium per dm^3 of solution:	(0.2 − x)/1	excess	x/1	x/1

Given that $pK_a = 4.82$, to find out the value of K_a we use $K_a = \text{antilog}_{10}(-pK_a)$. So, $K_a = \text{antilog}_{10}(-4.82) = 1.513 \times 10^{-5}$ mol dm^{-3}.

The expression for the dissociation constant

$$K_a = \frac{[CH_3(CH_2)_2COO^-(aq)]\,[H_3O^+(aq)]}{[CH_3(CH_2)_2COOH(aq)]}$$

Never put water into this expression – examiners will not forgive you if you do!

Substituting the values we know gives $1.513 \times 10^{-5} = \dfrac{x^2}{0.2 - x}$

At this stage, we can produce a quadratic equation that we solve for x. Two roots will result and the positive root is the value for x or the concentration of hydrogen ions.

However, we are able to make an assumption that we must state:

If, $1.513 \times 10^{-5} = \dfrac{x^2}{0.2 - x}$ then $1.513 \times 10^{-5} = \dfrac{x^2}{0.2}$

Remember the simplification: if the acid is a weak acid, the degree of dissociation is slight compared to the starting number of moles. This means that 0.2 – x is very close to 0.2. This simplifies the mathematics. You must state this simplification.

Making x^2 the subject of this equation gives: $x^2 = 1.513 \times 10^{-5} \times 0.2$
So, $x = \sqrt{(1.513 \times 10^{-5} \times 0.2)} = 1.740 \times 10^{-3}$ mol dm^{-3}
This is equal to the hydrogen ion concentration, $[H_3O^+(aq)]$
Therefore, $pH = -\log_{10}(1.740 \times 10^{-3}) = \mathbf{2.759}$

You must also be able to work backwards from the pH to the value of K_a or pK_a.

- **Given the pH of a solution of concentration 0.15 mol dm^{-3} is 5.38, calculate K_a for the acid.**

If the pH is 5.38, then it should be straightforward to calculate the corresponding hydrogen ion concentration using:

$$[H_3O^+(aq)] = \text{antilog}_{10}(-pH) = \text{antilog}_{10}(-5.38) = 4.169 \times 10^{-6}\ \text{mol dm}^{-3}$$

In these types of responses in which a structured answer is required, lay out your calculation very clearly so that the examiner can follow your working. If one of these questions carries 3 marks, 1 mark is normally for the answer and 2 are for clear and easy-to-follow working.

Writing the dissociation for the reaction in general terms gives:

	$HA(aq)$ +	$H_2O(l)$ ⇌	$A^-(aq)$ +	$H_3O^+(aq)$
Starting moles:	0.15	excess	0	0
Moles at equilibrium:	0.15 – x	excess	x	x
Concentration at equilibrium per dm^3 of solution:	(0.15 – x)/1	excess	x/1	x/1

But we know that the concentration of hydrogen ions at equilibrium, x, is 4.169×10^{-6} mol dm^{-3} (this is the value for x).

Substituting the known values gives:

$$K_a = \frac{[A^-(aq)]\,[H_3O^+(aq)]}{[HA(aq)]} \quad \text{then } K_a = \frac{x^2}{0.15 - x} = \frac{(4.169 \times 10^{-6})^2}{(0.15 - 4.169 \times 10^{-6})}$$

Note that the denominator of the fraction is very close to 0.15 (see earlier approximation).

So, $K_a = 1.158 \times 10^{-10}$ mol dm^{-3} or $pK_a = -\log_{10}(K_a)$

$= -\log_{10}(1.158 \times 10^{-10}) = \mathbf{9.936}$

F The weak base dissociation constant, K_b

A base, B, will interact with water molecules by accepting a proton from the water molecule in a reversible process in which the hydroxide ion is formed as well as the relatively strong conjugate acid of the base, $BH^+(aq)$.

Again, water is omitted from the expression since its concentration is constant.

$$\mathbf{B(aq) + H_2O(l) \rightleftharpoons BH^+(aq) + OH^-(aq)}$$

$$\textbf{and } K_b = \frac{[BH^+(aq)][OH^-(aq)]}{[B(aq)]} \quad \textbf{units} = \textbf{mol dm}^{-3}$$

$$\textbf{and } pK_b = -\log_{10}(K_b)$$

For example, using methyl amine, CH_3NH_2, and its protonation by water molecules:

$$CH_3NH_2(aq) + H_2O(l) \rightleftharpoons CH_3NH_3^+(aq) + OH^-(aq)$$

$$\text{and } K_b = \frac{[CH_3NH_3^+(aq)][OH^-(aq)]}{[CH_3NH_2(aq)]}$$

Compare the rules regarding strength of bases with K_b and pK_b with those for acids, i.e. K_a and pK_a; they are identical but in different contexts.

The stronger the base, the greater is the value of K_b and the lower the value for pK_b.

$K_w = K_a \times K_b$

Taking $\log_{10}$ of both sides of this equation and multiplying by −1 gives:

$pK_w = pK_a + pK_b$

where pK_w = **14 at 298 K**

1 *Examples of calculations involving weak bases in solution*

Some data books will quote this value for ammonia in terms of the dissociation constant for the conjugate acid: the ammonium ion. In this case, calculate $14 - pK_a$ to deduce the pK_b value for the base.

- **What is the pH of a solution of ammonia of concentration 0.45 mol dm^{-3}? The acid dissociation constant, pKa, for the ammonium ion, $NH_4^+(aq)$, is 9.25.**

Write down the relevant equation for the dissociation of ammonia in water:

$NH_3(aq) + H_2O(l) \rightleftharpoons NH_4^+(aq) + OH^-(aq)$

The equation, as written, refers to ammonia acting as a base.

The pK_b for this process is calculated using $pK_a + pK_b = 14$
or $9.25 + pK_b = 14$, so $pK_b = 4.75$

We also know that:
$pK_b = -\log_{10}(K_b)$, so, $K_b = \text{antilog}_{10}(-4.75) = 1.778 \times 10^{-5}\,\text{mol dm}^{-3}$.

Given the value for K_b, we can now calculate a value for the pH of the ammonia solution.

	$NH_3(aq)$	+ $H_2O(l)$	$\rightleftharpoons NH_4^+(aq)$	+ $OH^-(aq)$
Starting concentration/mol dm^{-3}:	0.45	excess	0	0
Equilibrium concentration/mol dm^{-3}:	0.45 − x	excess	x	x

Substituting into the expression:

$$K_b = \frac{[NH_4^+(aq)][OH^-(aq)]}{[NH_3(aq)]} \text{ gives: } \frac{x^2}{(0.45 - x)} = 1.778 \times 10^{-5}$$

Assuming that $0.45 \gg x$ gives $x^2 = \dfrac{1.778 \times 10^{-5}}{0.45}$

Solving for x gives x as $2.829 \times 10^{-3}\,\text{mol dm}^{-3}$.

x refers to the concentration of hydroxide ions,
so, $pOH = -\log_{10}[OH^-(aq)] = -\log_{10}(2.829 \times 10^{-3}) = 2.55$
Using $pH + pOH = 14$, the pH of the solution is therefore $14 - 2.55 =$ **11.45**

Always ask yourself whether this answer is reasonable for a weak base.

G Salt hydrolysis

When a salt is added to water, the ions separate from the lattice structure and they may be **hydrated** by water molecules. In a hydration process, water molecules surround the respective ions so that the slightly positive hydrogen

Stronger interactions will take place between ligands, like water molecules and transition metal ions. These cations are often more highly polarising and they have vacant d-orbitals that may be occupied by electrons from ligands (this would make the bonding stronger).

Solutions containing the ammonium ion (a strong conjugate acid) tend to be acidic because the ammonium ion donates a proton to a water molecule, forming acidic $H_3O^+(aq)$ ions.

atoms in the water molecule are pointing towards the negative ions (anions) and the slightly negatively charged oxygen atoms in the water molecule (and their lone pairs of electrons) are pointing towards the positive ions (cations). In general, hydration of this type involves a **weak interaction** between ions and the dipoles within the water molecule.

It is also possible with some ions that are regarded as being either strong conjugate acids or bases for **hydrolysis** to take place in which the water molecule is forced to dissociate. For example, the ethanoate ion (a strong conjugate base), CH_3COO^-, may interact with a water molecule by accepting a proton and leaving residual hydroxide ions:

$$CH_3COO^-(aq) + H_2O(l) \rightleftharpoons CH_3COOH(aq) + OH^-(aq)$$

Such a solution will be alkaline since residual hydroxide ions will be present. Such processes are said to involve **salt hydrolysis**.

- **Calculate the pH of a 0.5 M solution of the salt sodium ethanoate, $CH_3COO^-Na^+$ (pK_a for ethanoic acid is 4.25)**

The pH of the solution will be dependent on the basic nature of the ethanoate ions rather than the sodium ion. Sodium ions only **weakly interact** with water molecules and do not affect the hydrogen ion concentration within the solution.

If pK_a for ethanoic acid is 4.25, then pK_b for the ethanoate ion (the process being considered) is:

$14 - 4.25 = 9.75$, so $K_b = \text{antilog}_{10}(-9.75) = 1.79 \times 10^{-10}\,\text{mol dm}^{-3}$

Salt hydrolysis:	$CH_3COO^-(aq)$ +	$H_2O(l) \rightleftharpoons$	$CH_3COOH(aq)$ +	$OH^-(aq)$
Starting concentration/mol dm^{-3}:	0.5	excess	0	0
Equilibrium concentration/mol dm^{-3}:	0.5 – x	excess	x	x

$$K_b = \frac{[CH_3COOH(aq)][OH^-(aq)]}{[CH_3COO^-(aq)]} = 1.79 \times 10^{-10}\,\text{mol dm}^{-3}$$

substituting in gives $1.79 \times 10^{-10} = x^2$

and assuming that $0.5 \gg x$ gives $1.79 \times 10^{-10} = \dfrac{x^2}{0.5}$

Solving for x gives 9.429×10^{-6} mol dm^{-3}. This is equal to the hydroxide ion concentration.

Therefore, $pOH = -\log_{10}(9.429 \times 10^{-6}) = 5.03$ and so $pH = 14 - 4.78 =$ **9.22**

H pH titration curves

Titration curves form a well-trodden line of questioning in examinations in all types of question paper. Know them well!

A titration curve is a measurement of the recorded pH in a solution (on the y-axis) and volume of base added (on the x-axis).

There are four main types of titration curve, as shown in Figure 8.1 (overleaf).

When dibasic acids (acids that possess two available protons) are titrated with a base, two equivalence points are obtained. The first equivalence point would take place when one of the protons from the acid has reacted completely with the base, whereas the second equivalence point would occur when all of the available (both) protons have combined with the hydroxide ions.

- **Strong acid–strong base**
  e.g. hydrochloric acid and sodium hydroxide solution

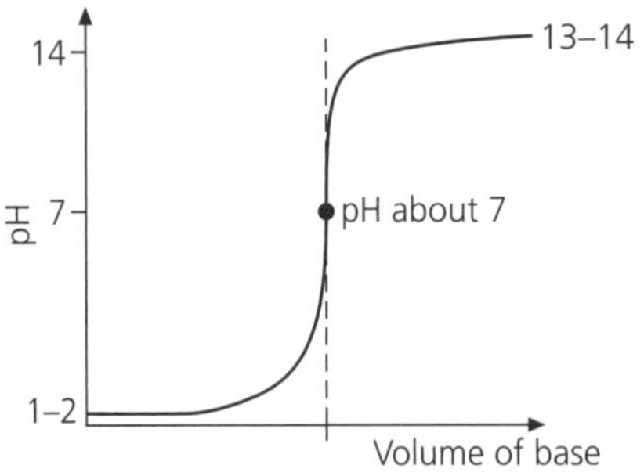

- **Weak acid–strong base**
  e.g. ethanoic acid and sodium hydroxide solution

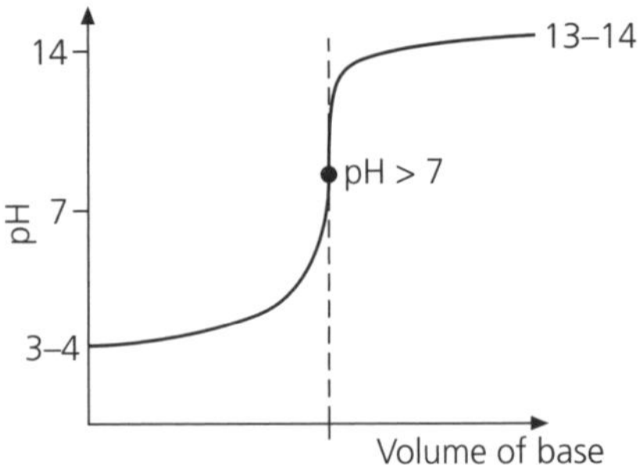

- **Strong acid–weak base**
  e.g. sulphuric(VI) acid and ammonia solution

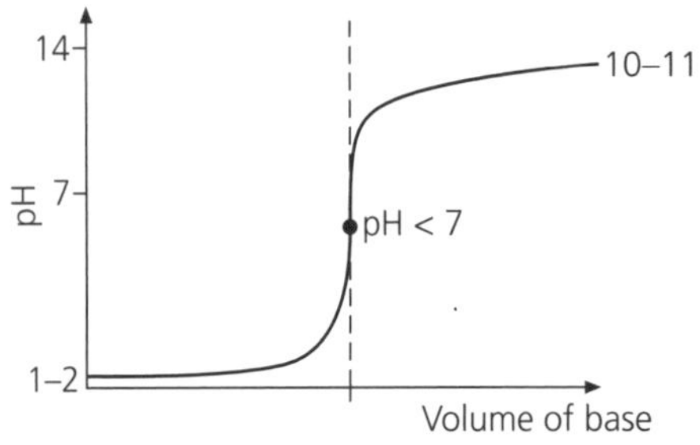

- **Weak acid–weak base**
  e.g. ethanoic acid and ammonia solution

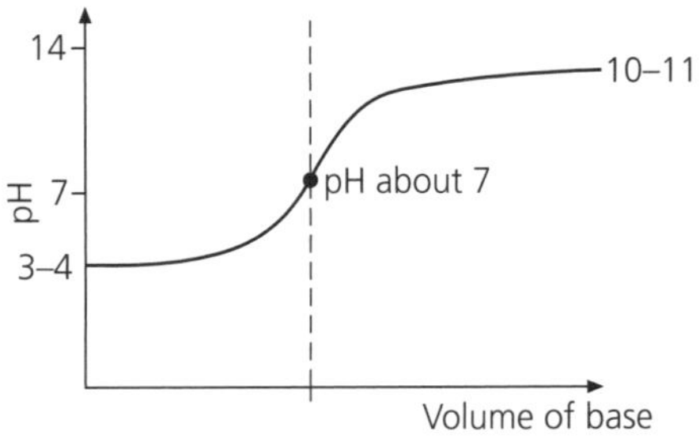

Figure 8.1

Note the following points about the titration curves:

- The starting pH and final pH are predictable from the strength of the acid and base being used.
- The pH remains virtually constant while the base is added and then the pH changes dramatically as equivalence is approached. The pH reaches a plateau in the excess alkaline region.
- The regions on the graph in which the pH remains approximately constant are called **buffer regions**.
- When the base reacts exactly with the measured amount of acid, we call this point the equivalence point. Its pH depends on the acid and base nature of the components in the solution formed at the equivalence point (see Table 8.2).

The pH of a solution of a salt depends on the acid or base nature of the ions in solution and how they interact with water molecules. This process is called salt hydrolysis (see above).

Table 8.2

Type	pH	Example
strong acid–strong base	about 7	sodium chloride solution
strong acid–weak base	lower than 7	ammonium chloride
weak acid–strong base	greater than 7	sodium ethanoate solution
weak acid–weak base	about 7	ammonium ethanoate

- If sodium hydroxide solution of concentration $0.5\,mol\,dm^{-3}$ is added to hydrochloric acid of the same concentration, the pH at the end point, about 7, will be the pH of a solution of sodium chloride of concentration $0.5/2\,mol\,dm^{-3}$. This is because, at the equivalence point, the sodium chloride formed is in twice the volume of solution compared with the original acid and base concentration.

Indicators

Indicators are substances that are either weak acids or weak bases. The relative concentrations of the acid and base forms of the indicators, and therefore the perceived colour of the indicator in solution, are dependent on the pH of the solution.

During an acid–base titration, we normally add only a few drops of the indicator. This is because the indicator has acid–base properties and will affect the titrated volume if too much is added.

If we represent the indicator as HIn (a weak acid), this could dissociate in water as an ordinary acid would be expected to behave when in solution:

$HIn(aq) + H_2O(l) \rightleftharpoons In^-(aq) + H_3O^+(aq)$

If the acid and conjugate base forms are of a different colour, then the pH of the solution will affect the colour that we see:

$HIn(aq) + H_2O(l) \rightleftharpoons In^-(aq) + H_3O^+(aq)$
colour A colour B

On 'lowering the pH', the pH falls to a smaller numerical value, e.g. pH 7 → 3.

- In acid solution, or on lowering the pH, the equilibrium will shift (using Le Chatelier's principle) to the left-hand side, producing more of the unionised or undissociated acid, and we will therefore see colour A in solution.
- If base is added, $OH^-(aq)$ ions react with the $H_3O^+(aq)$ base to form water. The equilibrium shifts to the right-hand side to produce more hydrogen ions (and maintain the same value for the equilibrium constant), and hence colour B is seen for the indicator.
- If the acid form of the indicator is red and the basic form is yellow, the point at which equal amounts of the basic and acid form are present will be perceived as orange.

- **When does an indicator change colour from one form to the other?**

For the reaction: $HIn(aq) + H_2O(l) \rightleftharpoons In^-(aq) + H_3O^+(aq)$, we can write down that:

$$K_{ind} = \frac{[In^-(aq)]\,[H_3O^+(aq)]}{[HIn(aq)]}$$

When the values of $[In^-(aq)]$ and $[HIn(aq)]$ are equal, $K_{ind} = [H_3O^+(aq)]$.

Taking log to the base 10 and multiplying both sides by −1 gives:

$\mathbf{pK_{ind} = pH}$

This is only true when the concentrations of both forms of the indicator are equal.

At this stage, you will have come across the terms pH, pOH, pK_w, K_w, K_a, pK_a, K_b, pK_b and now K_{ind} and pK_{ind}. Make sure that you can distinguish between these terms and, more particularly, the situations in which they are of use.

However, human eyesight will actually detect a colour change, on average, when one form of the indicator is ten times the concentration of the other and vice versa.

So, the colour change will start to be detected when the concentration of the base form is ten times the concentration of the acid form:

$$K_{ind} = \frac{(10 \times [In^-(aq)]\,[H_3O^+(aq)])}{[HIn(aq)]}$$

The different coloured forms will be in equal proportions when the following is true:

$K_{ind} = [H_3O^+(aq)]$, i.e. $[In^-(aq)] = [HIn(aq)]$

and when the acid form is producing a perceived colour change when the following is true:

$$K_{ind} = \frac{[In^-(aq)]\,[H_3O^+(aq)]}{(10 \times [HIn(aq)])}$$

Taking log to the base 10 of both sides puts a 1 on either side of the pK_{ind} value and this is the **pH range** over which you perceive the coloured forms changing.

For this reason, indicator pK_{ind} values are quoted together with **pH ranges** over which the indicator is perceived to be operating:

indicator pH range = $pK_{ind} \pm 1$

1 Choice of indicator for a titration

The choice of indicator depends on the pH at the equivalence point in the titration.

Indicators are themselves weak acids or bases and the relative concentrations of their acid–base pairs depend on the pH of the solution.

Do not choose an indicator that changes colour at too low a pH, i.e. before the equivalence point, or too high a pH, i.e. after the equivalence point. The point is that an indicator should be seen to be changing colour when the pH changes most dramatically (± 1pH unit of equivalence point). The point at which the indicator changes colour is referred to as the **end point** for the titration and this should be the same as the pH at the equivalence point for the acid–base process taking place.

1.1 Choice of indicators

The indicators that would be of use in common acid–base titrations are shown in Table 8.3.

There is more than one choice of an indicator for a titration. As long as the indicator changes colour over a dramatic pH change, it should be adequate.

Strength of acid and base	pH at equivalence point	Choice of indicator
strong acid–strong base:	pH about 7	phenolphthalein (8.3–10.0) bromothymol blue (6.0–7.6)
strong acid–weak base:	pH lower than 7	methyl orange (3.1–4.4) bromophenol blue (3.0–4.6) bromocresol green (3.8–5.4)
weak acid–strong base:	pH greater than 7	phenolphthalein (8.3–10.0) thymolphthalein (9.3–10.5)
weak acid–weak base:	pH about 7	no indicator suitable

Table 8.3

J Buffers

Buffer solutions are defined as solutions that resist a change in pH on adding small amounts of either acid or base.

This is true when only small amounts of acid or base are added.

Buffers exist as one of two main types according to their components:

- **Acid buffers:** a mixture of a weak acid and a solution of the strong conjugate base. The pH of the buffer solution is less than 7.
- **Basic buffers:** a mixture of a weak base and a solution of the strong conjugate acid. The pH of the buffer solution is greater than 7.

The pH at which a buffer operates most effectively depends on the pK_a of the acidic component present. Table 8.4 summarises two of the main types of buffer with an example that you must know, as well as the active components in the buffer solution. Note that for a buffer to operate well when base or acid is added, it is crucial that a mixture containing a **large** reservoir of both the base and acid forms is present.

pH range of buffer	Example of buffer solution	Active components in the mixture
4–6 Acid buffer	**A mixture of ethanoic acid and sodium ethanoate solution**	The weak acid, ethanoic acid, CH_3COOH (pK_a = 4.76), and the relatively strong conjugate base, the ethanoate ion, CH_3COO^-
8–10 Base buffer	**A mixture of ammonia solution and ammonium chloride**	The weak base, ammonia (NH_3), and the relatively strong conjugate acid, the ammonium ion, NH_4^+ (pK_a = 9.25)

Table 8.4

1 How does a buffer work?

Make sure that you are familiar with this section of work if you must know about buffers.

Consider the effect of adding acid and base to the **ethanoic acid–sodium ethanoate buffer system** (an acid buffer system).

The equilibrium operating is:

$$CH_3COOH(aq) + H_2O(l) \rightleftharpoons CH_3COO^-(aq) + H_3O^+(aq)$$

large quantity — large quantity

On the addition of base

- From the added base, the extra hydroxide ions react with the hydrogen ions, $H_3O^+(aq)$, in the above equilibrium, therefore reducing the hydrogen ion concentration ($H_3O^+(aq) + OH^-(aq) \rightarrow 2H_2O(l)$) and disturbing the equilibrium.
- The reaction opposes this change in hydrogen ion concentration by dissociating some of its large reservoir of ethanoic acid and producing more hydrogen ions to replace most of those removed by adding the base and thereby restoring the equilibrium.
- The final pH in the new equilibrium mixture is similar to its starting pH and the value for K_a in the above equilibrium is preserved (remember that concentration changes do not affect K_a or any other equilibrium constant).

On adding acid

- Adding acid increases the concentration of the hydrogen ions in the equilibrium above.

- This disturbs the equilibrium.
- The reaction uses its large reservoir of ethanoate ions to react with the excess hydrogen ions: $CH_3COO^-(aq) + H_3O^+(aq) \rightarrow CH_3COOH(aq) + H_2O(l)$.
- The concentration of hydrogen ions in the new equilibrium mixture will be similar to that at the start and the pH remains about the same.

The mechanism for buffer operation is similar for other buffer systems, so do learn the points above to make it easier for you to produce a good answer, full of relevant information, in the examination.

It is very common to see either the ethanoic acid–sodium ethanoate or the ammonium chloride–ammonia systems quoted as recognised buffer systems in examinations.

The other main buffer system is the **ammonia–ammonium chloride system** and the equilibrium operating is:

$$NH_3(aq) + H_2O(l) \rightleftharpoons NH_4^+(aq) + OH^-(aq)$$

On increasing the concentration of acid, the reaction shifts to the right-hand side; on increasing the concentration of base, the reaction shifts to the left-hand side. (The details will be the same as those of the ethanoic acid–sodium ethanoate system.)

2 Quantitative buffer considerations

If we consider the general dissociation of the weak acid, HA as:

$$HA(aq) + H_2O(l) \rightleftharpoons A^-(aq) + H_3O^+(aq)$$

Then we may derive $pK_a = \log_{10}\left(\frac{[HA(aq)]}{[A^-(aq)]}\right) + pH$

or buffer pH $= \mathbf{pK_a - \log_{10}\left(\frac{[HA(aq)]}{[A^-(aq)]}\right) = pK_a - \log_{10}\frac{[ACID]}{[BASE]}}$

In other words, the pH of a buffer solution depends on:

- the acid dissociation constant, pK_a
- the **ratio** of the acid to the base forms within the solution (not the absolute values for the concentrations)

When asked to deduce a change, it is important to indicate the magnitude of the change and its direction, either positive or negative.

- **Calculate the change in pH when (a) 50 cm^3 of 1 mol dm^{-3} hydrochloric acid and (b) 50 cm^3 of 1 mol dm^{-3} sodium hydroxide solution are added in two separate stages to a 1000 cm^3 solution that is 0.3 mol dm^{-3} with respect to ethanoic acid, and 0.2 mol dm^{-3} with respect to sodium ethanoate (pK_a for ethanoic acid is 4.76).**

The initial pH will be given by

$$pH = pK_a - \log_{10}\frac{[ACID]}{[BASE]} = 4.76 - \log_{10}(0.3/0.2) = \mathbf{4.58}$$

On adding 50 cm^3 of 1 mol dm^{-3} hydrochloric acid (5×10^{-2} moles), the number of moles of ethanoic acid increases by 5×10^{-2} moles and the number of moles of ethanoate ions decreases by 5×10^{-2} moles. Since the total volume will be increased but both the [ACID] and [BASE] will be affected equally, the total volume consideration is not important (the total volumes will cancel).

Changing the relative concentrations of the acid–base pairs in a buffer system by 10 will change the pH by only 1 unit. Remember that the pH depends not solely on the ratio [ACID]/[BASE] but the $\log_{10}$ of this ratio.

The pH will be given by:

$$pH = pK_a - \log_{10}\frac{[ACID]}{[BASE]} = 4.76 - \log_{10}\frac{(0.3 + 0.05)}{(0.2 - 0.05)} = \mathbf{4.57}$$

A change of only –0.01 of a pH unit!

On adding 50 cm^3 of 1 mol dm^{-3} sodium hydroxide solution (0.05 moles), the [ACID] decreases by 0.05 moles and the [BASE] increases by 0.05 moles. Therefore, the pH will be given by:

$$pH = pK_a - \log_{10}\frac{[ACID]}{[BASE]} = 4.76 - \log_{10}\frac{(0.3 - 0.05)}{(0.2 + 0.05)} = \mathbf{4.60}$$

A change of +0.02 of a pH unit!

UNIT 9 Redox reactions

At the end of this unit, you should be familiar with:

- redox reactions
- the oxidation number concept
- writing half equations for redox reactions
- the electrode potential, $E^{\ominus}$

A What are redox reactions?

The two most useful definitions can be summarised using 'OILRIG': Oxidation Is the Loss of electrons; Reduction Is the Gaining of electrons.

Many reactions are classed as **redox** reactions since they involve both **reduction** and **oxidation** of different species.

Oxidation is the loss of electrons. It is also, less usefully, defined as the gaining of oxygen or the loss of hydrogen.

Reduction is the gaining of electrons. It, too, is defined in simple terms as the losing of oxygen or the gaining of hydrogen.

Metal atoms react by **losing electrons** to form positive ions **(cations)**; this process is an oxidation. Metals donate their electrons to other substances and, because of this, metals are normally **reducing agents**.

Non-metal atoms react by **gaining electrons** to form negative ions **(anions)**; this process is a reduction. Non-metals gain their electrons from other substances and so are termed oxidising agents.

B The oxidation number concept

On the assumption that all substances are composed of ions, it is possible to view reactions in terms of what transformations these ions undergo. Of course, not all substances are made up of ions, but it is a useful model nevertheless. For example, carbon dioxide is known to exist as carbon dioxide molecules, CO_2. The assumption that it could be viewed as consisting of C^{4+} ions and O^{2-} ions may seem strange, yet it can yield some important chemical information, particularly in redox processes.

The oxidation number can be seen as the charge on an ion (when assumed to be solely ionic).

Oxidation number is defined as the number of electrons that must be either added to or removed from an ion to form a neutral atom.

1 *Working out oxidation numbers from chemical formulae*

In carrying out this type of routine calculation, we assume that we know all of the oxidation numbers of the elements in the compound apart from the one that we are trying to find out. There are some elements, however, that seem to have the same oxidation number in their compounds, or behave according to certain rules.

All elements in their standard states have an oxidation number of zero.

- **Main group metals** have an oxidation number in their compounds dictated by the number of electrons in their outer shells in their atoms that are then removed to leave a full outer shell of electrons. For example, Group I metals always possess +1 as an oxidation number, Group II as +2, Group III as +3, etc.
- **Main group non-metals** have one oxidation number determined by the number of electrons they must gain to fill their outer electron shell. In Group VII, elements react by gaining one electron per atom and therefore have an oxidation number of −1 (Group VI as −2, Group V as −3, etc). The only non-metal that has the same oxidation number in all of its compounds is fluorine as −1. Therefore, non-metals are not as easy as metals in knowing exactly which oxidation number they will exhibit, although you will learn to recognise particular oxidation states as characteristic of them.
- **Hydrogen** always takes the oxidation number +1 except when bonded to a metal; then it will be −1.
- **Oxygen** is nearly always −2 except if bonded to a more electronegative element like chlorine or fluorine, e.g. in Cl_2O and F_2O in which oxygen is +2 and the halogen is −1. In the compound hydrogen peroxide, the oxidation number is −1 for oxygen.
- **Transition metals** can vary their oxidation number and we must indicate, in the name of the compound, exactly which oxidation number we are considering. For example, iron may be either +2 or +3 and manganese may commonly be +2, +4 or +7 in its common compounds. The name of the transition metal compound will therefore have, written in Roman numerals after it, the metal's oxidation number – for example, manganese(II) fluoride, manganese(VII) oxide, iron(III) chloride or iron(II) sulphate, etc.
- The **total sum** of all the oxidation numbers in any **compound** is **zero**.
- The **sum** of the oxidation numbers for an ion equals the **charge** on the **ion**.
- **What is the oxidation number of the elements in the following?**

Remember the rules about which elements have fixed oxidation states and which are likely to vary.

Na_2S	Na = +1,	S = −2	Cl^-	Cl = −1	
MgO	Mg = +2,	O = −2	ClO_3^-	Cl = +5,	O = −2
AlF_3	Al = +3,	F = −1	SO_4^{2-}	S = +6,	O = −2
VI_2	V = +2,	I = −1	SO_3^{2-}	S = +4,	O = −2
Mn_2O_7	Mn = +7,	O = −2	$Cr_2O_7^{2-}$	Cr = +6,	O = −2
H_2O_2	H = +1,	O = −1	MnO_4^-	Mn = +7,	O = −2

2 Naming compounds and ions using oxidation numbers

As mentioned above, there are many elements that have different oxidation numbers depending on the nature of the compound or ion. We therefore include **oxidation numbers in the name** of the compound or ion to signify the oxidation number of the element:

Note that ions containing oxygen and another element are not referred to as oxides, e.g. MnO_4^- is the manganate(VII) ion and SO_4^{2-} is the sulphate(VI) ion.

$MgSO_4$	magnesium sulphate(VI)	SO_3^{2-}	sulphate(IV) ion
SO_4^{2-}	sulphate(VI) ion	$NaClO_4$	sodium chlorate(VII)
$CuSO_4$	copper(II) sulphate(VI)	OsO_4	osmium(VIII) oxide
$FeCl_3$	iron(III) chloride	$Cr(NO_3)_3$	chromium(III) nitrate(V)

C Writing half equations for redox reactions

In a redox reaction there are two processes taking place: one species loses electrons (is oxidised) and the other gains electrons (is reduced). A half equation is a convenient way of representing each separate process so that we can see exactly what is happening.

This set of balancing rules is always the same (when in acid conditions), so try to learn it: add the water, add the hydrogen ions and then add the electrons.

Use the following steps when balancing half equations:

- balance the number of the reduced or oxidised element first
- add the correct number of **waters** to balance up the oxygens
- add the correct number of **hydrogen ions** to balance up the hydrogens
- balance the charge by adding the correct number of **electrons**

Examples

Complete the following half equations, indicating which feature oxidations and which feature reductions:

- **manganate(VII) to manganate(II)**

  $MnO_4^- \rightarrow Mn^{2+}$

  $MnO_4^- \rightarrow Mn^{2+} + 4H_2O$ balancing the oxygens

  $MnO_4^- + 8H^+ \rightarrow Mn^{2+} + 4H_2O$ balancing the hydrogens

  $MnO_4^- + 8H^+ + 5e^- \rightarrow Mn^{2+} + 4H_2O$ balancing the electrons

  This is a reduction since electrons have been added or the oxidation number of manganese has been reduced (from +7 to +2). Manganate(VII) has been reduced to manganate(II).

- **chromate(VI) to chromate(III)**

  $Cr_2O_7^{2-} \rightarrow 2Cr^{3+}$ balance the Cr first

  $Cr_2O_7^{2-} \rightarrow 2Cr^{3+} + 7H_2O$

  $Cr_2O_7^{2-} + 14H^+ \rightarrow 2Cr^{3+} + 7H_2O$

  $Cr_2O_7^{2-} + 14H^+ + 6e^- \rightarrow 2Cr^{3+} + 7H_2O$

  This too is a reduction since the chromium has been reduced from +6 to +3. Chromate(VI) has been reduced to chromium(III).

MnO_4^- and $Cr_2O_7^{2-}$ are oxidising agents since they both remove electrons from other species. They themselves are reduced. Notice how acid is needed to enable each to exhibit its oxidising power. The oxygen in the oxidising agent always ends up in the water.

1 *Writing overall balanced equations by combining half equations*

Produce balanced equations using the half equations given:

- **Example 1**

  Equation 1 $MnO_4^- + 8H^+ + 5e^- \rightarrow Mn^{2+} + 4H_2O$

  Equation 2 $Fe^{2+} \rightarrow Fe^{3+} + e^-$

  Before adding the half equations together, the number of electrons in each half equation must be the same.

Multiplying Equation 2 by 5 gives:
$5Fe^{2+} \rightarrow 5Fe^{3+} + 5e^-$
Then, adding the multiplied equation to Equation 1, gives (the electrons cancel):
$\mathbf{5Fe^{2+} + MnO_4^- + 8H^+ \rightarrow 5Fe^{3+} + Mn^{2+} + 4H_2O}$

- **Example 2**
Equation 1 $IO_3^- + 6H^+ + 6e^- \rightarrow I^- + 3H_2O$
Equation 2 $2I^- \rightarrow I_2 + 2e^-$
Multiply Equation 1 by Equation 2 and then add together the two half equations:
$IO_3^- + 6H^+ + 6I^- \rightarrow I^- + 3H_2O + 3I_2$
Note that we can cancel one of the iodide ions on the right-hand side:
$\mathbf{IO_3^- + 6H^+ + 5I^- \rightarrow 3I_2 + 3H_2O}$

Electrons are never written into the overall ionic equation for a chemical process; they only appear in the half equations.

Notice how the number of electrons, that needs to be added or removed, is equal to the change in oxidation number. This means that you should be able to balance equations using oxidation number change alone.

For example, balance the ionic equation:

$Fe^{3+} + Zn \rightarrow Zn^{2+} + Fe$

Using your data book, you should practise, the following important skills: balancing half equations; adding any two half equations together by multiplying the equations by a number so that the numbers of electrons are the same; and adding to form an overall equation.

The zinc moves **up 2** in oxidation number from 0 to +2, whereas the iron(III) ion moves **down 3** from +3 to 0. To balance the 'up and down' oxidation number change, multiply the zinc half by 3 and the iron half by 2 so that the up and down change is 6. The resulting equation is then:

$2Fe^{3+} + 3Zn \rightarrow 3Zn^{2+} + 2Fe$

D The electrode potential, E⊖

The oxidising ability or the reducing ability of various substances differs according to the nature of the substance being used. The way in which we measure the tendency of substances to be oxidising agents, or the tendency to accept electrons, is by measuring a substance's electrode potential or, more particularly, its standard electrode potential (if measured under standard conditions).

Remember that an equilibrium exists between the metal and the metal ions – many students omit this fact.

For a metal, $M^{n+}(aq) + ne^- \rightleftharpoons M(s)$ E⊖ = electrode potential

However, the standard electrode potential is measured using the **hydrogen electrode** as the reference and this is assigned an **arbitrary** E⊖ of **zero volts**.

The standard electrode potential of an element, E⊖, is defined as the potential difference between a standard hydrogen half cell and a half cell of the element, both half cells containing solutions of 1 mol dm^{-3} at 298 K and 1 atm.

1 *How do we measure the standard electrode potential of a substance?*

It is important to realise that we cannot measure the potential difference of an isolated half cell, for example the electrical charge on a piece of copper that arises when the metal is dipped into a solution of its own ions. We must use a standard reference, a hydrogen electrode, to allow a valid comparison to be made and also to enable us to record a potential **difference** between two cells (see Figure 9.1).

Make sure that you know this diagram and that you can draw it and label it fully.

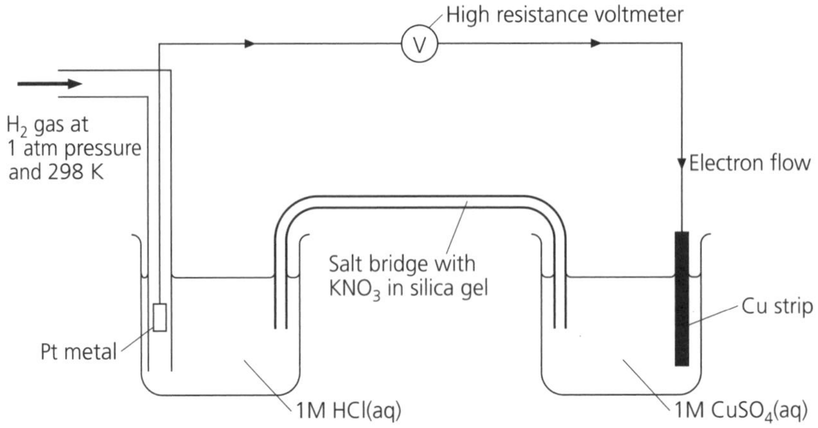

Figure 9.1 How the standard electrode potential for copper is measured

- The standard conditions are 298 K, 1 atmosphere pressure, solutions of concentration 1 mol dm^{-3}.
- The materials of which the salt bridge is made are potassium nitrate in silica gel.
- **Ions** pass through the salt bridge and **electrons** pass through the external circuit.
- A high resistance voltmeter is used so that the current flowing is at a minimum. If a current is allowed to flow, chemical change will occur in the beakers and the potential difference will then change.
- The electrode with the more positive electrode potential (written with electrons added to the left-hand side) is the positive electrode and the more negative is the negatively charged electrode.
- The electrons flow from the negative pole to the positive pole (if electrons were allowed to move).
- The terms cathode and anode create problems in this context since many students expect the positive electrode to be called the anode. This is not the case. To be clear, remember the following:

  Cathode is where redu**c**tion occurs and **anode** is where oxid**a**tion occurs.

	Electrolysis	Electrochemical cells (as in this case)
Anode	+	–
Cathode	–	+

2 *Cell diagrams*

For all cells (a combination of two half cells), a cell diagram may be written. The cell diagram is a symbolic form of representation of chemical processes taking place in the cell.

The cell diagram normally takes the form:

What has been oxidised? | To what? ¦¦ What has been reduced? | To what?

- the symbol '|' represents a solid–liquid or gas–liquid interface
- the symbol '¦¦' represents the salt bridge
- the half cell part for the hydrogen electrode, which is normally the left-hand part of the cell diagram, is written as: $Pt(s) \mid H_2(g) \mid 2H^+(aq)$ ¦¦
- each half cell must be balanced and does not include electrons

3 Calculating overall electrode potentials of cells using individual cell potentials

The right-hand electrode, as written in the cell diagram, is connected to the positive terminal on the voltmeter, and the left-hand cell to the negative terminal.

The overall cell potential, $\mathbf{E^\ominus = E_{rhs} - E_{lhs}}$ where E_{rhs} and E_{lhs} are the two electrode potentials for the half equations written as reductions, i.e. as they are written in most data books.

If the overall electrode potential is positive, then the redox process being considered is spontaneous (it will work) but the rate is not predictable.

Do not try to remember a clockwise or anticlockwise rule: this is not a rule and it shows little understanding of the ideas involved. Talk about the magnitudes of the electrode potentials involved and their differing equilibrium positions.

Remember, the more positive electrode potential moves to the right and this forces the other to move to the left.

- As an example, consider the two half equations:
  $Ag^+(aq) + e^- \rightleftharpoons Ag(s)$ $\quad E^\ominus = +0.80\,V$
  $Ni^{2+}(aq) + 2e^- \rightleftharpoons Ni(s)$ $\quad E^\ominus = -0.25\,V$
- Since the $Ag^+ \mid Ag$ electrode potential is more positive than the nickel electrode potential, the silver process will proceed from left to right as written. In this process, electrons are required and these are gained from the nickel metal. This forces the nickel half equation to the left-hand side. So, the processes that will occur are:
  $Ag^+(aq) + e^- \rightarrow Ag(s)$ and $Ni(s) \rightarrow Ni^{2+}(aq) + 2e^-$
- The cell diagram for the spontaneous process will be:
  What has been oxidised? | To what? ¦¦ What has been reduced? | To what?
  $Ni(s) \mid Ni^{2+}(aq)$ ¦¦ $Ag^+(aq) \mid Ag(s)$
- The overall electrode potential, $E^\ominus$, is equal to $E_{rhs} - E_{lhs} = +0.80 - (-0.25) =$ $\mathbf{+1.05\,V}$
- The silver is the positive terminal in the cell (since its electrode potential is more positive than the nickel half); the nickel half is the negative terminal.
- $E^\ominus$ is the maximum voltage obtainable from this cell under standard conditions.

UNIT 10 Periodicity

At the end of this unit you should be familiar with:

- the idea of periodicity
- element structure

and periodicity in:

- the melting points of the elements
- first ionisation enthalpy
- atomic and ionic radius
- electronegativities of the elements
- electrical conductivity of the elements
- the chlorides and oxides of Period 3 elements in the Periodic Table

A The idea of periodicity

Periodicity is the regular and repeating pattern of various physical or chemical properties. Since the outer electronic configuration of atoms is a periodic function, we therefore expect other properties to change accordingly.

B Periodicity in element structure

(See also Unit 4, where structure and bonding are discussed in more detail.)

1 *Metals*

A metallic structure is sometimes described as a close packed structure of cations encasing a sea of mobile electrons.

All metals consist of a close packed arrangement of positively charged ions surrounded by a 'sea' of mobile electrons. The presence of the negatively charged electrons provides a force of attraction between the positively charged ions in the structure. The resulting structure is bonded electrostatically and is called a **giant metallic structure**.

2 *Semi-metals (metalloids)*

The covalent bond is a strong bond, so to disrupt a giant structure will require a lot of energy.

Many semi-metals, e.g. silicon and carbon (and graphite as diamond), exist as **giant molecular (giant covalent) structures**. These structures consist of an arrangement of millions of atoms all covalently bonded together to produce a giant structure.

3 *Non-metals*

Most non-metals exist as molecules, in which the molecules are strongly covalently bonded together. The molecules formed do not have an overall charge and, as a result, the intermolecular forces acting between molecules tend to be

The f... n mole... rong but ... between molecu... are weak.

significantly weaker that the covalent bonds themselves. Example molecules include: O_2, N_2, H_2, F_2, S_8, P_4, etc. When these molecules are weakly packed together in the solid state, the structure is called a **simple molecular structure**. The noble gases consist of single atoms bonded only by very weak van der Waals interactions. These structures, in the solid state, are called **simple atomic structures**.

C The melting points of the elements

The trend in melting points of the elements across Periods 2 and 3 mirror each other since melting point is a periodic function (there is a regular, repeating pattern).

When a substance melts, the forces between the particles are disrupted, but not all of them. When the substance boils, all of the available intermolecular forces or inter-ionic forces are broken.

The melting points are determined by the structures of the elements. The general trend in melting points across a period is shown in Table 10.1 and Figure 10.1.

Table 10.1

	Metals			Non-metals
Group:	I II III	IV	V VI VII	VIII
Structural type:	giant metallic	giant molecular	simple molecular	simple atomic
Melting point:	increases	very high →	drops → generally increases	→ decreases

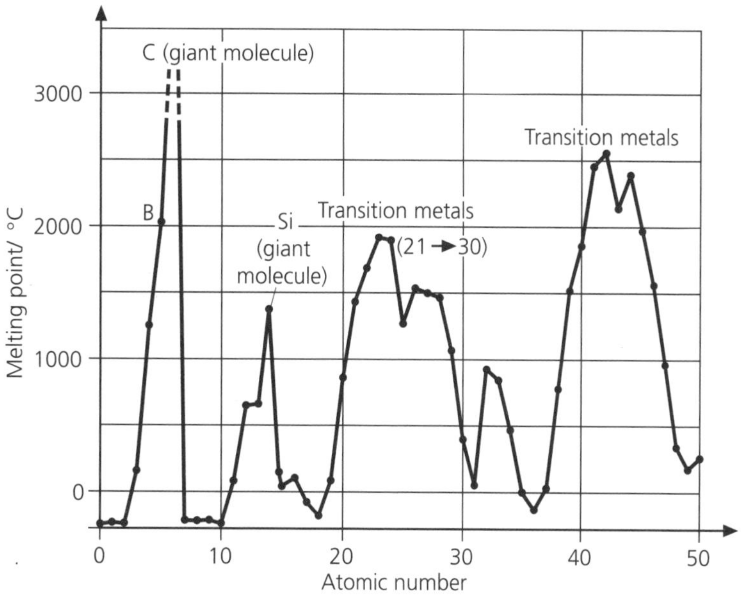

Figure 10.1 Graph of melting point vs. atomic number

D First ionisation enthalpy

See Unit 2, section D where this important variation is discussed in detail.

E Atomic and ionic radius

1 Atomic radius

The radius of an atom or an ion is very difficult to measure since the probability of finding an electron at any distance from the nucleus is never zero. We normally use contour lines to represent a probability of finding the electron within the atom boundary.

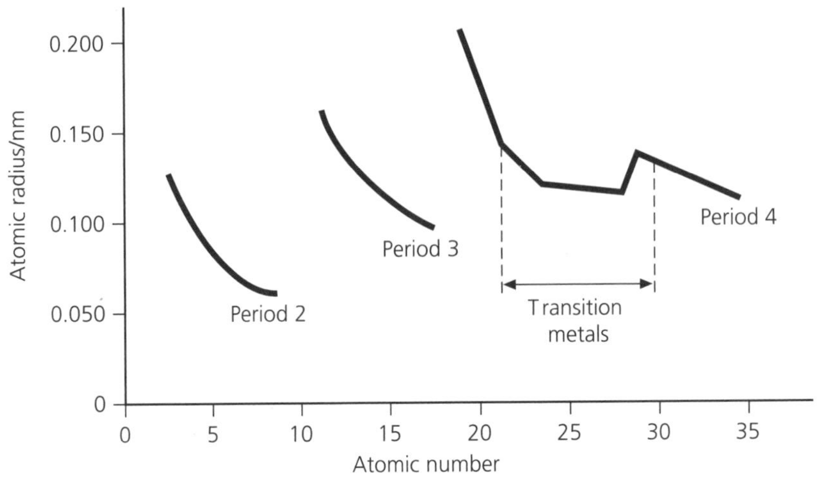

Figure 10.2 Graph of atomic radius vs. atomic number

Atomic radius generally decreases, moving from left to right across a period.

Moving across a period

The trend in atomic radius, moving from left to right across a period, is to generally **decrease** since, within a period, the electrons are being added (as the atomic number increases) to the same shell **but** the positive charge of the nucleus is increasing by 1 each time. The overall effect is that the charge of the nucleus causes a contraction of the outer shell of electrons in towards the nucleus.

Moving down a group

Although the nuclear charge increases down a group, the electrons are being added to a different shell (higher in energy and further from the nucleus). The overall effect is to increase the atomic radius.

2 Ionic radius

Positive ions (cations)

Positive ions have smaller radii than their respective atoms and, as the positive charge increases, the ionic radius becomes even less. The electrons being removed may be the only electron in that shell, so the effect of removing these electrons can be a dramatic decrease (removal of a shell). Also, the attractive force acting on the outer electrons increases when more electrons are removed since the balance of protons to electrons increases (we often say that the effective nuclear charge increases when more electrons are removed).

Positive ions have lower ionic radii compared with their corresponding atoms, whereas negative ions have greater ionic radii.

Negative ions (anions)

Negative ions have larger radii compared with their respective atoms. The addition of extra electrons (i) increases the repulsion in the outer shell of electrons and (ii) decreases the effective nuclear charge. As the negative charge increases, so too does the ionic radius.

F Electronegativities of the elements

Fluorine is the most electronegative element in the Periodic Table. Its nucleus binds onto the bonding electrons very tightly when present in a covalent bond.

Electronegativity is defined as the tendency for an atom to attract a bonded pair of electrons towards it. (Remember the bonded pair part in this definition.)

The electronegativity is determined by the same factors as atomic radius so you will see that nuclear charge acting on electrons in the same shell and shells further from the nucleus are two important ideas.

1 *Trends in electronegativity*

Increase – moving from left to right across the period

Across a period the bonded electrons are in the same shell. The increasing nuclear charge therefore increases the ability of the nucleus to attract the bonded pair. The electronegativity thus increases.

Decrease – on descending a group

On descending a group, the bonded electrons are further from the nucleus since they reside in a shell further from the nucleus (despite the increased nuclear charge). Shielding from inner electron shells also shields the outer electrons from the positively charged nucleus. The tendency for atoms to be able to attract the bonded pair decreases, i.e. the electronegativity therefore decreases.

Figure 10.3 Variation of electronegativity in the Periodic Table

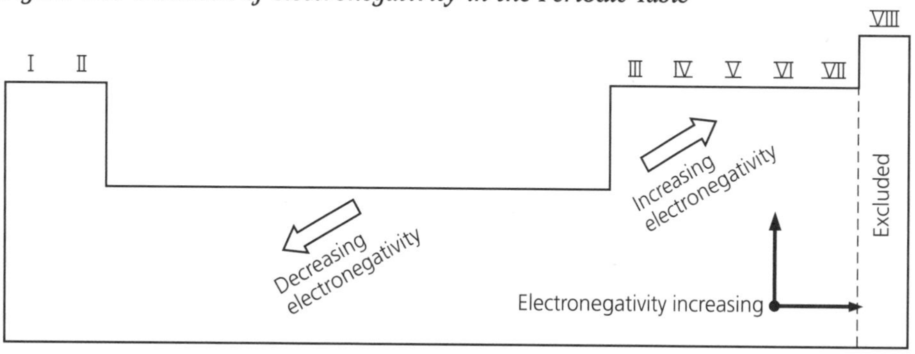

G Electrical conductivity of the elements

Electrical conductivity in an element is dependent on the existence of mobile electrons (not ions).

Electrical conductivity is a measure of the mobility of electrons in the structure being considered. As mentioned earlier, metals are good electrical conductors since they have a sea of delocalised electrons moving through the structure, and hence metals will carry electrical charge very well. However, non-metals in general are poorer electrical conductors since the electrons are more likely to be confined to covalent bonds. Exceptions include graphite and, to a lesser extent, silicon which both conduct electricity as non-metals.

H The chlorides and oxides of Period 3 elements

The study of the physical and chemical properties of the oxides and chlorides of the elements in Period 3 yields some important trends in behaviour. These trends are similar across Period 2.

Table 10.2 summarises the following properties for Period 3 elements:

1 The formulae of the simplest oxides together with their physical states.
2 The bonding and structure of the oxides at room temperature and pressure.
3 The reaction, if any, of the oxide with water.
4 The formulae of the common chlorides together with their physical states.
5 The bonding and structure of the chlorides at room temperature and pressure.
6 The reaction, if any, of the chlorides with water.

Make sure that you can remember these equations.

Metal ions are hydrated by water molecules – they may then undergo hydrolysis.

Table 10.2

	Properties					
Element	**1**	**2**	**3**	**4**	**5**	**6**
Na	$Na_2O(s)$ $Na_2O_2(s)$	ionic giant ionic	$Na_2O + H_2O$ $\rightarrow 2NaOH$	$NaCl(s)$	ionic, giant ionic	dissolves to form hydrated Na^+ and Cl^-
Mg	$MgO(s)$	ionic giant ionic	$MgO + H_2O$ $\rightarrow Mg(OH)_2$	$MgCl_2(s)$	ionic, giant ionic	dissolves with mild hydrolysis $MgCl_2 + 2H_20$ $\rightarrow Mg(OH)_2 + 2HCl$
Al	$Al_2O_3(s)$	ionic/ covalent giant ionic	no reaction	$Al_2Cl_6(s)$	covalent/ ionic, simple molecular/ giant ionic	$Al_2Cl_6 + 12H_2O \rightarrow$ $2[Al(H_2O)_6]^{3+} + 6Cl^-$ then hydrolysis
Si	$SiO_2(s)$	covalent giant molecular	no reaction	$SiCl_4(l)$	covalent, simple molecular	$SiCl_4 + 4H_2O$ $\rightarrow SiO_2.2H_2O$ $+ 4HCl$ hydrolysis
P	$P_4O_6(s)$ $P_4O_{10}(s)$	covalent simple molecular	$P_4O_6 + 6H_2O$ $\rightarrow 4H_3PO_3$ $P_4O_{10} + 6H_2O$ $\rightarrow 4H_3PO_4$	$PCl_3(l)$ $PCl_5(s)$	covalent, simple molecular	$PCl_3 + 3H_2O$ $\rightarrow H_3PO_3 +$ $3HCl$ $PCl_5 + H_2O \rightarrow$ $POCl_3 + 2HCl$ Then: $POCl_3 + 3H_2O$ $\rightarrow H_3PO_4 + 3HCl$ hydrolysis
S	$SO_2(g)$ $SO_3(s)$	covalent simple molecular	$SO_2 + H_2O$ $\rightarrow H_2SO_3$ $SO_3 + H_2O$ $\rightarrow H_2SO_4$	$S_2Cl_2(l)$ $SCl_2(l)$	covalent, simple molecular	$S_2Cl_2 + 3H_2O$ $\rightarrow 2HCl + H_2S$ $+ H_2SO_3$ hydrolysis
Cl	$Cl_2O(g)$	covalent simple molecular	$Cl_2O + H_2O$ $\rightarrow 2HOCl$			

Hydration is the binding of a water molecule onto an ion where the water molecule remains intact.

Hydrolysis represents the chemical decomposition of a substance in the presence of water; the water molecule is also broken down.

1 Reactions of the chlorides with water

Ionic substances with a high degree of ionic character dissolve in water and the ions become surrounded with water molecules. This process is called **hydration**.

As the degree of covalency in the compound increases, so does the tendency for **hydrolysis** (reaction with water) to occur. As a result, **the pH of the chlorides of Period 3 elements decreases on moving from left to right in the Periodic Table, i.e. the solutions become more acidic.**

2 Reactions of the oxides with water

The oxides of elements on the left-hand side form **alkaline solutions** and those on the right form **acidic solutions**. The elements in between form **amphoteric oxides**.

Generally, the basic and acidic nature of the oxides varies according to a regular trend.

A base is a substance that reacts with an acid to form a salt and water only.

- **On moving from left to right across a period, the oxides become more acidic and less basic.**
- **On moving down any group, the oxides become more basic and less acidic.**

3 Structure and bonding of the oxides and chlorides

- **Bonding trend within period:**

ionic ⟶ covalent
increase in covalent character →

The negative ion is polarised by the positive ion (not the other way round).

Positive ions in Group I tend to be moderately large and have a single positive charge on the ion – **they have a low charge density on their ions**. The ability of these ions to distort or deform (polarise) a spherical ion is dependent on the charge density of the cation. Therefore, Group I metal ions (e.g. Na^+) are not able to polarise the spherical chloride or oxide ion as effectively as Group II metal ions (e.g. Mg^{2+}).

Aluminium chloride is largely covalent in its bonding character. The aluminium atom can therefore be viewed as electron deficient since it will only possess six electrons around the central atom if covalently bonded.

The Group III metal aluminium forms a +3 charge on its ion and the ion has a very small ionic radius. As a result, Al^{3+} polarises the chloride ion and the oxide ion effectively and the resulting compounds tend to display a significant degree of covalent character (lower melting points and boiling points, more soluble in non-polar solvents, etc.).

After and including silicon, the oxides and chlorides are largely covalent and tend to exist as either giant molecules (e.g. SiO_2) or simple molecules (e.g. SO_2, P_4O_{10}, $SiCl_4$, etc), and they have correspondingly covalent characteristics.

- **Structure trend within period:**

giant ionic structures ⟶ simple covalent structures
increase in covalent character →

Polarising power is a very important concept. Make sure that you understand how it is used to explain ideas in chemical bonding.

The polarising power of the positive ion and its ability to polarise or distort the negatively charged ion and thereby induce covalent character is important – see Table 10.3.

Table 10.3

Bonding type	Ionic	Covalent
Name of particles present:	Ions	Molecules
Deviations from the pure case:	Polarising power of the positive ion increases ⟶	
	⟵	Electronegativity difference increases

UNIT 11 Extraction of metals

This unit deals with some of the major extraction techniques required by most syllabuses. Check that you are aware of the methods of metal extraction needed for your syllabus.

At the end of this unit, you should be familiar with industrial techniques for obtaining:

- aluminium
- iron
- chromium
- sodium and the chlor-alkali industry
- titanium

A Aluminium

Aluminium is extracted from bauxite which is impure aluminium oxide, Al_2O_3. The main impurities in bauxite are silicon dioxide and iron(III) oxide. Before the aluminium oxide is electrolysed, it must first be separated from the impurities within the bauxite.

Aluminium has a relatively negative electrode potential: $Al^{3+} + 3e^- \rightleftharpoons Al$; $E^\ominus = -1.66\,V$. This means that conventional reduction of the aluminium ion using metal with more negative electrode potentials is unlikely and, if possible, tends to be very expensive and hazardous. For this reason, electrolysis is used.

1 *The purification of bauxite*

This process relies on the fact that aluminium oxide is **amphoteric** and will therefore not just react with acids (as normal bases do) but will also react with bases to form a salt and water.

The bauxite is added to hot, concentrated sodium hydroxide solution. The sodium hydroxide dissolves the aluminium oxide as well as the silicon dioxide, but other impurities are insoluble and so are filtered off and disposed of sensibly.

$$Al_2O_3(s) + 2NaOH(aq) + 3H_2O(l) \rightarrow 2NaAl(OH)_4(aq)$$

aluminium oxide + sodium hydroxide solution + water → sodium aluminate(III) solution

$$SiO_2(s) + 2NaOH(aq) \rightarrow Na_2SiO_3(aq) + H_2O(l)$$

silicon dioxide + sodium hydroxide solution → sodium silicate solution + water

The filtrate is cooled and the aluminate(III) solution hydrolysed by diluting with water and adding a little freshly prepared aluminium hydroxide (or bubbling through carbon dioxide gas). This addition induces more precipitation to occur of aluminium hydroxide in a process known as 'seeding'. The sodium silicate solution remains unaffected by the seeding process and so the silicon containing impurity stays in solution.

$$[Al(OH)_4]^-(aq) + 3H_2O(l) \rightleftharpoons Al(OH)_3(H_2O)_3(s) + HO^-(aq)$$

aluminate ions + water aluminium ⇌ hydroxide (hydrated) + hydroxide ions

The aluminium hydroxide is then filtered off and heated to form the pure aluminium oxide.

$$2Al(OH)_3 \rightarrow Al_2O_3(s) + 3H_2O(l)$$

aluminium hydroxide → aluminium oxide + water

2 *The electrolysis*

The aluminium oxide is now dissolved in molten cryolite (Na_3AlF_6) and electrolysed at 950°C (from 2045°C for pure aluminium oxide). The addition of cryolite (a naturally occurring mineral found, for example, in Greenland) lowers the melting point of the aluminium oxide and thus lowers the energy consumption and cost of the electrolytic process. A low voltage is used so that the cryolite itself does not decompose. Figure 11.1 shows the cell used – this type of cell is called the Hall–Heroult cell.

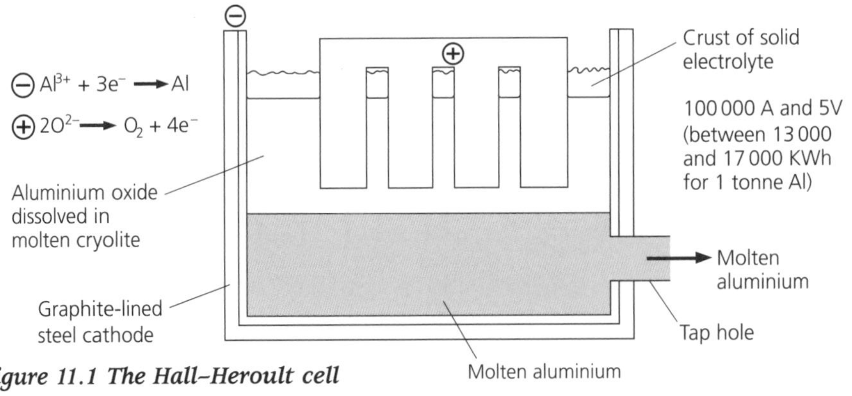

Figure 11.1 The Hall–Heroult cell

During the electrolysis, the positive and negatively charged ions in the molten aluminium oxide are free to move and migrate towards the oppositely charged electrode where they are discharged.

The cathode is made of steel and it is lined with graphite. The molten aluminium forms at the cathode.

At cathode: Al^{3+} **+** $3e^-$ **→ Al; a reduction**
(cation)

Remember these important half equations that summarise the discharge of aluminium and oxygen gas at the electrodes.

The anodes are made of graphite. Oxygen is formed at the anode. The anodes need replacing regularly (this increases the cost) as they erode due to reaction with the oxygen formed. This results in the formation of oxides of carbon.

At anode: $2O^{2-}$ **→** $2O_2$ **+** $4e^-$**; an oxidation**
(anion)

Then C(s) + O_2**(g) →** CO_2**(g) and 2C(s) +** O_2**(g) → 2CO(g)**

The molten aluminium is then vacuum pumped out of the cell where it is used to form alloys or it is allowed to cool to form ingots.

The extraction of aluminium is only economic where cheap electricity is available, normally from hydro-electric water power.

B Iron

Iron is a less reactive metal ($Fe^{2+} + 2e^- \rightleftharpoons Fe$; $E^\ominus = -0.44$ V) than aluminium, so electrolysis is not necessary; carbon is used in conventional reduction techniques.

Iron is the second most abundant metal in the Earth's crust. It occurs in the earth in various chemical forms: haematite (Fe_2O_3) and magnetite (Fe_3O_4) are two examples.

1 *The blast furnace*

There are impurities in the iron ore and these may be silicon dioxide, various metallic sulphides and phosphides. The impurities are not separated initially, as they are in the production of aluminium, but are extracted at the end of the process. A diagram of the blast furnace is shown in Figure 11.2.

The furnace is made of brick on the inside (a good thermal insulator) and strengthened with steel. There are inlet pipes (tuyeres) at the base of the furnace and these inject hot air into the furnace. The inlets at the top of the furnace consist of hoppers into which the charge of solid raw materials is added – these materials are the iron ore, limestone and coke. Coke is coal that has been heated in the absence of air, and this process removes any sulphur impurities that may be present and gives the coke a larger surface area.

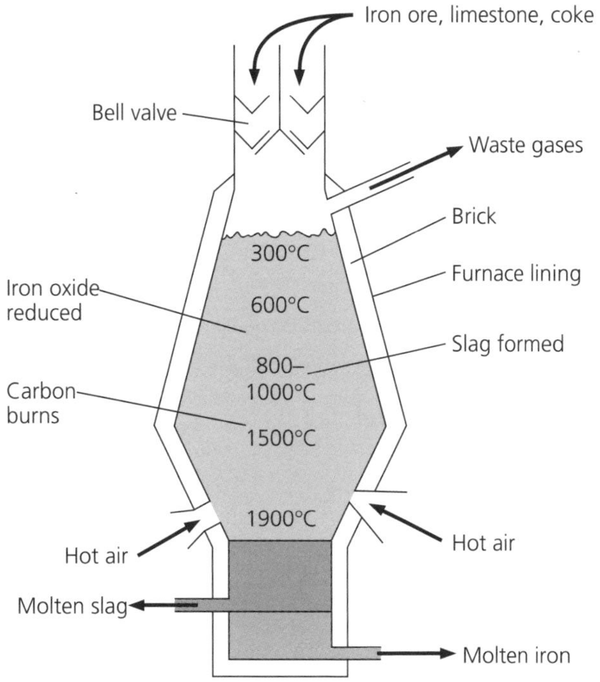

Figure 11.2 The blast furnace

At the heart of the furnace, the temperature is approximately 1200 °C and the temperature decreases steadily on ascending the furnace.

The **combustion** of the coke in the hot air provides the thermal energy in the furnace (therefore facilitating the necessary reactions) as well as producing the gas (carbon monoxide) required for the actual reduction of the iron ore.

$$C(s) + O_2(g) \rightarrow CO_2(g) \qquad \Delta H^\ominus = -396\ kJ\ mol^{-1}$$
$$\text{and } 2C(s) + O_2(g) \rightarrow 2CO(g) \qquad \Delta H^\ominus = -111\ kJ\ mol^{-1}CO(g)$$
$$\text{and } CO_2(g) + C(s) \rightarrow 2CO(g)$$

The reduction of the iron ore

$$Fe_2O_3(s) + 3CO(g) \rightleftharpoons 2Fe(l) + 3CO_2(g)$$

It is also possible in the hotter parts of the furnace for carbon to reduce the iron(III) oxide directly to form iron and more carbon monoxide.

$$2Fe_2O_3(s) + 3C(s) \rightarrow 3CO_2(g) + 4Fe(l)$$

Removal of the impurities

At about 800 °C, limestone decomposes to produce calcium oxide and carbon dioxide, and then the basic calcium oxide reacts with the acidic silicon dioxide to produce a slag called calcium silicate.

Make sure that you know these equations.

$$CaCO_3(s) \rightarrow CaO(s) + CO_2(g)$$
$$CaO(s) + SiO_2(s) \rightarrow CaSiO_3(s)$$

The carbon monoxide gas not used during the process is combusted when it is removed from the furnace, and the heat generated by this combustion is used to heat the air entering the furnace.

Removing the iron and treatment

The molten iron falls to the bottom of the furnace where it is tapped off and used to make various forms of iron and steel. The calcium silicate that is less dense than the iron floats on the molten iron and can be removed and used to make concrete or it can be converted to make a woolly form of slag used for insulation.

2 *Manufacture of steel*

One method for removing the impurities from the molten iron obtained from the blast furnace is to blow pure oxygen through the molten iron. The oxygen reacts with the impurities to form gaseous compounds that will then leave the molten iron. This process is called the Basic Oxygen Steel making process (BOS) and the vessel used is called a Bessemer converter.

These oxides will all consist of simple molecules with relatively weak intermolecular forces. They are produced as volatile compounds (as gases) and are removed from the mixture.

$2Mn + O_2 \rightarrow 2MnO$
$Si + O_2 \rightarrow SiO_2$
$P_4 + 5O_2 \rightarrow P_4O_{10}$
$2C + O_2 \rightarrow 2CO$

Sulphur is normally removed prior to the BOS process and this is done by blowing magnesium powder into the molten iron via a lance. The magnesium metal combines ferociously with the impurities, forming ionic impurities that float on the iron to produce a slag. They are then scraped off to leave the purer iron.

Remember some common steels and their compositions.

Table 11.1 lists some different types of steel that are commonly used, together with their approximate composition and their desirable physical properties.

Table 11.1

Steel	% composition	General properties
cast iron	< 3.5% C	brittle, tough, low thermal expansion
mild steel	< 0.1% C	ductile, high tensile strength
high carbon steel	0.6%–1.5% C	tough and hard-wearing
stainless steel	18% Cr 8% Ni	corrosion resistant

C Chromium

Chromium has uses as a metallic element, in alloys with other metals, e.g. with iron in stainless steels, and in its compounds, e.g. sodium chromate(VI).

The process of extracting pure chromium from the ore chromite is very demanding. This process occurs in several steps, the final displacement reaction being reduction of the chromium(III) oxide by aluminium metal to form metallic chromium.

Aluminium possesses a more negative electrode potential than chromium. It is therefore a more powerful reducing agent.

$$Cr_2O_3(s) + 2Al(s) \rightarrow 2Cr(s) + Al_2O_3(s)$$

chromium(III) oxide + aluminium metal → chromium metal + aluminium oxide

D Sodium and the chlor–alkali industry

The extraction of sodium and chlorine from the widely available sodium chloride is of great importance to the chemical industry, not just in the potential uses of the elements sodium and chlorine but also in other products like sodium hydroxide, sodium chlorate(I) and hydrogen gas.

There are several methods used for electrolysing sodium chloride. Make sure that you know which is required for your syllabus.

The methods frequently used are shown in Table 11.2.

Table 11.2

Name of cell	Products from cell
Downs cell	sodium metal and chlorine gas
Castner-Kellner cell	sodium hydroxide, hydrogen and chlorine
diaphragm cell	sodium hydroxide, hydrogen and chlorine
membrane cell	sodium hydroxide, hydrogen and chlorine

Note that sodium chlorate(I) is a product that is easily obtained by the reaction of chlorine gas with dilute and cold sodium hydroxide solution and can therefore be formed from any of the processes above, particularly cells 2, 3 and 4.

Although all four cells are not discussed in this text, you must make sure that you are aware of the cell required for your syllabus. The Downs cell and the diaphragm cell are discussed below as two cells in which different chemical processes operate.

1 The Downs Cell

The current, not the voltage, determines the number of moles of product produced per unit time.

A diagram of the Downs Cell is shown in Figure 11.3. A typical Downs Cell operates at 30 000 A and 7 V and a temperature of about 600 °C.

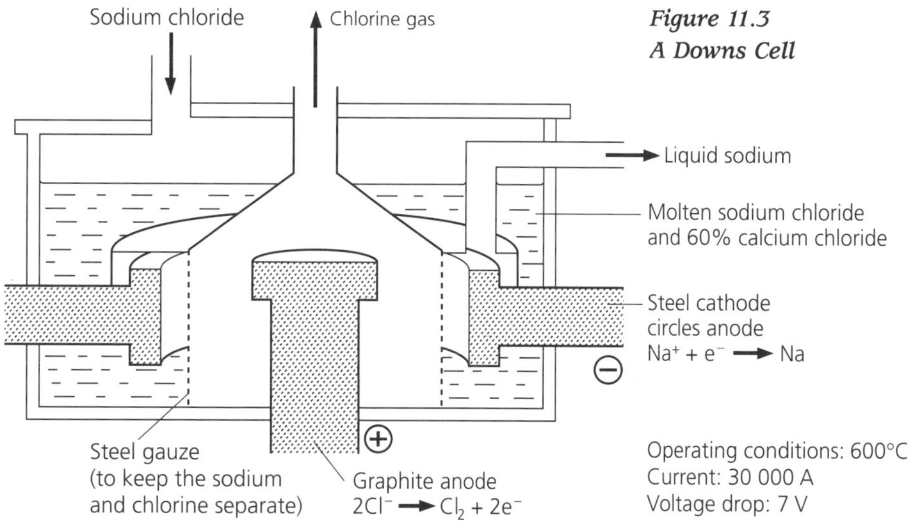

Figure 11.3
A Downs Cell

Salt (sodium chloride) may be obtained by mining rock salt, obtaining salt solution (brine) by pumping water from the surface to dissolve the salt and then evaporating it, or by evaporation of salt water by the sun.

Sodium chloride melts at about 800°C. The problem with these high temperatures is that the metallic electrodes will corrode rapidly, leading to high operating costs.

Calcium chloride is added to the molten electrolyte in order to reduce the melting point and to prevent the sodium, once it forms, from dissolving in the electrolyte and therefore acting as a more efficient electrical conductor than the sodium chloride. The melting point of the mixture is about 600 °C. There is a steel gauze to prevent the sodium reacting with the chlorine in this process. The equations for the discharge of chloride and sodium ions are:

(−) At cathode: $Na^+(l) + e^- \rightarrow Na(l)$; a reduction
(+) At anode: $2Cl^-(l) \rightarrow Cl_2(g) + 2e^-$; an oxidation

2 The diaphragm cell

This process consists of a similar set up to that shown before, but no mercury is used (see Figure 11.4). In the cell, titanium anodes (chemically inert to chlorine gas) discharge the chloride ions, producing chlorine gas. It should be noted that although the electrode potential for the discharge of the hydroxide ions is less, therefore implying that they will form on thermodynamic grounds, the concentration of the chloride ions far exceeds the hydroxide ions so the rate at which chloride ions will form will be greater.

You should know that electrode potentials predict the chance of a product being discharged in this context; they do not tell us about the rate of discharge (the concentration of the ions is an important factor here).

(+) At anode reaction: $4OH^- \rightleftharpoons O_2 + 2H_2O + 4e^-$; $E^\ominus = -0.40\,V$
Actual reaction that occurs: $2Cl^- \rightleftharpoons Cl_2 + 2e^-$; $E^\ominus = -1.36\,V$

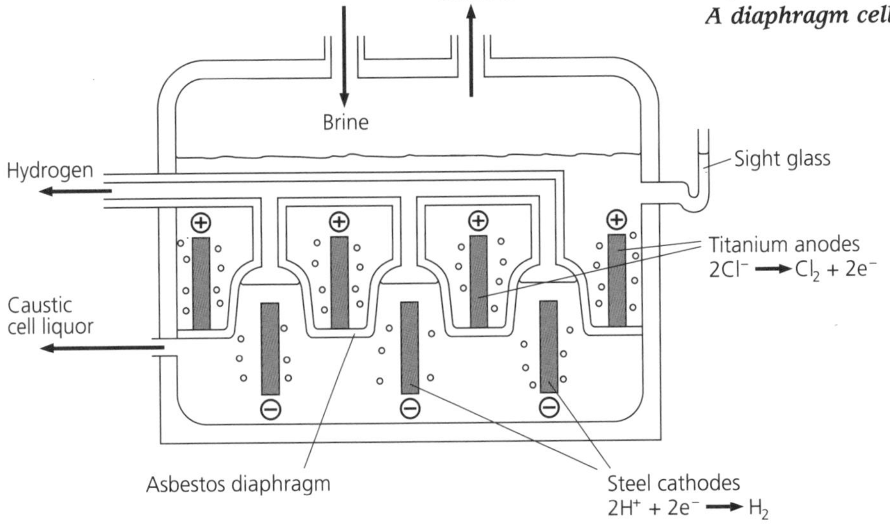

Figure 11.4
A diaphragm cell

The cathodes are made of steel. Hydrogen ions and sodium ions migrate towards these electrodes, and the hydrogen gas is produced (not sodium metal). The hydrogen ions are therefore preferentially discharged over the sodium ions.

(−) At cathode reaction: $2H^+(aq) + 2e^- \rightarrow H_2(g)$

We know that $[H^+(aq)] \times [OH^-(aq)] = K_w$ so if the hydrogen ion concentration is decreasing, the hydroxide ion concentration must be increasing to make K_w the same.

Around the cathode, hydrogen ions are being removed from the solution. So around the cathode, a solution containing hydroxide ions, $OH^-(aq)$, and sodium ions, $Na^+(aq)$, will form, i.e. sodium hydroxide solution. The diaphragm prevents the sodium hydroxide solution reacting with the chlorine gas.

The sodium hydroxide solution produced from the cathode compartment also contains some sodium chloride solution; this results from some chloride ions that can pass through the diaphragm. This solution is concentrated by evaporation and the less soluble sodium chloride crystallises out. The resulting solution is 50% by mass sodium hydroxide and 1% by mass sodium chloride (the rest is water).

3 The production of sodium chlorate(I)

Chlorine gas, produced from the electrolytic process with sodium chloride, may be deliberately reacted with cold and dilute sodium hydroxide solution. This results in the formation of sodium chlorate(I).

$$Cl_2(g) + 2NaOH(aq) \rightarrow NaCl(aq) + NaOCl(aq) + H_2O(l)$$

chlorine gas + sodium hydroxide solution → sodium chloride solution + sodium chlorate(I) solution + water

E Titanium

The extraction of titanium from a titanium oxide based ore consists of two main stages.

Formation of the covalent chloride of titanium

This is achieved by mixing the titanium ore with carbon and heating the mixture in a stream of chlorine gas.

$$TiO_2(s) + C(s) + 2Cl_2(g) \rightarrow TiCl_4(l) + CO_2(g)$$

titanium(IV)oxide + carbon + chlorine gas → titanium(IV) chloride + carbon dioxide

The volatile titanium(IV) chloride is then extracted from the reaction mixture using fractional distillation ready for the next stage.

Production of the metal from titanium(IV) chloride

Either magnesium or sodium is used to displace titanium from the chloride. This reaction is carried out in a steel vessel at 700 °C under an argon atmosphere. Argon is used as an inert atmosphere since other gases, like gases in the air, nitrogen and oxygen, will be absorbed into the titanium metal and, as a result, the titanium will be brittle (compare this with the effect of carbon in steels). Liquid titanium(IV) chloride is then poured into the vessel containing bars of heated magnesium metal. A vigorous reaction results, producing titanium metal.

$$TiCl_4(l) + 2Mg(s) \rightarrow Ti(s) + 2MgCl_2(s)$$

titanium(IV) chloride + magnesium → titanium metal + magnesium chloride

The process for making titanium is very expensive and this restricts its use.

UNIT 12 Inorganic group chemistry

At the end of this unit, you should be familiar with the main chemical reactions and physical properties of the elements in Groups I, II, III (aluminium) and VII.

A Group I: the alkali metals

1 *Li, Na, K, Rb, Cs, Fr*

Group I elements are all reactive and are kept under oil to prevent reaction with oxygen or water vapour in the air. On descending the group, the outer electron is further from the positively charged nucleus and is therefore more easily removed. This leads to increasing reactivity.

All are soft and silvery and the melting points decrease on descending the group since the radius of the positive ion within the metallic structure is becoming larger and so the nucleus is less effective in its ability to bond electrostatically to the sea of delocalised electrons.

All form ionic compounds, although the small and highly charged lithium ion may polarise spherical, negatively charged ions and therefore induce more covalent character in these particular compounds. On descending the group, the polarising ability decreases and compounds become ionic and less covalent in their properties. Some anomalous properties of lithium include:

- lithium hydroxide is sparingly soluble in water
- lithium hydroxide is thermally unstable, $2LiOH(s) \rightarrow Li_2O(s) + H_2O(l)$
- lithium carbonate is unstable, $Li_2CO_3(s) \rightarrow Li_2O(s) + CO_2(g)$

Lithium compounds are often atypical (different) because the high charge density of the lithium ion causes it to polarise anions (distort their electron distribution) and induces covalent character.

All form the +1 state in their compounds by losing their outer s electron to form a singly charged cation. Since this outer electron is relatively easily removed, they are all good reducing agents (with negative standard electrode potentials).

Reactions with oxygen result in various oxides forming. Lithium forms the ordinary oxide containing the O^{2-} ion, whereas sodium forms the peroxide containing the O_2^{2-} ion and the larger cations form the superoxide ion in their compounds, O_2^-.

You may not need to be aware of the existence of more than one oxide with Group I metals (check your syllabus).

$4Li(s) + O_2(g) \rightarrow 2Li_2O(s)$
$2Na(s) + O_2(g) \rightarrow Na_2O_2(s)$
$K(s) + O_2(g) \rightarrow KO_2(s)$

Group I metals react directly, on heating with hydrogen and halogens to form ionic products.

$2Na(s) + H_2(g) \rightarrow 2NaH(s)$; **sodium hydride**
$2K(s) + Cl_2(g) \rightarrow 2KCl(s)$; **potassium chloride**

All of the elements react with water, forming alkaline solutions.

For example, $2Na(s) + 2H_2O(l) \rightarrow 2Na^+(aq) + 2OH^-(aq) + H_2(g)$

Lithium reacts with water more exothermically than sodium but it reacts more slowly – the hydration energy of the lithium ion, Li^+, is more exothermic than the sodium ion, Na^+.

The anions of Group I compounds are sometimes good bases, so after hydration they are hydrolysed to form alkaline solutions.

- **hydration**
  $$Na_2O(s) \xrightarrow{H_2O(l)} 2Na^+(aq) + O^{2-}(aq)$$
  $$Na_2CO_3(s) \xrightarrow{H_2O(l)} 2Na^+(aq) + CO_3^{2-}(aq)$$

- **hydrolysis**
  $$O^{2-}(aq) + H_2O(l) \rightarrow 2OH^-(aq)$$
  $$CO_3^{2-}(aq) + H_2O(l) \rightarrow HCO_3^-(aq) + OH^-(aq)$$

The water molecule undergoes a decomposition (the O–H bond breaks) in a hydrolysis process.

Virtually all Group I compounds are soluble in water.

Thermal stability compounds. Most compounds are thermally resistant compared with the corresponding Group II compounds.There are some notable exceptions:

$$2NaNO_3(s) \rightarrow 2NaNO_2(s) + O_2(g)$$

sodium nitrate(III)

The decomposition of the nitrates (as well as others) can be explained in terms of either polarising power or the difference in lattice energies between the nitrates and the corresponding oxides.

B Group II: the alkaline earth metals

1 Be, Mg, Ca, Sr, Ba, Ra

All the metals are reactive but not as reactive as Group I metals. They are silvery in appearance, although they are harder than the metals in Group I.

They all react by losing their outer two s electrons to form a positive ion (a cation) with a +2 charge.

Since Group II metals donate two electrons to the metallic structure whereas Group I metals only donate one electron per atom, the strength of the metallic bonding is consequently greater. Group II metals have higher melting points, higher densities and higher tensile strengths than Group I metals.

The size of the cation increases down Group II so, in the metallic structure, the sea of delocalised electrons is further from the nucleus in each case. As a result, the strength of the metallic bonding decreases as the group is descended.

They all form ionic compounds but, like lithium, the beryllium ion, Be^{2+}, has a lower ionic radius and a higher charge than the lithium ion. Beryllium polarises negatively charged ions to induce a higher degree of covalent character in the compounds. The oxide of beryllium is amphoteric.

The oxide of beryllium is amphoteric so it may react with either acids or bases.

As a base: $BeO(s) + 2H_3O^+(aq) \rightarrow Be^{2+}(aq) + 3H_2O(l)$

As an acid: $BeO(s) + 2OH^-(aq) + H_2O(l) \rightarrow Be(OH)_4^{2-}(aq)$

The covalent chloride of beryllium, $BeCl_2$, forms a layered structure like aluminium chloride.

They all react with oxygen and halogens directly to form the corresponding oxides (containing the O^{2-} ion) and halides respectively (although those of beryllium are predominantly covalent in bonding and structure).

Group II compounds tend to be less thermodynamically stable compared with Group I compounds, e.g. $MgCO_3(s) \rightarrow MgO(s) + CO_2(g)$, and the degree of thermal dissociation decreases as the group is descended.

Lattice and hydration energies are useful in explaining solubility trends.

Group II compounds tend to be less soluble than Group I compounds. Some Group II compounds are notably more insoluble in water compared with Group I metals, e.g. carbonates, hydroxides, some sulphates(VI). Note that the hydroxides **increase** in solubility as the group is descended, whereas the solubility of the sulphates(VI) **decreases**. This is explained in terms of the effects of the relative sizes of the smaller hydroxide and the larger sulphate(VI) ion on the lattice and hydration energies of these compounds (see Figure 12.1). Both energy quantities decrease as the group is descended but, for hydroxides, the lattice energy decreases more rapidly than the hydration energy (since any change made to the cation affects the lattice energy significantly). For sulphates(VI), the lattice energy decreases less rapidly compared to the hydration energy since the changes made to the metal ion radius affect the lattice energy only slightly because the sulphate(VI) ion is a larger ion.

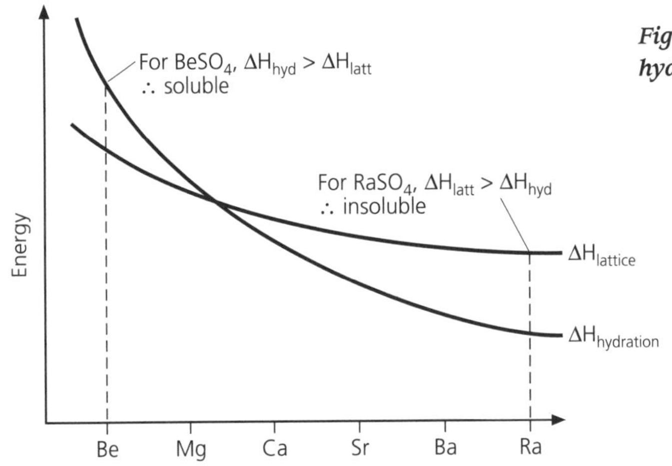

Figure 12.1 Lattice and hydration energies graph

Group II sulphates increase in solubility down the group. Group II hydroxides decrease in solubility.

All react with water to form alkaline solutions, although the reaction is slower and less energetic than the same reaction with a Group I element.

$$Ca(s) + 2H_2O(l) \rightarrow Ca(OH)_2(aq) + H_2(g)$$

Group II hydroxides may only be slightly soluble in water, so the resulting concentration of hydroxide ions is less than with a Group I metal hydroxide and the pH is lower. Group II metal hydroxides are less alkaline or weaker alkalis than those in Group I.

C Group III: aluminium

Aluminium has many uses as a metal. These uses reflect its high tensile strength-to-weight ratio and its ability to form a resistant oxide coating on its surface that protects itself against chemical attack.

The metal is a strong reducing agent. It reduces hydrogen when it reacts with both acids and bases to form a salt and water.

Aluminium compounds tend to display a high degree of covalent character (greater than with beryllium and lithium) because the aluminium ion has a +3 charge and its ionic radius is very low. As a result, the aluminium ion is very polarising and it will distort negatively charged ions and therefore induce covalency in many of its compounds. Although the smaller fluoride ion does not undergo much polarisation, the larger chloride ion is distorted by a greater amount and is therefore more covalent.

The hexaaquaaluminium ion, $[Al(H_2O)_6]^{3+}(aq)$, undergoes hydrolysis in solution. The polarising aluminium ion distorts the water molecules so that the aluminium–oxygen bonds are strengthened and the oxygen–hydrogen bonds in water are weakened. As a result, the hydrated aluminium ion is acidic in solution.

Although these equations look complicated, they involve breaking the O–H bond in a coordinated water molecule and the subsequent protonation of a free water molecule.

$$[Al(H_2O)_6]^{3+}(aq) + H_2O(l) \rightleftharpoons [Al(H_2O)_5(OH)]^{2+}(aq) + H_3O^+(aq)$$

The resulting ion may undergo further hydrolysis according to:

$$[Al(H_2O)_5(OH)]^{2+}(aq) + H_2O(l) \rightleftharpoons [Al(H_2O)_4(OH)_2]^+(aq) + H_3O^+(aq)$$

When base is added to a solution of aluminium ions in water, the equilibria above are displaced to the right-hand side, encouraging more deprotonation in the aluminium complex. This process continues until the aluminium complex has a zero charge, $[Al(H_2O)_3(OH)_3](s)$. If more hydroxide ions are added to this precipitate, the complex dissolves to form aluminate ions, $[Al(OH)_4]^-(aq)$.

Aluminium oxide is amphoteric. It will react with both acids and bases to form a salt.

As a base: $Al_2O_3(s) + 6H_3O^+(aq) \rightarrow 2Al^{3+}(aq) + 9H_2O(l)$
As an acid: $Al_2O_3(s) + 2OH^-(aq) + 3H_2O(l) \rightarrow 2\,[Al(OH)_4]^-(aq)$ the aluminate ion

Aluminium chloride exists in two forms: the hydrated form, $[Al(H_2O)_6]^{3+}3Cl^-$, and the anhydrous form, $AlCl_3$ or Al_2Cl_6 (in its dimeric form). The anhydrous form behaves as a Lewis acid in that it will accept a lone pair of electrons from another species (see Figure 12.2).

- **Lewis acids will accept a lone pair of electrons.**
- **Lewis bases donate a lone pair of electrons.**

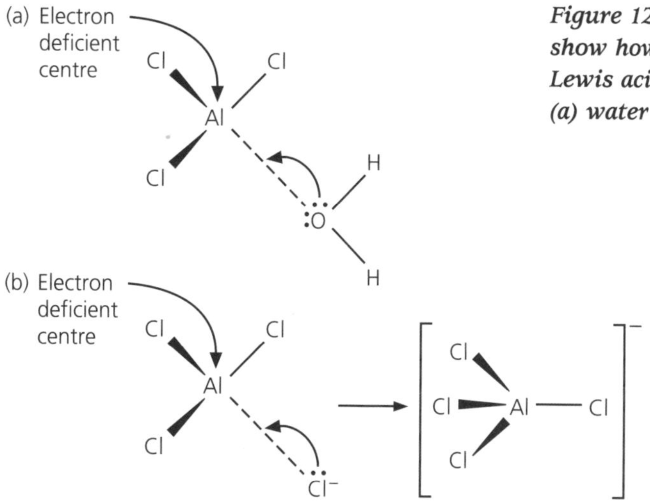

Figure 12.2 Diagrams to show how $AlCl_3$ behaves as a Lewis acid in reactions with (a) water and (b) chloride ions

or symbolically as $AlCl_3 + Cl_2 \rightarrow [AlCl_4]^-Cl^+$

D Group VII: the halogens

1 F, Cl, Br, I, At

Table 12.1

Halogen	Appearance at room temperature	Formula as the element	mpt/°C
Fluorine	pale yellow gas	F_2	−220
Chlorine	pale green gas	Cl_2	−101
Bromine	orange liquid	Br_2	−7
Iodine	dark grey solid	I_2	114

Iodine, as an element, is a dark grey shiny solid – not a brown solution.

The melting and boiling points increase down the group since the number of electrons is also increasing, so increasing the number and strength of the van der Waals interactions.

All halogens exist as diatomic molecules, X_2. The X–X bond length increases down the group as more electron shells shield the nucleus from the bonding electrons. The bond strength therefore decreases down the group, but the F–F bond strength is very weak: $E(F\text{–}F) = +158\ kJ\ mol^{-1}$.

This anomolous value for fluorine is explained in terms of the close proximity of the lone pairs of electrons on adjacent fluorine atoms in the molecule repelling each other and weakening the covalent bond.

Halogens are powerful oxidising agents. They possess seven electrons in their outer electron shell and they will gain one electron (either by sharing or by electron transfer) to complete their outer shell. Their ability to oxidise or gain electrons decreases down the group; this can be illustrated using the electrode potentials:

$$F_2(g) + 2e^- \rightleftharpoons 2F^-(aq) \quad E^\ominus = +2.87\ V$$
$$Cl_2(g) + 2e^- \rightleftharpoons 2Cl^-(aq) \quad E^\ominus = +1.36\ V$$
$$Br_2(g) + 2e^- \rightleftharpoons 2Br^-(aq) \quad E^\ominus = +1.06\ V$$
$$I_2(g) + 2e^- \rightleftharpoons 2I^-(aq) \quad E^\ominus = +0.54\ V$$

Less positive electrode potential as the group is descended

As the electrode potential increases, the equilibrium position shifts to the right-hand side, indicating that the tendency to gain electrons increases. The halogens become more reactive on **ascending** the group. Using the energy cycle in Figure 12.3, it can be seen that the two major reasons for the reactivity of fluorine are the weakness of the F–F bond and the hydration energy of the resulting fluoride ion.

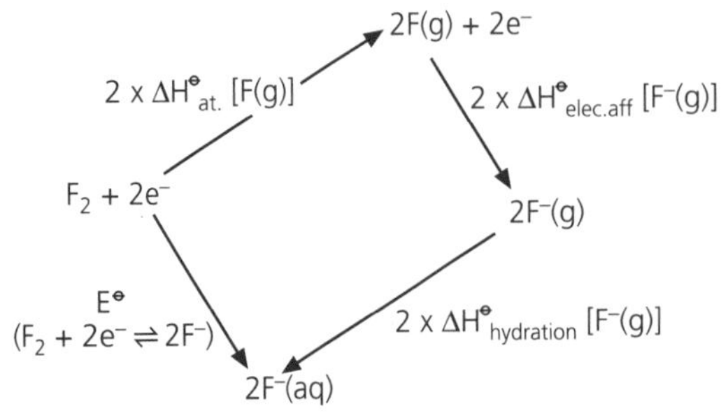

Figure 12.3 Energy cycle that can be used to relate various energy terms to the electrode potential

The halide ions have the ability to act as reducing agents. The ability for a halide ion to lose an outer electron increases on descending the group since the outer electron is shielded more by the extra electron shells:

$2X^-(aq) \rightleftharpoons X_2(aq) + 2e^-$

Reducing power: $I^- > Br^- > Cl^- > F^-$

A halogen with a more positive electrode potential will displace (or oxidise in this case) a halogen, with a less positive electrode potential, from solution:

Bromine is produced from seawater by bubbling chlorine though a concentrated solution containing the bromide ion.

$Cl_2(aq) + 2I^-(aq) \rightarrow 2Cl^-(aq) + I_2(aq)$ or
$Br_2(aq) + 2I^-(aq) \rightarrow 2Br^-(aq) + I_2(aq)$

Concentrated sulphuric(VI) acid undergoes a redox reaction with bromide and iodide ions. (Chloride and fluoride ions are not oxidised by this reagent.) The reactions are complex, so only the major processes are mentioned. In practice, a mixture of products (especially for iodide and bromide) is formed.

All of these equations involve a proton transfer followed by (in the case of HBr and HI) a redox reaction; these can be balanced by using oxidation numbers.

- **With fluoride:**
  $F^-(s) + H_2SO_4(l) \rightarrow HF(g) + HSO_4^-(s)$ acid/base process
- **With chloride:**
  $Cl^-(s) + H_2SO_4(l) \rightarrow HCl(g) + HSO_4^-(s)$ acid/base process
- **With iodide:**
  $I^-(s) + H_2SO_4(l) \rightarrow HI(g) + HSO_4^-(s)$ acid/base process
  then $8HI(g) + H_2SO_4(l) \rightarrow 4I_2(s) + H_2S(g) + 4H_2O(l)$; redox.
  I: −1 to 0, S: +6 to −2
- **With bromide:**
  $Br^-(s) + H_2SO_4(l) \rightarrow HBr(g) + HSO_4^-(s)$ acid/base process
  then: $2HBr(g) + H_2SO_4(l) \rightarrow Br_2(l) + SO_2(g) + 2H_2O(l)$; redox
  Br: −1 to 0, S: +6 to +4

The halogens are all electronegative elements when in a covalent bond. They are able to attract a bonded pair of electrons towards themselves. The electronegativity decreases down the group (as more electron shells are added). As a result of this, molecules containing halogens tend to be polar.

In solution, HF is a weak acid but, in its pure state, HF is one of the strongest acids in existence.

The hydrogen halides are all strong acids, except hydrogen fluoride, HF. Most dissociate completely in water to form halide ions and hydrogen ions.

$HCl(g) + H_2O(l) \rightleftharpoons H_3O^+(aq) + Cl^-(aq)$

The order of strength of hydrogen halides as acids is determined largely by the strength of the H–X bond (H–F > H–Cl > H–Br > H–I). The strength of acidity in solution is HI > HBr > HCl ≫ HF. Hydrogen fluoride is a weak acid as a result of the strength of the hydrogen–fluorine covalent bond.

The relative boiling points of the hydrogen halides are explained by hydrogen bonding (in hydrogen fluoride only) and van der Waals interactions (HI > HBr > HCl due to a greater number of electrons within the molecules).

The halide ions can be identified by testing with silver(I) nitrate solution acidified with nitric(V) acid and then adding ammonia solution. Table 12.2 lists the resulting coloured silver halide precipitates seen.

Halide ion $X^-(aq)$	Addition of acidified silver nitrate solution to form coloured precipitate	Solubility in dil. $NH_3(aq)$	Solubility in conc. $NH_3(aq)$
$Cl^-(aq)$	white: silver(I) chloride, AgCl(s)	dissolves	dissolves
$Br^-(aq)$	cream: silver(I) bromide, AgBr(s)	insoluble	dissolves
$I^-(aq)$	yellow: silver(I) iodide, AgI(s)	insoluble	insoluble

Table 12.2

An ionic equation for these precipitations would be:

$Ag^+(aq) + X^-(aq) \rightarrow AgX(s)$

- **For example:**

  $Ag^+(aq) + Cl^-(aq) \rightarrow AgCl(s)$

  and then:

  $AgCl(s) + 2NH_3(aq) \rightleftharpoons [Ag(NH_3)_2]^+(aq)$ the diamminesilver(I) ion (a linear complex)

Iodides are more covalent in character than other halides since the large spherical electron distribution of the halide ion may be easily polarised (or distorted) by a cation.

The radius of the X^- ion increases down the group. Therefore the polarisability also increases as the group is descended. As a result, the tendency of the spherical electron distribution to be distorted by cations increases, so the degree of covalent character increases down the group. Hence lithium fluoride, LiF, would be more ionic than lithium chloride, LiCl, than lithium bromide, LiBr, than lithium iodide, LiI. This is due to the high charge density of the lithium ion polarising the larger iodide ion more than the smaller and more tightly-bound electron cloud of the fluoride ion. The corresponding physical properties set out in Table 12.3 should also be predictable.

Table 12.3

Physical properties	LiF	LiCl	LiBr	LiI
melting point and boiling point	decreases →→→→→→→→			
electrical conductivity when molten	decreases →→→→→→→→			
solubility in polar solvents	decreases →→→→→→→→			
solubility in non-polar solvents	increases →→→→→→→→			

Disproportionation is the process of simultaneous oxidation and reduction of the same species. Chlorine disproportionates in cold, dilute and aqueous alkali:

$Cl_2(g) + 2NaOH(aq) \rightarrow NaOCl(aq) + NaCl(aq) + H_2O(l)$

chlorine: 0 to +1 and from 0 to −1

Sodium chlorate(I) is used as a bleach as the chlorate(I) ion oxidises germs and bacteria:

HOCl is a much better oxidising agent than OCl^-.

$ClO^-(aq) + 2H^+(aq) + 2e^- \rightleftharpoons Cl^-(aq) + H_2O(l)$

The chlorate(I) ion disproportionates in hot and concentrated hydroxide ions according to:

$3ClO^-(aq) \rightarrow 2Cl^-(aq) + ClO_3^-(aq)$ (the ClO_3^- ion is the pyramidal chlorate(V) ion)

Chloric(I) acid, HOCl(aq), is a bleaching and oxidising agent and it will decompose in the presence of visible light to form oxygen:

$2HOCl(aq) \rightarrow 2HCl(aq) + O_2(g)$

UNIT 13 Transition metals

At the end of this unit, you should be familiar with:
- properties of the transition metals
- what a transition metal is
- the colour of transition metal compounds
- complex formation
- variable oxidation state
- catalytic behaviour

A Properties of the transition metals

The metals are all denser, have higher tensile strengths and have higher melting and boiling points compared to other main group metals. Transition metals are able to delocalise both their s and d electrons into the metallic structure. Since the d orbitals shield poorly the delocalised electrons from the nuclear charge, the positively charged nucleus has a significant attraction towards the electron cloud. The effect of this poor shielding by the 3d electrons is to contract the outer electrons in towards the nucleus, thus making the atoms relatively small compared with main group metallic elements. As a result of the increased number of delocalised electrons and the smaller size of the ions formed, the strength of the metallic bonding is larger with these metals.

In the first series of the transition metals (Sc to Zn), an extra proton is being added into the nucleus but an extra electron is being added to the 3d sub-shell, thus shielding the outer 4s electrons. The effect of these two competing factors is that the outer 4s electrons all experience similar nuclear pulls. Therefore, the transition metals all have similar first ionisation energies, reactivity and atomic radii.

They are of relatively low reactivity. The outer s electrons being removed are very much under the influence of the positively charged nucleus since the d electrons are relatively ineffective at shielding (see above). As a result, the outer electrons are more tightly bound to the nucleus than with, for example, a Group I metal. The electrode potentials for the metals are therefore not as negative as for main group metals, which explains their relative reluctance to be oxidised to form cations.

For example: $K^+(aq) + e^- \rightleftharpoons K(s)$; $E^\ominus = -2.92\,V$
whereas $Cu^+(aq) + e^- \rightleftharpoons Cu(s)$; $E^\ominus = +0.52\,V$

B What is a transition metal?

A transition metal is defined as a metal that forms at least one ion which has a partially filled d orbital.

Scandium and zinc are not often considered to be transition metals since they do not form one stable ion in which there is a partially filled d sub-shell. Sc^{3+} and Zn^{2+} do not have partially filled sub-shells.

1 *Electronic configuration of transition metal atoms*

The electronic configurations of the first series of transition metals are shown below. The box diagrams on the right-hand side show the electrons in the 4s and 3d orbitals only.

		4s	3d				
Sc	$1s^2, 2s^2, 2p^6, 3s^2, 3p^6, \mathbf{4s^2, 3d^1}$	↑↓	↑				
Ti	$1s^2, 2s^2, 2p^6, 3s^2, 3p^6, \mathbf{4s^2, 3d^2}$	↑↓	↑	↑			
V	$1s^2, 2s^2, 2p^6, 3s^2, 3p^6, \mathbf{4s^2, 3d^3}$	↑↓	↑	↑	↑		
*Cr	$1s^2, 2s^2, 2p^6, 3s^2, 3p^6, \mathbf{4s^1, 3d^5}$	↑	↑	↑	↑	↑	↑
Mn	$1s^2, 2s^2, 2p^6, 3s^2, 3p^6, \mathbf{4s^2, 3d^5}$	↑↓	↑	↑	↑	↑	↑
Fe	$1s^2, 2s^2, 2p^6, 3s^2, 3p^6, \mathbf{4s^2, 3d^6}$	↑↓	↑↓	↑	↑	↑	↑
Co	$1s^2, 2s^2, 2p^6, 3s^2, 3p^6, \mathbf{4s^2, 3d^7}$	↑↓	↑↓	↑↓	↑	↑	↑
Ni	$1s^2, 2s^2, 2p^6, 3s^2, 3p^6, \mathbf{4s^2, 3d^8}$	↑↓	↑↓	↑↓	↑↓	↑	↑
*Cu	$1s^2, 2s^2, 2p^6, 3s^2, 3p^6, \mathbf{4s^1, 3d^{10}}$	↑	↑↓	↑↓	↑↓	↑↓	↑↓
Zn	$1s^2, 2s^2, 2p^6, 3s^2, 3p^6, \mathbf{4s^2, 3d^{10}}$	↑↓	↑↓	↑↓	↑↓	↑↓	↑↓

2 *Electronic configuration of transition metal ions*

When a transition metal atom forms a positive ion, the electrons are removed from the 4s first and then the 3d.

Since most transition metals have two electrons in the 4s orbital, loss of these two electrons tends to result in the most common oxidation state being +2. For this reason, zinc and scandium are not normally defined as transition metals. They form no other ion apart from Zn^{2+} and Sc^{3+} (both of which have a complete and vacant 3d orbital respectively).

3 *Electronic configurations for ions of transition metals*

		4s	3d				
Ti^{4+}	$1s^2, 2s^2, 2p^6, 3s^2, 3p^6$						

(this ion is colourless since it possesses no 3d partially filled)

		4s	3d				
V^{3+}	$1s^2, 2s^2, 2p^6, 3s^2, 3p^6, \mathbf{3d^2}$		↑	↑			
Cr^{2+}	$1s^2, 2s^2, 2p^6, 3s^2, 3p^6, \mathbf{3d^4}$		↑	↑	↑	↑	
Mn^{2+}	$1s^2, 2s^2, 2p^6, 3s^2, 3p^6, \mathbf{3d^5}$		↑	↑	↑	↑	↑
Fe^{3+}	$1s^2, 2s^2, 2p^6, 3s^2, 3p^6, \mathbf{3d^5}$		↑	↑	↑	↑	↑
Co^{3+}	$1s^2, 2s^2, 2p^6, 3s^2, 3p^6, \mathbf{3d^6}$		↑↓	↑	↑	↑	↑
Ni^{2+}	$1s^2, 2s^2, 2p^6, 3s^2, 3p^6, \mathbf{3d^8}$		↑↓	↑↓	↑↓	↑	↑
Cu^{+}	$1s^2, 2s^2, 2p^6, 3s^2, 3p^6, \mathbf{3d^{10}}$		↑↓	↑↓	↑↓	↑↓	↑↓

(the Cu^+ ion is colourless since it has a filled 3d orbital)

It is very difficult to predict the ion that is likely to form by considering electronic configurations alone. However, the +2 state is common and this is because most of these metals possess an outer $4s^2$ configuration. The maximum oxidation state is the sum of the outer s and d electrons.

C Colour of transition metal compounds

Colour is the result of incomplete d sub-shells in transition metal compounds.

Most transition metal ions in complexing medium, e.g. water, are coloured. The hydrated metal ion has **unpaired electrons** that are able to interact with visible light and impart colour to the solution or the crystalline solid. For this reason, ions with no or completed 3d orbitals tend not to be coloured. The half-filled d sub-shell seems to possess a degree of stability. It is dangerous to talk of half-filled p or half-filled s orbitals having any extra stability since this is not the case. The stability of the ions Mn^{2+} and Fe^{3+} can be tentatively explained in terms of a half-filled 3d sub-shell.

D Complex formation

Transition metal ions react with ligands to form complexes.

A ligand is a lone pair electron donor; this is sometimes called a Lewis base. In an organic context, it will be called a nucleophile.

- A complex is a species in which a group of ligands are datively bonded to a central metal ion.
- A ligand is a molecule or ion with the capacity to donate an electron pair and form a dative bond (see Table 13.1 for examples).

Table 13.1

Ligand	Name of complex formed from ligand
NH_3	ammine-
H_2O	aqua-
Cl^-	chloro-
CN^-	cyano-
$S_2O_3^{2-}$	thiosulphato-

- Ligands are Lewis bases since they are electron pair donors.
- A dative bond is a polar covalent bond formed when one atom donates **both** electrons towards the formation of the bond.
- Ligands are also named according to the number of dative bonds that they form per ligand. Ligands that form one dative bond are called **monodentate** ligands (e.g. H_2O, NH_3, Cl^-) and those that form two bonds are called **bidentate** ($H_2N(CH_2)_2NH_2$, $C_2O_4^{2-}$). EDTA has the capacity to be a **hexadentate** ligand (see Figure 13.1).

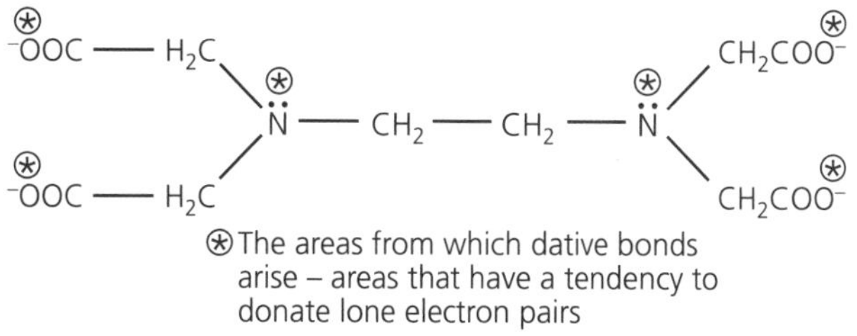

***Figure 13.1* EDTA with its available lone pairs shown**

Examples of transition metal complexes and their corresponding three-dimensional shapes include:

$[Ag(NH_3)_2]^+$	diamminesilver(I)	linear
$[Ag(S_2O_3)_2]^{3-}$	dithiosulphatoargentate(I)	linear
$[CuCl_4]^{2-}$	tetrachlorocuprate(II)	tetrahedral
$[CoCl_4]^{2-}$	tetrachlorocobaltate(II)	tetrahedral
$[Fe(H_2O)_6]^{2+}$	hexaaquairon(II)	octahedral
$[Fe(CN)_6]^{3-}$	hexacyanoferrate(III)	octahedral
$[Cu(NH_3)_4(H_2O)_2]^{2+}$	tetraaminediaquacopper(II)	distorted octahedral

Negatively charged complexes containing metals end in '-ate'. The metallic part of the name may have to change according to the Latin stem, e.g. copper to cuprate, iron to ferrate, etc.

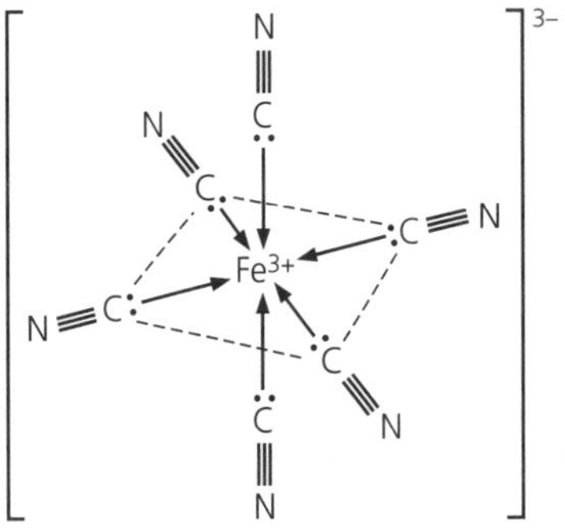

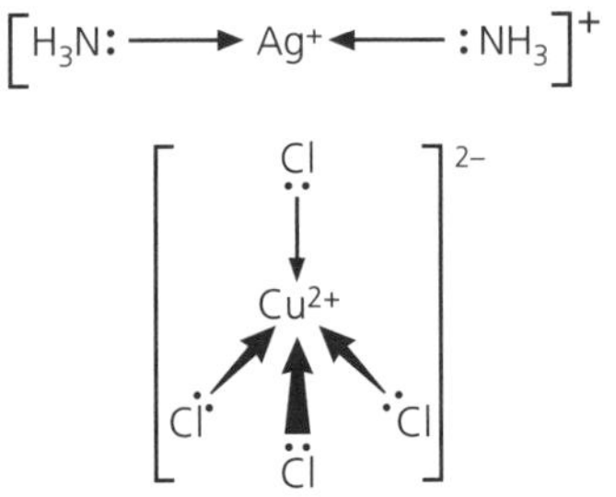

Figure 13.2 *$[Fe(CN)_6]^{3-}$, $[Ag(NH_3)_2]^+$ and $[CuCl_4]^{2-}$*

1 *Structural, geometrical and optical isomers of transition metal complexes*

Inorganic complexes may sometimes display geometrical isomerism and optical isomerism. These types of isomerism are not just confined to organic chemistry.

Organic structures are able to exist in different isomeric forms. This is also true of the octahedral complexes of some of the transition metals (see Figure 13.3).

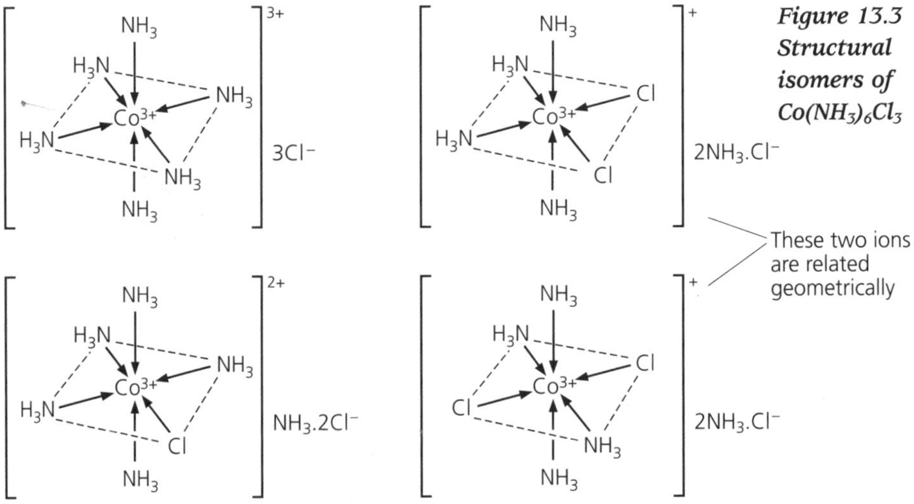

Figure 13.3 Structural isomers of $Co(NH_3)_6Cl_3$

Silver(I) nitrate solution will distinguish the various structural isomers since silver(I) ions will react and precipitate out the chloride ions that are **not** bonded to the central metal ion. The other chloride ions will not combine with silver ions since they will be strongly bonded to the central metal ion. By analysing the number of moles of silver chloride obtained from one mole of each complex, the number of moles of datively bonded and externally bonded chloride ions may be assessed (Table 13.2).

In all of these complexes, the coordination number of the metal ion is 6, that is the number of nearest neighbours is 6.

Empirical formula	Colour of solid	% ionic chlorine	Formula of complex
(i) $CoCl_3(NH_3)_6$	orange-yellow	100	$[Co(NH_3)_6]^{3+}.3Cl^-$
(ii) $CoCl_3(NH_3)_6$	violet	67	$[Co(NH_3)_5Cl]^{2+}.NH_3.2Cl^-$
(iii) $CoCl_3(NH_3)_6$	violet	33	$[Co(NH_3)_4Cl_2]^+.2NH_3.Cl^-$
(iv) $CoCl_3(NH_3)_6$	green	33	$[Co(NH_3)_4Cl_2]^+.2NH_3.Cl^-$

Note that (iii) and (iv) are geometrically related.

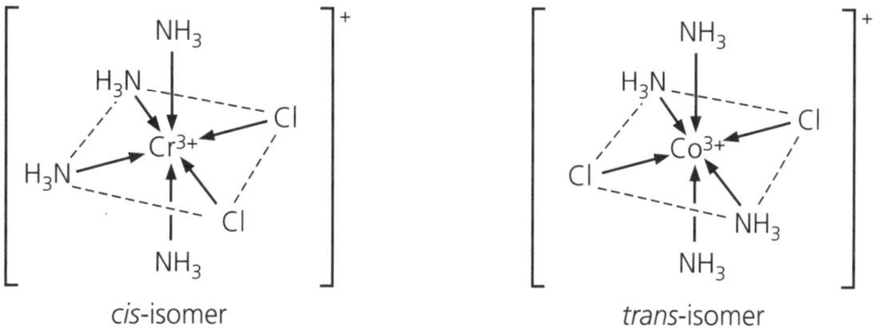

Figure 13.4 The cis and trans forms of $[Cr(NH_3)_4Cl_2]^+$

cis-isomer

trans-isomer

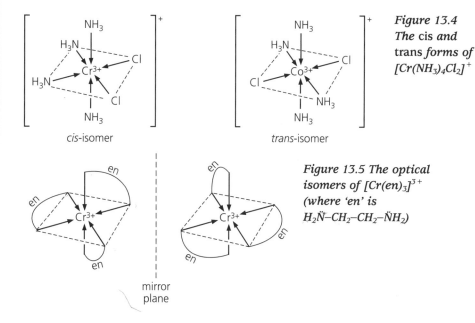

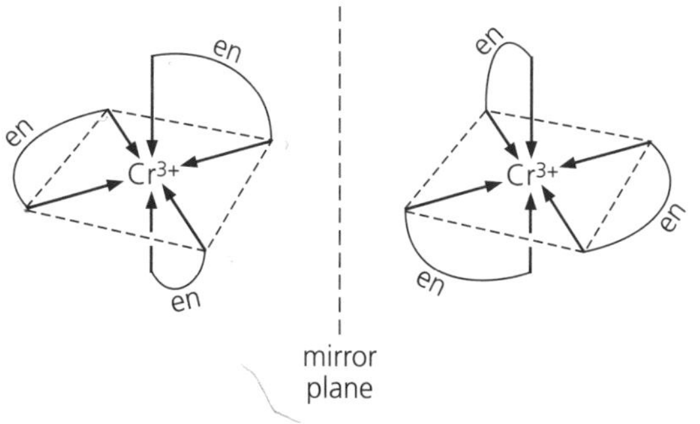

Figure 13.5 The optical isomers of $[Cr(en)_3]^{3+}$ (where 'en' is $H_2\ddot{N}-CH_2-CH_2-\ddot{N}H_2$)

mirror plane

The reactions of hydrated transition metal ions is often misunderstood and unfamiliar. Make sure that you are aware of the reactions that you must know.

All hydrated ions react initially by a step-wise process called deprotonation. As this process occurs, the charge on the complex becomes less positive until it reaches zero. Then the complex forms as an insoluble species.

2 Reactions of hydrated transition metal ions

2.1 TRANSITION METAL IONS IN THE +2 OXIDATION STATE

All form M^{2+} as the most common oxidation state (loss of both s electrons). All aqueous ions consist of the octahedral $[M(H_2O)_6]^{2+}(aq)$ ion (Table 13.3).

Table 13.3

V^{2+}	Cr^{2+}	Mn^{2+}	Fe^{2+}	Co^{2+}	Ni^{2+}	Cu^{2+}
lavender	blue	pale pink	pale green	pink	green	blue

2.1a Reactions

- **With sodium hydroxide solution, $Na^+OH^-(aq)$**
 All aqueous ions are deprotonated in a stepwise process until the zero charged hydroxide precipitate is formed.
 $[M(H_2O)_6]^{2+}(aq) + 2OH^-(aq) \rightarrow [M(H_2O)_4(OH)_2](s) + 2H_2O(l)$
 The colours of the precipitates are generally the same as corresponding aqua ions except for cobalt in which blue $[Co(H_2O)_4(OH)_2](s)$ forms.

- **With excess sodium hydroxide solution**
 All the hydroxides are only slightly soluble and these reactions are of little importance here.

- **With ammonia solution**
 Step one: deprotonation using $OH^-(aq)$ from $NH_3 + H_2O \rightleftharpoons NH_4^+ + OH^-$ (see above).

Step two: some hydroxide precipitates dissolve in excess ammonia solution. This process is known as **ligand exchange** or **ligand substitution**.

$$[M(H_2O)_4(OH)_2](s) + 6NH_3(aq) \rightleftharpoons [M(NH_3)_6]^{2+}(aq) + 4H_2O(l) + 2OH^-(aq)$$

This happens for Co^{2+}, Ni^{2+} and Cu^{2+} in which yellow, blue and aquamarine amine complexes form. Copper(II) forms complexes with only four ammonia ligands and two water ligands, i.e. $[Cu(NH_3)_4(H_2O)_2]^{2+}(aq)$: tetraamminediaqua copper(II) ion (distorted octahedron).

If an ammine complex forms, the metal ion is normally bonded to six ammonia molecules. However, copper(II) normally forms strong bonds to only four ammonia molecules and two weak bonds to water molecules.

Special case: cobalt(II). When $[Co(NH_3)_6]^{2+}(aq)$ is formed, this yellow complex will turn dark brown due to the formation of hexaammine cobalt(III) in an oxidation process:

$$2[Co(NH_3)_6]^{2+}(aq) + 2H^+(aq) + \tfrac{1}{2}O_2(g) \rightarrow 2[Co(NH_3)_6]^{3+}(aq) + H_2O(l)$$

- **With sodium carbonate solution, $Na_2CO_3(aq)$**
  This solution is mildly alkaline due to the basic carbonate ion: $CO_3^{2-} + H_2O \rightleftharpoons HCO_3^- + OH^-$, however the concentration of OH^- is small. **The carbonate ions react with aqua ions to form insoluble carbonate precipitates** (colours are similar to those of hydroxide precipitates):
  $[M(H_2O)_6]^{2+}(aq) + CO_3^{2-}(aq) \rightarrow MCO_3(s) + 6H_2O(l)$
  Basic hydroxy-carbonate complexes are also likely.

2.2 Transition metal ions in the +3 oxidation state

Most transition metal elements form M^{3+}. Although the stable and well-documented ions are Cr^{3+} (green but red when non-hydrolysed) and Fe^{3+} (yellow but pale violet when non-hydrolysed), their chemistry is very similar to that of Al^{3+} (similar radius to charge ratio). In aqueous solution, all exist as the $[M(H_2O)_6]^{3+}$ ion, although hydrolysis always occurs to form the ion $[M(H_2O)_5(OH)]^{2+}$ (this explains the colour change). The high polarising ability of M^{3+} is due to the high positive charge, small ionic size and lack of shielding ability of the 3d electrons. This reveals the nuclear charge to ligands like water molecules and these are consequently strongly held.

$$[M(H_2O)_6]^{3+}(aq) + H_2O(l) \rightleftharpoons [M(H_2O)_5(OH)]^{2+}(aq) + H_3O^+(aq)$$

As a result of this reaction, solutions of Cr^{3+} and Fe^{3+} tend to be acidic (compared with Al^{3+}) and have a pK_a close to ethanoic acid.

2.2a Reactions

- **With sodium hydroxide solution, $Na^+OH^-(aq)$**
  When hydroxide ions are added from the reaction above, it shifts progressively over to the right-hand side and more water molecules are deprotonated until the zero charged complex is formed (see M^{2+} complexes).

  $[Cr(H_2O)_6]^{3+}(aq) + 3OH^-(aq) \rightleftharpoons [Cr(OH)_3(H_2O)_3](s) + 3H_2O(l)$
  green solution — grey/green precipitate

  $[Fe(H_2O)_6]^{3+}(aq) + 3OH^-(aq) \rightleftharpoons [Fe(OH)_3(H_2O)_3](s) + 3H_2O(l)$
  yellow solution — brown precipitate

  However, like $Al(OH)_3(H_2O)_3(s)$, further reaction takes place to form $[Cr(OH)_6]^{3-}(aq)$, hexahydroxochromate(III), a green solution; ($[Fe(OH)_3(H_2O)_3](s)$ does not react in this way):

  $[Cr(OH)_3(H_2O)_3](s) + 3OH^-(aq) \rightleftharpoons [Cr(OH)_6]^{3-}(aq) + 3H_2O(l)$

Chromium(III) hydroxide is the main complex that dissolves in excess hydroxide ions; the rest do not tend to do this.

If an examination question asks for an equation, you must make sure that it balances. It is very common to see chemical transformations represented by writing substances on arrows, etc. and the final 'equation' does not balance.

- **With ammonia solution**
  The reactions take place involving OH^- (see above). Little further reaction takes place to form $[M(NH_3)_6]^{3+}(aq)$ with $M^{3+}(aq)$, although chromium can form slowly the $[Cr(NH_3)_6]^{3+}(aq)$ complex.

- **With sodium carbonate solution, $Na_2CO_3(aq)$**
  Since this solution is alkaline, reaction initially takes place to form hydroxide precipitates. Carbon dioxide gas also forms because the aqueous solution of M^{3+} is acidic, i.e.
  $CO_3^{2-}(aq) + H_3O^+(aq) \rightarrow CO_2(g) + H_2O(l)$
  So, $\mathbf{2[Cr(H_2O)_6]^{3+}(aq) + CO_3^{2-}(aq) \rightarrow 2[Cr(H_2O)_5(OH)]^{2+}(aq) + CO_2(g) + H_2O(l)}$
  etc.
  the overall reaction is:
  $\mathbf{2[Cr(H_2O)_6]^{3+}(aq) + 3CO_3^{2-}(aq) \rightarrow 2[Cr(H_2O)_3(OH)_3](s) + 3CO_2(g) + 3H_2O(l)}$
  Further dissolving of the $[Cr(H_2O)_3(OH)_3](s)$ is not often possible since the concentration of OH^- is not great enough in aqueous carbonate solutions. $[Fe(H_2O)_6]^{3+}(aq)$ tends to react in the same way as $[Cr(H_2O)_6]^{3+}(aq)$, as does $[Al(H_2O)_6]^{3+}(aq)$.

E Variable oxidation state

The number of possible oxidation states varies according to the number of unpaired electrons in the transition metal atom. From the left to the right, the number of possible states increases and peaks at Mn. After this, electrons start to pair up, reducing the number of unpaired electrons.

Transition metals can form ions in more than one oxidation state. There are many alternative electronic configurations for transition metal ions that are reasonably stable. We must indicate the oxidation state of the metal ion in the name of the substance being considered, e.g. copper(II) sulphate (contains the Cu^{2+} ion), copper(I) oxide (contains the Cu^+ ion), chromium(III) fluoride (contains the Cr^{3+} ion).

1 *Electrode potential considerations*

Electrode potentials yield some important information regarding the relative stability of various transition metal ions when in aqueous solution. It is possible to assess the tendency of some metal ions to disproportionate in water, e.g. copper(I), $Cu^+(aq)$.

Using the electrode potentials:

$Cu^{2+}(aq) + e^- \rightleftharpoons Cu^+(aq);\ E^\ominus = +0.15\,V$ and
$Cu^+(aq) + e^- \rightleftharpoons Cu(s);\ E^\ominus = +0.52\,V$

Combining these two gives: $2Cu^+(aq) \rightleftharpoons Cu(s) + Cu^{2+}(aq)$
where the overall electrode potential is $+0.52 - 0.15 = \mathbf{+0.37\,V}$.

Copper(I) compounds normally disproportionate in aqueous solution to form copper metal and copper(II) ions. However, the presence of iodide ions stabilises the copper(I) by forming the insoluble copper(I) iodide and this reduces the concentration of Cu(I) ions in solution.

The positive value for the electrode potential means that the disproportionation should take place (is spontaneous) and so copper(I) ions (colourless or white in appearance) tend to produce a blue solution of aqueous copper(II) ions and a precipitate of pinky-brown copper metal. Mn(VI) and Au(I) also disproportionate in aqueous solution.

Disproportionation is the simultaneous oxidation and reduction of the same species.

2 Ligand stabilisation of oxidation states

Ligands like cyanide ions, CN^-, if added to a particular transition metal ion in aqueous solution, may affect the electrode potential for a particular process. Consider the following electrode potentials:

$Fe^{3+}(aq) + e^- \rightleftharpoons Fe^{2+}(aq)$; $E^\ominus = +0.77$ V and
$I_2(aq) + 2e^- \rightleftharpoons 2I^-(aq)$; $E^\ominus = +0.54$ V

These two potentials suggest that a reaction will take place between iron(III) ions, Fe^{3+}, and iodide ions, I^-, resulting in the formation of iron(II) ions, Fe^{2+}, and iodine, I_2. However, if cyanide ions are added to a solution containing iron(II) and iron(III) ions, then the following equilibrium will operate:

$[Fe(CN)_6]^{3-} + e^- \rightleftharpoons [Fe(CN)_6]^{4-}$; $E^\ominus = +0.36$ V

So, if the iron(III)-containing complex $[Fe(CN)_6]^{3-}$ is added to iodide ions, no reaction should *take* place this time ($E^\ominus = -0.18$ V). However, if iodine, I_2, is added to hexacyanoferrate(II) ions, $[Fe(CN)_6]^{4-}$, a reaction should occur, forming hexacyanoferrate(III) ions, $[Fe(CN)_6]^{3-}$, and iodide ions ($E^\ominus = +0.18$ V). It can be seen therefore that in the presence of cyanide ions, the Fe^{3+} state is stabilised more than if in an aqueous solution. In other words, iron(III) ions, Fe^{3+}, are more powerfully oxidising in water than in cyanide, and iron(II), Fe^{2+} ion, becomes appreciably more reducing in cyanide systems than in water systems.

The stability of one oxidation state over another may depend on the type of ligands involved and the pH of the solution.

3 Redox processes involving transition metal ions

Below are some well-known interconversions which you may need to know (some fine details may be omitted; you can find these in your text).

3.1 Chromium, Cr

Chromium can form ions in the +2, +3 and +6 oxidation states (Table 13.4).

Table 13.4

Ion	Cr(II)	Cr(III)	Cr(VI)
Colour	blue	green	orange in $Cr_2O_7^{2-}$ yellow in CrO_4^{2-}

Chromium(III) ions are red and not green when non-hydrolysed $[Cr(H_2O)_6]^{3+}$.

- **The chromate(VI)–dichromate(VI) interconversion (CrO_4^{2-}(yellow)/$Cr_2O_7^{2-}$ (orange))**
  This is not a redox reaction but, in alkaline and acidic conditions, the equilibrium position in the following process is affected:
  adding acid (H^+) ⟶
  $$2CrO_4^{2-}(aq) + 2H^+(aq) \rightleftharpoons Cr_2O_7^{2-}(aq) + H_2O(l)$$
  ⟵ adding alkali (OH^-)

- **Cr(III) → Cr(VI)**
  Chromium(III) can be converted into the Cr(VI) species (CrO_4^{2-}) by warming a solution containing the chromium(III) ion and sodium hydroxide solution with aqueous hydrogen peroxide:
  $2Cr^{3+}(aq) + 4OH^-(aq) + 3O_2^{2-}(aq)$ (from H_2O_2) $\rightarrow 2CrO_4^{2-}(aq) + 2H_2O(l)$

Chromium(II) ions are easily oxidised by oxygen in the air to form $[Cr(H_2O)_6]^{3+}$.

- **Cr(VI) → Cr(III)**
  Chromate (VI) is reduced to the green chromium(III) using an aqueous solution containing acidified iron(II) ions:
  $Cr_2O_7^{2-}(aq) + 14H^+(aq) + 6Fe^{2+}(aq) \rightarrow 2Cr^{3+}(aq) + 7H_2O(l) + 6Fe^{3+}(aq)$
- **Cr(VI) → Cr(II)**
  Chromium(VI), as orange $Cr_2O_7^{2-}(aq)$, is reduced to chromium(III) using zinc in hydrochloric acid solution:
  $Cr_2O_7^{2-}(aq) + 14H^+(aq) + 4Zn(s) \rightarrow 2Cr^{2+}(aq) + 7H_2O(l) + 4Zn^{2+}(aq)$

3.2 Vanadium, V

Vanadium can form ions in the +2, +3, +4 and +5 oxidation states (Table 13.5).

Table 13.5

Ion	V(II)	V(III)	V(IV)	V(V)
Colour	mauve	green	blue	yellow as VO_2^+ or VO_3^-

- **V(V) → V(IV)**
  Bubbling sulphur dioxide gas through a solution of yellow VO_3^- ions and warming produces the bright blue VO^{2+} ion:
  $2VO_3^-(aq) + 4H^+(aq) + SO_2(g) \rightarrow 2VO^{2+}(aq) + SO_4^{2-}(aq) + 2H_2O(l)$
- **V(V) → V(III)**
  Warming the $VO_3^-(aq)$ solution with iodide ions results in the formation of iodine and VO^{2+}. Then adding sodium thiosulphate solution forms the green V^{3+} ion.
  $2VO_3^-(aq) + 8H^+(aq) + 2I^-(aq) \rightarrow 2VO^{2+}(aq) + I_2(aq) + 4H_2O(l)$
  Then $VO^{2+}(aq) + 2H^+(aq) + e^- \rightleftharpoons V^{3+}(aq) + H_2O(l)$
- **V(V) → V(II)**
  If an acidified solution of $VO_2^+(aq)$ is warmed with zinc powder, the solution will turn green (this contains a mixture of V(V) and V(IV)), then blue, green and finally mauve due to (VII):
  $2VO_2^+(aq) + 3Zn(s) + 8H^+(aq) \rightarrow 2V^{2+}(aq) + 3Zn^{2+}(aq) + 4H_2O(l)$

Acidified potassium manganate(VII) solution will oxidise V(II) back up to V(V).

3.3 Manganese, Mn

Potassium manganate(VII) solution (potassium permanganate) is a well-known oxidising agent that is easily converted, in acidic conditions, to form the pale pink Mn^{2+} ion.

$MnO_4^-(aq) + 8H^+(aq) + 5e^- \rightleftharpoons Mn^{2+}(aq) + 4H_2O(l); E^\ominus = +1.51\,V$

Potassium manganate(VII) solution is of importance in titrations in determining the concentration or amounts of reducing agents, e.g. Fe(II), V(II) or V(III). In titrations of this type, potassium manganate(VII) solution is added from the burette and the end point is indicated by the first pale pink coloration in the solution.

Potassium manganate(VII) solution is self-indicating. The titration ends with the first pale pink coloration to the solution being titrated.

In acidic conditions, it is normally the lower oxidation state that is favoured and, in alkaline conditions, the higher oxidation state, e.g. Mn(VII) to Mn(II) in acidic conditions, Cr(III) to Cr(VI) in alkaline conditions.

3.4 Iron, Fe

Iron can form ions in the common +2 and +3 oxidation states (Table 13.6).

Table 13.6

Ion	Fe(II)	Fe(III)
Colour	pale green	yellow or brown

- **Fe(0) → Fe(II)**
  If hydrogen chloride gas is passed over heated iron, iron(II) chloride is formed:
  $\mathbf{Fe(s) + 2HCl(g) \rightarrow FeCl_2(s) + H_2(g)}$

- **Fe(0) → Fe(III)**
  If chlorine gas is passed over heated iron, iron(III) chloride is formed:
  $\mathbf{Fe(s) + 3Cl_2(g) \rightarrow Fe_2Cl_6(s)}$ **(or** $\mathbf{FeCl_3(s)}$**)**

- **Fe(II) → Fe(III)**
  Most oxidising agents can convert Fe(II) into Fe(III), e.g. Cl_2, H_2O_2, MnO_4^-, $Cr_2O_7^{2-}$, etc.
  The reduction potential for $Fe^{3+} + e^- \rightleftharpoons Fe^{2+}$ is $+0.77\,V$. Any system with a more positive voltage will, in theory, be able to convert Fe(II) into Fe(III).

- **Fe(III) → Fe(II)**
  Iodide ions will reduce iron(III) to iron(II):
  $\mathbf{2I^-(aq) + 2Fe^{3+}(aq) \rightarrow 2Fe^{2+}(aq) + I_2(aq)}$

Acidified potassium manganate(VII) is not used to oxidise Fe(II) to Fe(III) in, for example, $FeCl_2$, since the chloride ions will also be oxidised to form chlorine gas (this may be a problem).

F Catalytic behaviour

There are two main types of catalytic behaviour depending on the phases of the reactants and the catalysts. See Unit 6 for a more in-depth discussion of these two types of catalysis.

1 *Heterogeneous catalysis*

The reactants and the catalyst are in different physical states.

- the Haber process:
  $N_2(g) + 3H_2(g) \rightleftharpoons 2NH_3(g)$, catalyst: iron
- saturating alkenes, catalyst: finely divided nickel
- the synthesis of nitrogen(II) oxide as a precursor to forming nitric(V) acid:
  $4NH_3(g) + 5O_2(g) \rightarrow 4NO(g) + 6H_2O(g)$ catalyst: platinum/rhodium
- the removal of carbon monoxide and nitrogen(II) oxide in catalytic convertors in motor vehicles:
  $2NO(g) + 2CO(g) \rightarrow 2CO_2(g) + N_2(g)$ catalyst: platinum, palladium and rhodium

The unpaired electrons in a typical transition metal can be used to receive incoming electrons from other molecules, e.g. N_2 and CO, thus forming a bond on the surface of the metal.

2 *Homogeneous catalysis*

The reactants and the catalyst are in the same physical state.

- enzymic processes
- the reaction between $S_2O_8^{2-}$ ions and I^- ions, catalyst: Fe^{2+} or Fe^{3+}
- the reaction between potassium sodium tartrate and hydrogen peroxide, catalyst: Co^{2+}

Many homogeneous processes may be explained by using electrode potentials.

UNIT 14

Functional groups and isomerism in organic chemistry

The number of covalent bonds that atoms form is worth remembering:
carbon = 4,
nitrogen = 3,
hydrogen = 1,
oxygen = 2,
halogens = 1.

Organic chemistry involves the chemistry of compounds containing the element carbon. Carbon is able to form strong covalent bonds, both with itself to form chains and rings and with many other elements; these include hydrogen, oxygen, nitrogen and the halogens. A multitude of organic compounds is therefore possible. The small group of atoms that determine the associated reactions of an organic compound is called the functional group.

A Recognising functional groups

It is often frustrating to see students throw away marks due to poor recognition of simple organic functional groups. Table 14.1 lists the groups that you must remember.

Table 14.1

Name of functional group	Structure of functional group	Example with name	
Alkene	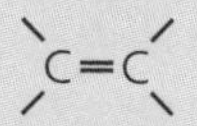	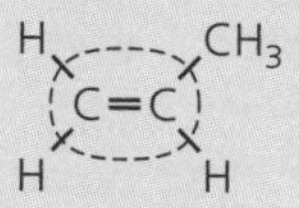	propene
Halogenoalkane	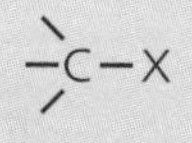	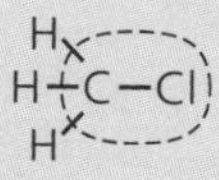	monochloromethane
Aldehyde	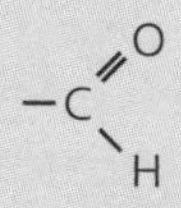	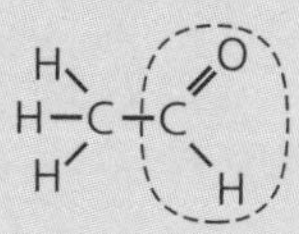	ethanal
Alcohol	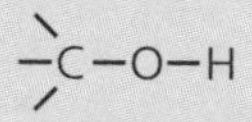	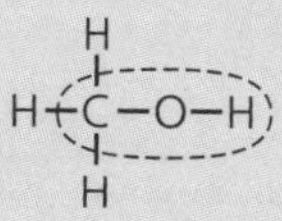	methanol
Carboxylic acid	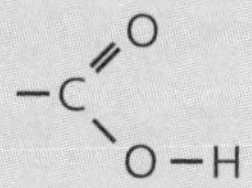	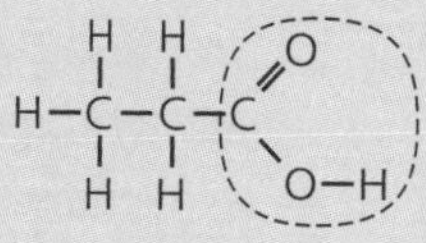	propanoic acid
Ester	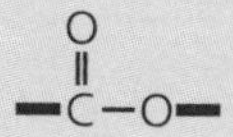	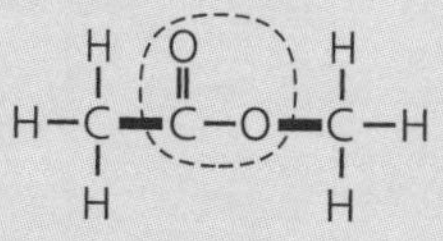	methyl ethanoate
Ketone	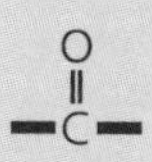	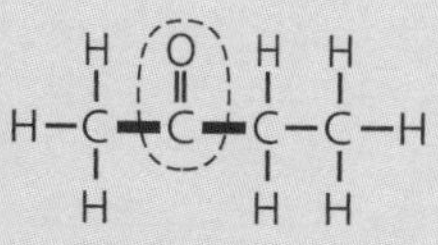	butanone
Amine	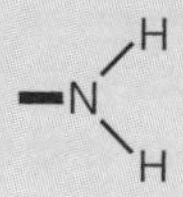	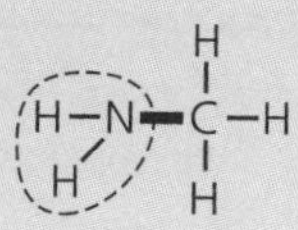	methyl amine

Amide	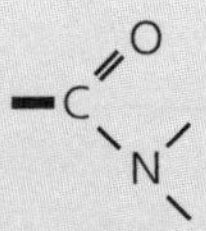	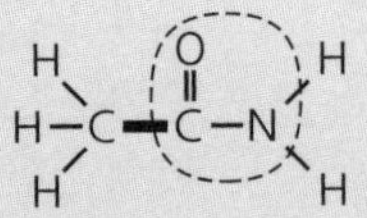	ethanamide
Acyl chloride	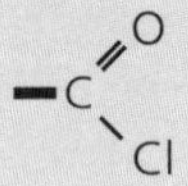	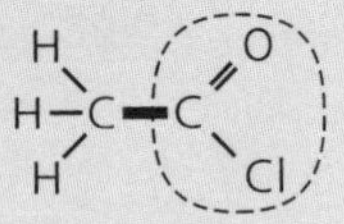	ethanoyl chloride
Acid anhydride		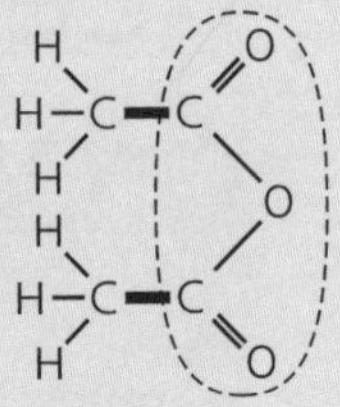	ethanoic anhydride
Epoxy		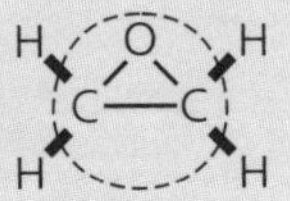	epoxyethane
Nitrile	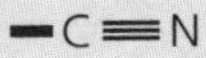	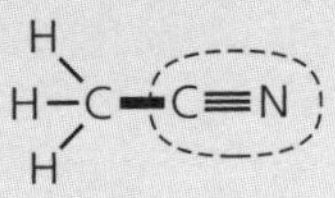	ethanonitrile

Make sure you know which of these functional groups you need to be familiar with.

B Isomerism

The two main types of isomerism are **structural isomerism** and **stereoisomerism**.

1 Structural isomerism

Structural isomers are molecules with the same molecular formula but different structural formulae.

- **Examples of structural isomers**
  Ethanol and methoxymethane both have the molecular formula, C_2H_6O, but they possess different structures.

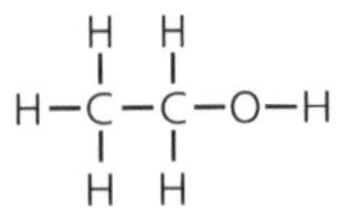

ethanol (an alcohol)

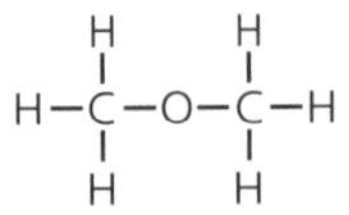

methoxymethane (an ether)

Notice that in ethanol the oxygen atom is covalently bonded to a hydrogen and a carbon atom, whereas in methoxymethane the oxygen atom is bonded to two carbon atoms. In structural isomers, atoms are joined to different neighbouring atoms.

2 Stereoisomerism

Molecules bonded to the same neighbours but differing in their arrangement in three-dimensional space are called **stereoisomers**.

There are two main types of stereoisomerism: **geometrical** and **optical** isomerism.

2.1 Geometric isomerism

In geometrical isomerism, the isomers differ in the **spatial arrangement** of their atoms/groups. Substituted alkenes are often used to illustrate this. The C=C bond prevents rotation and this means that two distinct forms are possible for some alkenes. These forms are called either the ***cis-*** form (in which two identical groups occupy the same side of the C=C bond) and the ***trans-*** form (in which the two groups are on opposite sides of the double bond). As an example of this, consider but-2-ene:

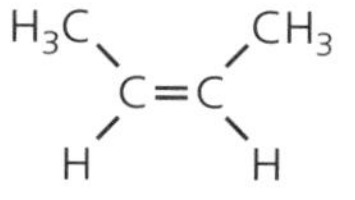

cis-but-2-ene

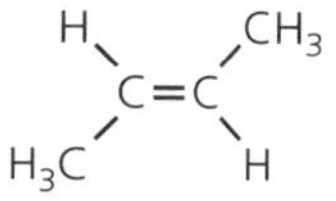

trans-but-2-ene

Geometrical isomers can differ in their physical properties, but their chemical properties tend to be similar. However, the rate at which one isomer reacts with a reagent may be different from the other isomer.

2.2 Optical isomerism

With this type of isomerism a molecule must have a mirror image that is **non-superimposible** upon itself. In other words, one molecule cannot be placed directly on top of the other so that corresponding atoms overlap. The two molecules are then related optically.

Structurally, the important feature within such organic molecules is that a carbon atom (known as the **chiral** carbon (*)) is attached to four different groups in a tetrahedral arrangement in space.

Optical isomerism is not confined solely to organic molecules. Transition metal complexes, e.g. the chromium(III)-ethanedioate complex, displays optical isomerism as $[Cr\,(C_2O_4)_3]^{3-}$.

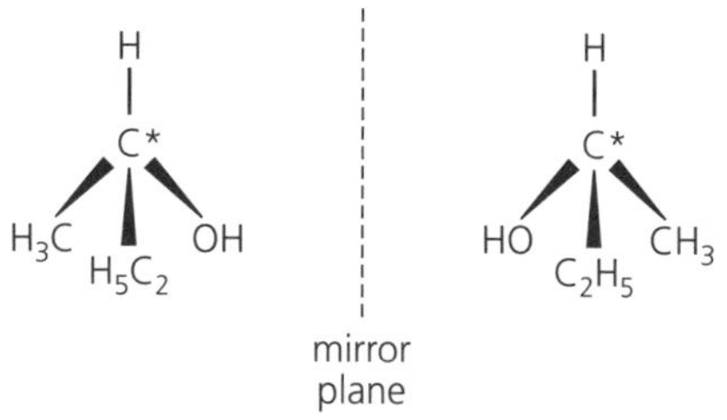

Optical isomers of butan-2-ol

These distinct forms may be identified by the effect they have on **plane polarised light**: one isomer **rotates** plane polarised light to the left (the – form) and the other isomer to the right (the + form).

Not 'reflect' or 'refract' but 'rotate'.

Some important features regarding this type of isomerism include the following:

- The optical isomers which are mirror images of each other are often called **enantiomers**.
- The process of separating one isomer from the other is called **resolution** (enzymes are sometimes of use in this process).
- A mixture of equal concentrations of both (+) and (–) forms is called a **racemic mixture**.
- A racemic mixture has no effect on plane polarised light since both enantiomers have an equal and opposite effect. There is therefore no overall effect on the rotation of the light.
- The chemical properties of optical isomers tend to be similar, although the rates of their reactions may differ markedly, especially in the case of enzymic processes.

UNIT 15 The alkanes, alkenes and benzene

A The alkanes

1 *What are alkanes?*

Alkanes are hydrocarbons. Hydrocarbons are compounds consisting of the elements hydrogen and carbon only.

The general formula for the alkanes is C_nH_{2n+2}.

The alkanes, like other organic families, are said to form a **homologous series**: CH_4, C_2H_6, C_3H_8, C_4H_{10}, C_5H_{12}, etc. In this series (in which each alkane differs from the next by a CH_2 unit) a gradual change in physical properties is expected, e.g. melting point, boiling point, enthalpy of combustion, enthalpy of formation, etc.

The term saturated refers to the presence of C–C bonds only. Unsaturated refers to the presence of C=C bonds and these are present in alkenes.

All are **saturated**: they have a carbon–carbon skeleton of single bonds only. In each alkane, the carbon is sp^3 hybridised. Each carbon atom forms four single covalent bonds and the configuration of these about each carbon is tetrahedral.

Alkanes are extracted from crude oil by fractional distillation into a range of boiling points called fractions. Alkanes with higher relative molecular masses also possess more electrons and the van der Waals forces, and boiling points, are therefore greater. Each fraction has a particular use: fuels (gases C_1 to C_4, petrol C_4 to C_8, diesel C_{10} to C_{16}), lubricants (lubricating oil C_{20} to C_{35}), tar on roads and roofs (over 35 carbon atoms per molecule), and as a source of other organic compounds (the naphtha fraction C_5 to C_{12}).

Crude oil is formed when microscopic sea creatures are deposited at the bottom of the sea where they are compressed and heated over many millions of years with the aid of anaerobic bacterial processes.

2 *Molecular structures for alkanes*

- **Simple straight chain alkanes – methane to pentane:**

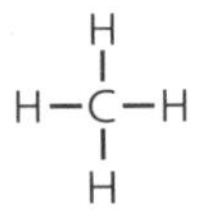
methane

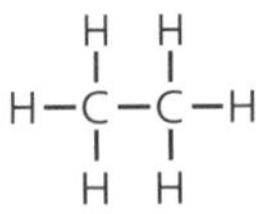
ethane

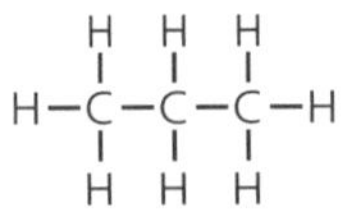
propane

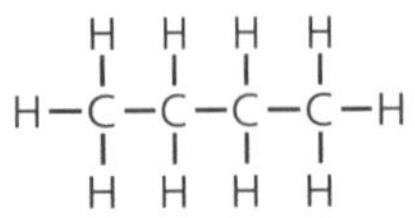
butane

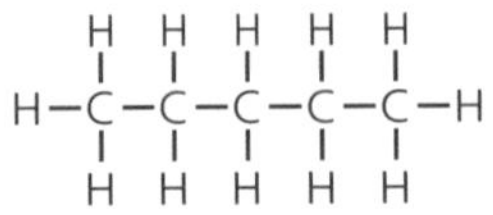
pentane

Alkanes are named according to:

- the number of carbon atoms in the longest chain
- the number of carbon atoms in any side chains (alkyl groups)
- the position of the side chain(s) along the main chain

The prefixes used to indicate the number of carbon atoms in the main chain are:

1 carbon atom:	meth-	5 carbon atoms:	pent-
2 carbon atoms:	eth-	6 carbon atoms:	hex-
3 carbon atoms:	prop-	7 carbon atoms:	hept-
4 carbon atoms:	but-	8 carbon atoms:	oct-

The symbol R represents an alkyl group, e.g. $-CH_3$, $-C_2H_5$, $-C_3H_7$, etc.

The alkyl groups attached to the main chain (viewed as covalently bonded radical (R) groups) are: $-CH_3$, methyl; $-C_2H_5$, ethyl; $-C_3H_7$, propyl; etc.

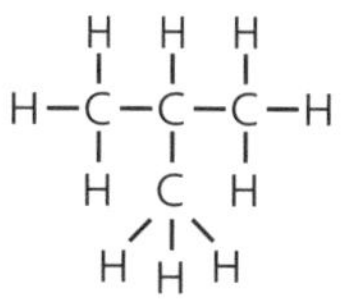

2-methylpropane

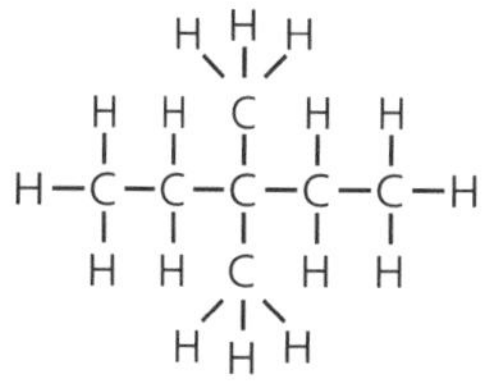

3,3-dimethylpentane

Alkanes with more than three carbon atoms per molecule can exist as structural isomers.

Do not confuse the terms isomer, isotope and allotrope (they all have completely different meanings).

Structural isomers are molecules with the same molecular formulae but different molecular structures, e.g. n-pentane and 2,2,-dimethylpropane.

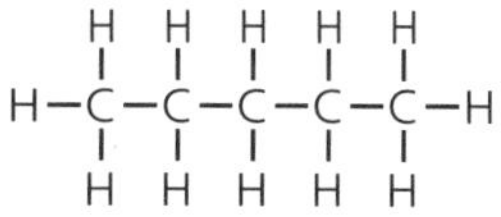

n-pentane

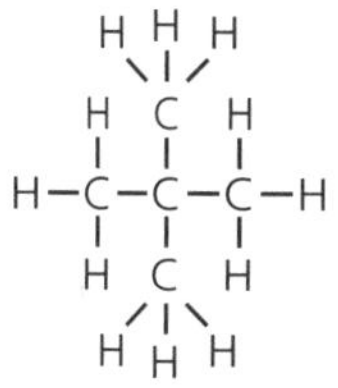

2,2,-dimethylpropane

3 Physical properties of alkanes

The carbon–carbon and the carbon–hydrogen bonds are strong covalent bonds. Alkanes are consequently seen as **relatively unreactive** because it is unlikely that these bonds will be broken and replaced with even stronger covalent bonds.

The C–H and C–C bonds are non-polar bonds since the elements forming the C–H bond are very similar in electronegativity (2.5 for carbon and 2.1 for hydrogen). As a result, **alkanes are non-polar molecules**.

Alkanes, which are non-polar, are almost completely insoluble in water, indicating the very poor interactions between the hydrocarbon chain and the water molecules. Hydrocarbons are often described as **hydrophobic** (water-hating) because of this property. However, non-polar alkanes are considerably more soluble in non-polar solvents like other alkanes or liquid alkenes or molecules containing benzene ring structures.

Alkanes are made up of **simple molecules** and these molecules are **weakly bonded together by van der Waals interactions**. As the number of electrons possessed by an alkane increases (as you ascend the homologous series), so does the number and strength of the van der Waals forces. As a result, the melting and boiling points increase with increasing relative molecular mass. Note that branches on the hydrocarbon chain inhibit close approach from other hydrocarbon molecules, therefore lowering the magnitude of the van der Waals interactions and lowering the melting and boiling points. For example, the boiling point of n-pentane is 36.3 °C and that of 2,2-dimethylpropane is 9.5 °C (see structures above).

4 Chemical reactions of alkanes

Reactions of alkanes, as a result of the strong covalent C–C and C–H bonds, often have high activation energies. They tend therefore to occur very slowly at room temperature and often severe conditions are needed in order to break the required bonds and facilitate reaction.

4.1 Combustion

All alkanes undergo combustion to produce water vapour and carbon dioxide or carbon monoxide (depending on the proportion of alkane to oxygen when burning).

Complete combustion gives carbon dioxide and water. Incomplete combustion occurs in a limited supply of oxygen; toxic carbon monoxide gas is normally formed.

- **complete combustion: $CH_4(g) + 2O_2(g) \rightarrow CO_2(g) + 2H_2O(l)$**
- **incomplete combustion: $2CH_4(g) + 3O_2(g) \rightarrow 2CO(g) + 4H_2O(l)$**

The combustion is exothermic. The greater the number of carbon atoms, the more exothermic is the combustion process.

4.2 With a halogen

*Conditions: chlorine or bromine in the presence of ultraviolet light.

In the presence of ultraviolet light, halogens will react with alkanes (and other organic molecules) in a process known as a **radical substitution.**

Radicals are very reactive species since they possess an unpaired electron that has the potential to form a covalent bond. Radicals are not regiospecific, that is they attack a molecule anywhere by substituting for other atoms.

A radical is a reactive species with an unpaired electron.

In this reaction, hydrogen atom(s) are substituted for halogen atom(s) and the organic product is called a halogenoalkane. An acidic hydrogen halide gas is also formed.

Examples:

$CH_4(g) + Br_2(g) \rightarrow CH_3Br(g) + HBr(g)$

$C_3H_8(g) + Cl_2(g) \rightarrow C_3H_7Cl(g) + HCl(g)$

The mechanism of a radical substitution reaction is divided into discrete steps.

- **Initiation:** the process of generating radicals from molecules. This process is also known as **homolytic fission**.
  The halogen molecule dissociates to form halogen radicals when ultraviolet light is incident:
  $Br_2 \rightarrow 2Br^\bullet$ or $Br{-}Br \rightarrow Br^\bullet + Br^\bullet$

- **Propagation:** the process of a molecule reacting with a radical to form another radical; in this process the concentration of radicals remains constant (the rate can increase in chain branching processes).
  The alkane molecule reacts with the halogen radical as follows:
  $CH_4 + Br^\bullet \rightarrow CH_3^\bullet + HBr$
  and then $CH_3^\bullet + Br_2 \rightarrow CH_3Br + Br^\bullet$
  It is also then possible for bromomethane to react with another radical, and so on.
  Note: due to bond energy considerations, hydrogen radicals do **not** form in this process. The following reaction is **unlikely** on bond energy grounds:
  $CH_4 + Br^\bullet \rightarrow CH_3Br + H^\bullet$

- **Termination:** the decrease in the radical concentration due to radicals forming molecules.
  There are many possible termination steps for the reaction being considered:
  $CH_3^{\bullet}$ + $Br^{\bullet}$ → CH_3Br
  or $CH_3^{\bullet}$ + $CH_3^{\bullet}$ → C_2H_6
  In this radical process, it is difficult to control the product composition since radicals are very reactive and are non-regiospecific regarding the site of attack. As a result, one property of radical processes is that the product consists of a complex mixture of molecules.

4.3 Cracking to form alkenes and shorter chain alkanes

*Conditions: either heat (450–700 °C) or, at a lower temperature (400–500°C), with a catalyst (Al_2O_3 mixed with either chromium(VI) oxide or silica).

This process involves **homolytic fission** and results in the formation of alkenes as well as shorter chain alkanes. The process is a very important one in the petrochemical industry since it enables more of the less-marketable longer chain alkanes to be converted into smaller, more-marketable alkanes (important in the manufacture of petrol – a fuel in high demand).

Cracking of alkanes is a radical process; smaller alkanes and alkenes are produced in this reaction.

The reaction involves the formation of radicals and the names of the stages in the mechanism are the same as with the radical substitution reactions of alkanes with halogens (in the presence of ultraviolet light).

Example: the cracking of a butane molecule, C_4H_{10}

- Initiation: homolytic fission (i.e when a bond breaks as )

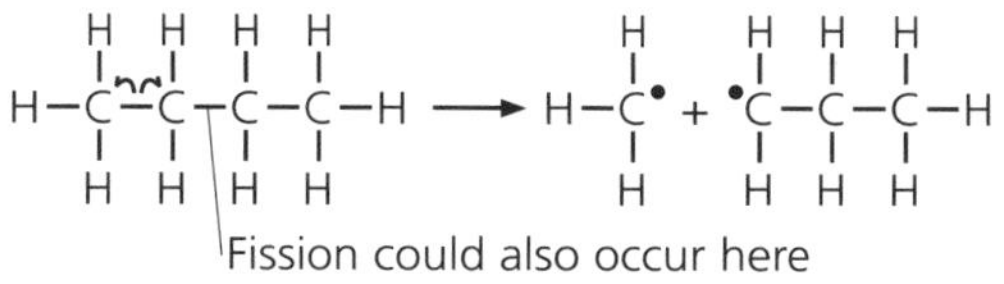

z

- Propagation: a radical approaches a molecule and produces another radical

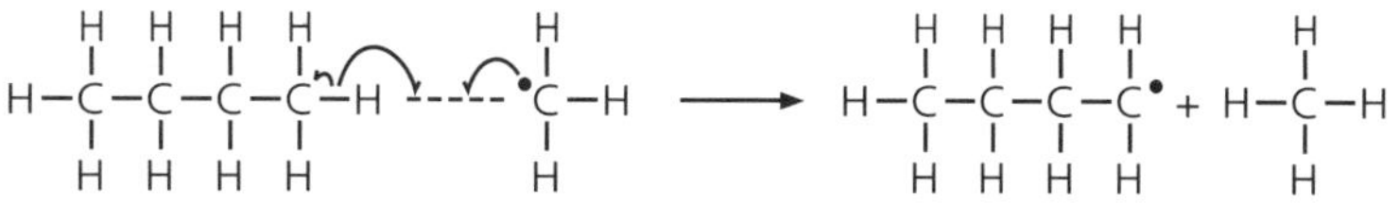

The radicals produced may then rearrange

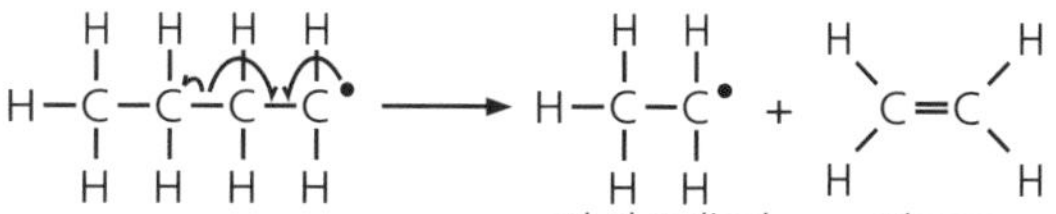

- Termination: two radicals react to form a molecule

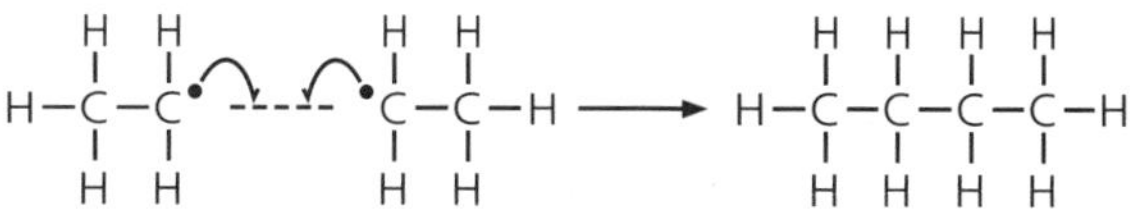

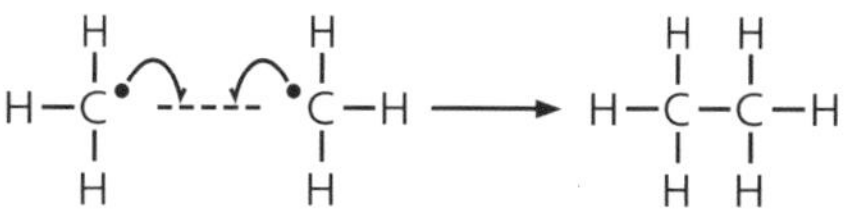

Cracking and halogenation of alkanes involves the formation of radicals.

B The alkenes

1 What are alkenes?

Alkenes are more reactive than alkanes due to the presence of a π (pi) bond. This is higher in energy than a σ (sigma) bond and is therefore more reactive.

Alkenes are hydrocarbons which contain one or more carbon–carbon double bonds (C=C).

- They are **unsaturated** since they contain double bonds.
- They have the general formula C_nH_{2n}.
- They are manufactured in the cracking process with alkanes.
- The carbon–carbon double bond makes the alkenes much more reactive than the alkanes.

Alkenes are very similar to alkanes in that both are relatively non-polar molecules and have solubility traits that reflect this (low solubility in polar solvents but appreciable solubility in non-polar solvents).

1.1 Molecular structures of alkenes

- **Ethene, propene, but-1-ene, but-2-ene and buta-1,3-diene**

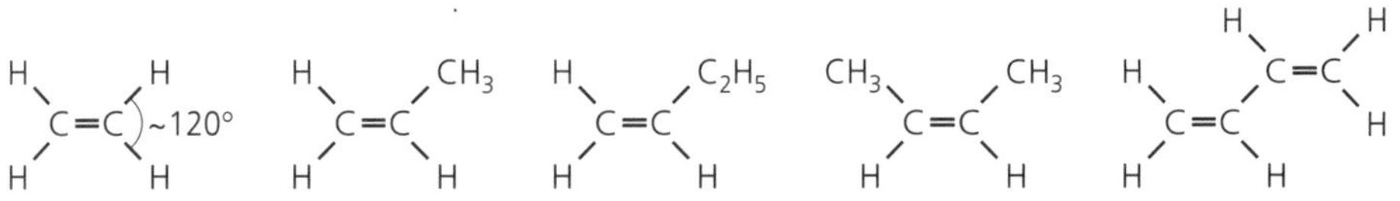

ethene | propene | but-1-ene | *cis*-but-2-ene | buta-1,3-diene

Notice that for butene, the double bond may either reside between the first two carbon atoms or between the central two carbon atoms. As a result, two **structural isomers** may exist called but-1-ene and but-2-ene.

2 Geometrical isomerism in alkenes

The double bond in an alkene consists of a σ and a π bond (Figure 15.1). The π bond is higher in energy (and therefore weaker) than the σ bond. The two electrons in the π bond unpair and form two σ bonds on each carbon atom, but the original σ bond remains intact.

Figure 15.1 Diagrammatic representation of the σ and π bond in a double bond

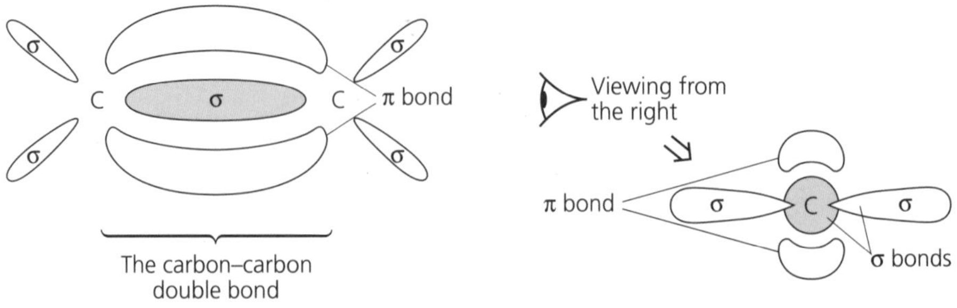

The presence of the π bond prevents rotation about the double bond and this means that two different molecules may exist for some alkenes, for example but-2-ene or with the halogenated alkene 1,2-dichloroethene. Isomers that

differ in their spatial arrangement about the double bond in this way are called **geometrical isomers**. (Geometrical isomers are also possible with transition metal complexes, e.g. $[Co(NH_3)_2Cl_4]^-$).

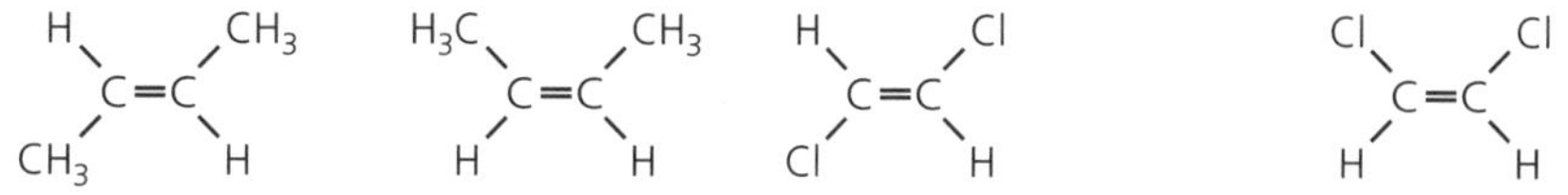

trans-but-2-ene | *cis*-but-2-ene | *trans*-1,2-dichloroethene | *cis*-1,2-dichloroethene

The prefix *cis*- refers to geometrical isomers in which the identical groups are on the same side of the double bond, whereas *trans*- refers to the same groups being on opposite sides of the double bond.

3 Chemical reactions of alkenes

An electrophile is an electron pair acceptor and a nucleophile is an electron pair donor.

The double bond facilitates reactions described as **electrophilic addition** reactions in which an **electrophile** (an electron pair acceptor) accepts the π electrons pair from the alkene and a new bond results. Alkenes themselves are defined as **nucleophiles** since they can donate a lone pair of electrons. Alkenes are also able to undergo radical process with halogens in the presence of ultraviolet light in which hydrogen atoms are substituted for halogen atoms (see this reaction mechanism with the alkanes).

In all of the following electrophilic addition reactions, ethene gas is used to illustrate the particular reaction being considered but, where necessary, other alkenes may be used.

3.1 With halogens

Reactions of alkenes tend to be very fast. In these reactions the alkene donates its electron pair (from the π bond) to a species that is prepared to accept it. The attacking species is called an electrophile.

The reaction of an alkene with the halogen bromine is used as a diagnostic test for the presence of unsaturation (the presence of a double bond). The orange bromine solution is decolorised in this reaction. For example:

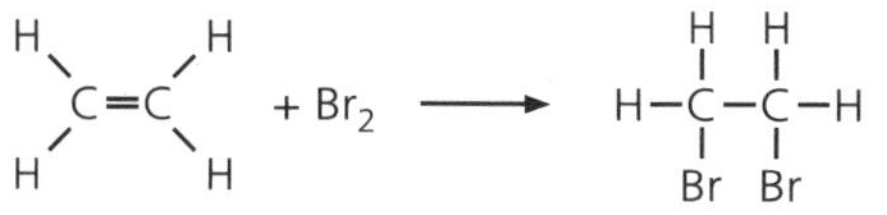

ethene 1,2-dibromoethane

- **Mechanism for the reaction of bromine with an alkene**

The bromine molecule approaches the π bond of the alkene and an induced dipole occurs in the bromine molecule. The bromine atom closest to the π bond then develops a slight positive charge.

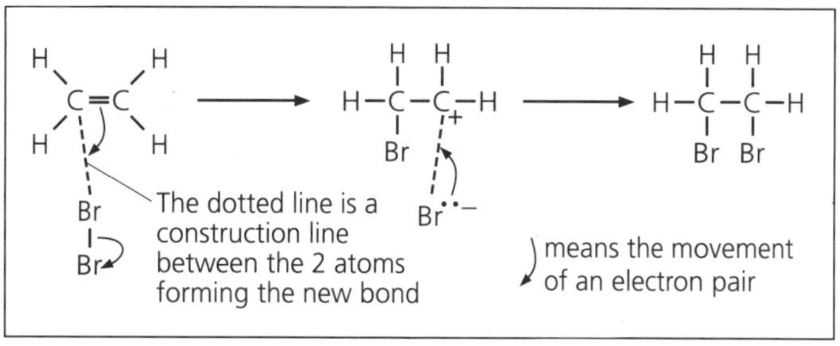

This is an electrophilic addition process

3.2 With hydrogen gas

*Conditions: hydrogen gas and a Raney nickel catalyst at 150 °C.

Carbon double bonds react with hydrogen in the presence of nickel as a catalyst to yield alkanes, e.g. ethene is converted to ethane. This is an **addition reaction** involving reaction on the surface of the heterogeneous nickel catalyst. This process is of particular importance in the **manufacture of margarine** since liquid oils are hardened into solid fats by part-saturation of the double bonds present.

● Conversion of ethene to ethane

$$
\underset{\text{ethene}}{\text{H}_2\text{C=CH}_2} + \text{H}_2 \xrightarrow[150°C]{\text{Ni}} \underset{\text{ethane}}{\text{CH}_3-\text{CH}_3}
$$

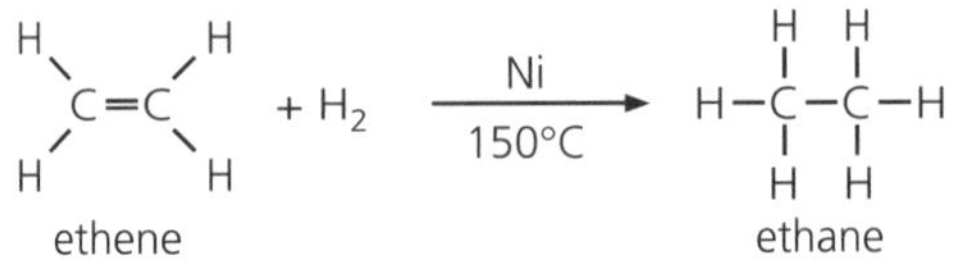

3.3 WITH HYDROGEN HALIDES

An addition reaction takes place and the halogenoalkane is formed.

$$
\underset{\text{ethene}}{\text{H}_2\text{C=CH}_2} + \text{HBr} \longrightarrow \underset{\text{bromethane}}{\text{CH}_3-\text{CH}_2-\text{Br}}
$$

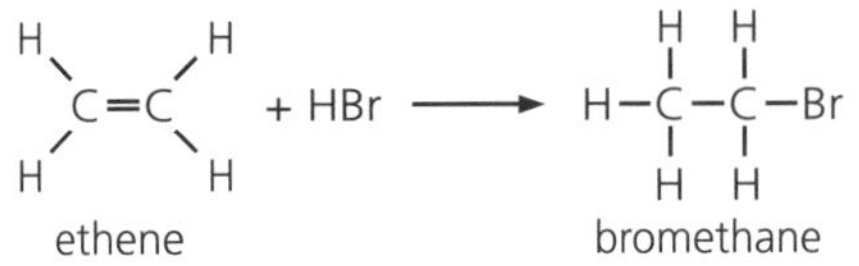

With unsymmetrical alkenes like propene, there are two possible products from this reaction: either 1-bromopropane or 2-bromopropane. However, 2-bromo-propane is the major product and this observation, as well as those with other alkenes, is summarised using **Markovnikov's Rule**.

● Markovnikov's Rule:
When a hydrogen halide is added to an unsymmetrical alkene, the bromine atom attaches itself to the carbon atom (in the double bond) that is attached to the fewer hydrogen atoms.

● Mechanism for reaction of hydrogen bromide with an alkene

Markovnikov's Rule is not an explanation, it is merely a rule. For an explanation, the mechanism for electrophilic addition is considered.

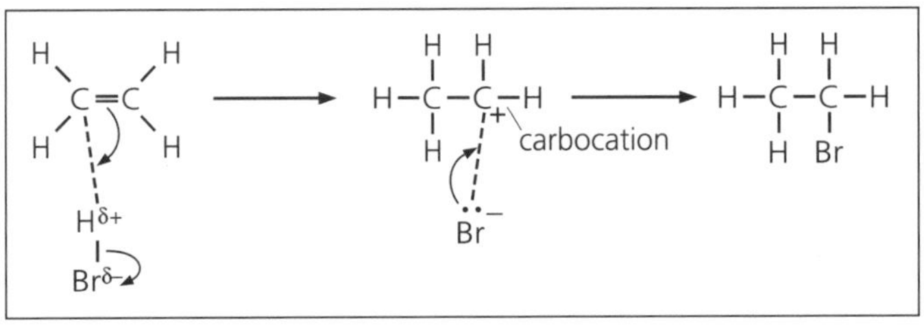

This is an electrophilic addition process

The double bond may be protonated in one of two different positions. A carbo-cation is formed, R^+, in both cases, but the relative stability of the carbocations differs. A tertiary carbocation is more stable than the secondary (and the primary) because of the electron-pushing (inductive) effect of the alkyl groups around the positively charged carbon atom. This delocalises the positive charge.

3.4 WITH CONCENTRATED SULPHURIC(VI) ACID

This reaction can be useful in the conversion of an alkene to an alcohol.

$$
\underset{\text{ethene}}{\text{H}_2\text{C=CH}_2} + \text{H}_2\text{SO}_4(l) \longrightarrow \underset{\substack{\text{ethyl hydrogen}\\\text{sulphate(VI)}}}{\text{CH}_3-\text{CH}_2-\text{O-SO}_3\text{H}} \xrightarrow{+\text{H}_2\text{O}} \underset{\text{ethanol}}{\text{CH}_3-\text{CH}_2-\text{OH}}
$$

Virtually all reactions of a carbon–carbon double bond are electrophilic addition processes.

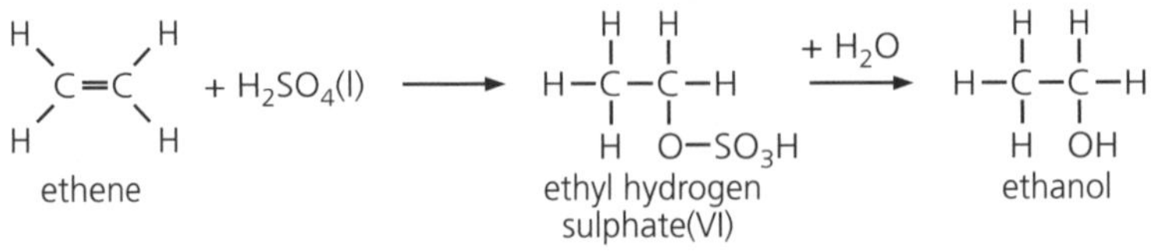

The ethyl hydrogen sulphate may be boiled with water to form the corresponding alcohol via a **nucleophilic substitution process**.

3.5 With steam

*Conditions: steam in the presence of phosphoric(V) acid catalyst at 300 °C and 70 atm.

This results in the formation of the corresponding alcohol:

$CH_2{=}CH_2 + H_2O \rightleftharpoons CH_3CH_2OH$

ethanol

You must recall your conditions for a reaction. Don't just remember the reagents. What about the presence of a catalyst? At what temperature does the reaction take place? What pressure? What about the concentrations of the reactants?

3.6 With oxygen

*Conditions: oxygen in the presence of a silver catalyst, 250–300 °C.

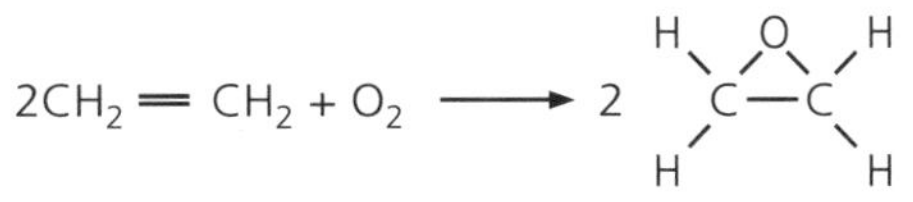

ethene epoxyethane

The epoxide may then react (via a nucleophilic addition process) with water or alcohols (at 200 °C with a trace of acid) to yield the following:

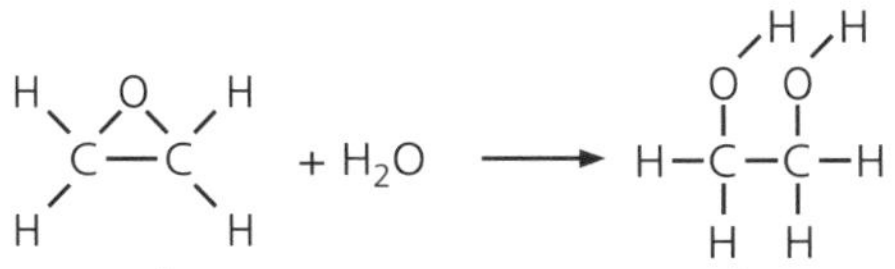

epoxyethane ethane-1,2-diol (used in antifreeze)

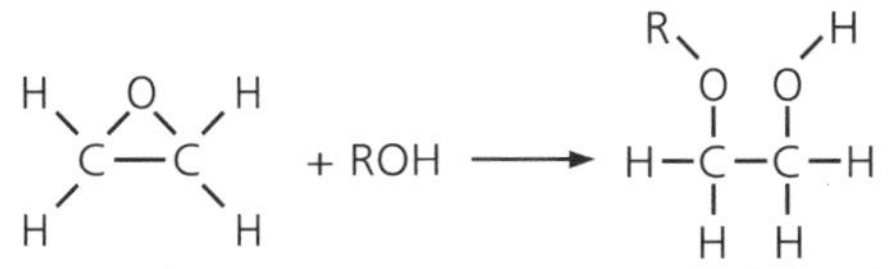

epoxyethane

An hydroxyether (this process may continue to form a polymeric hydroxyether – used in paints and printing inks)

Epoxides are very reactive due to the strain in the oxygen bridge over the two carbon atoms (this is called ring strain).

- **Mechanism for reaction of water with epoxyethane**

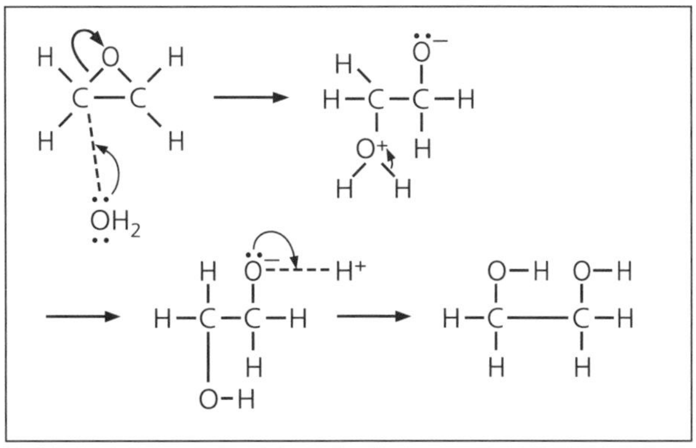

This is a nucleophilic addition process

3.7 With another alkene

Conditions:

- For low density polymers: pressure 1500 atm, 200 °C, organic peroxide initiator.
- For high density polymers: pressure 2–6 atm, 60 °C, titanium(IV) chloride–triethylaluminium ($TiCl_4.Al(C_2H_5)_3$), the Ziegler–Natta catalyst.

High or low density polymers may form, depending on the pressure and catalyst used. Low density (somewhat surprisingly) produces high density polymers, but this is largely due to the way that the Ziegler–Natta catalyst produces effective packing of the polymeric chains.

A molecule of alkene can react with other molecules of the same alkene to form long chain molecules. This process is called **polymerisation**. The product is a **polymer**. The single molecules are called **monomers**. The convention for naming the polymer is poly(name of monomer).

Examples:

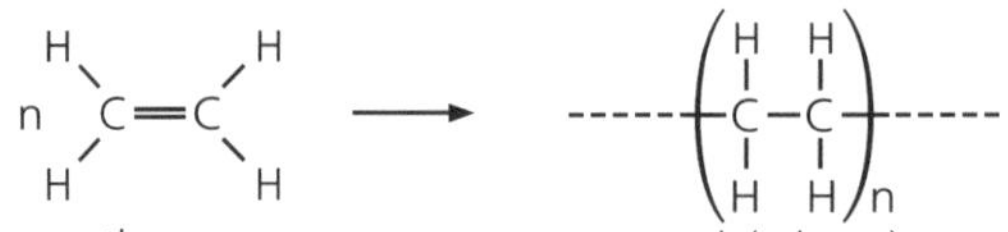

ethene → poly(ethene)

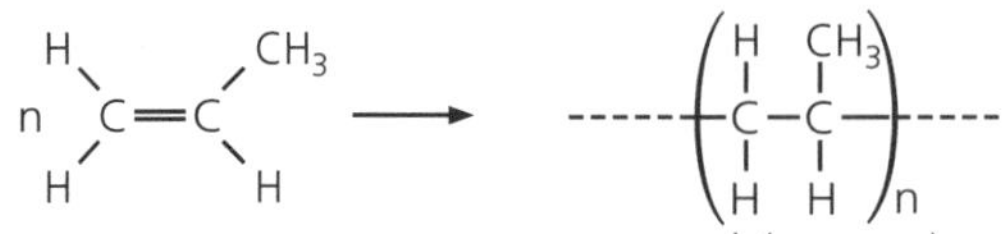

propene → poly(propene)

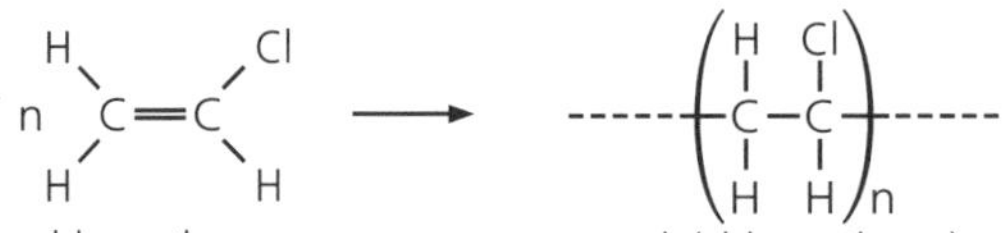

chloroethene → poly(chloroethene)

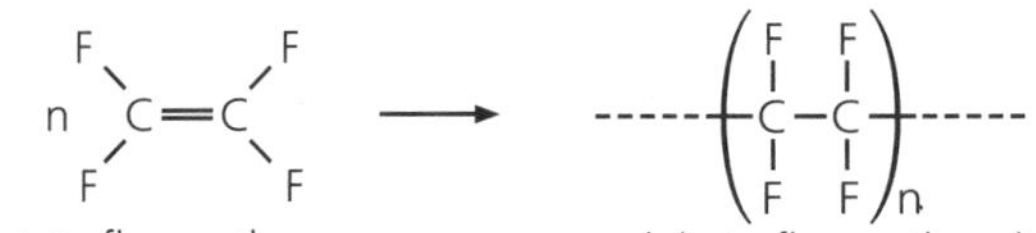

tetrafluoroethene → poly(tetrafluoroethene)

In addition polymerisations the π bond breaks and the two unpaired electrons are used to bond with other molecules that undergo the same process.

These reactions are known as addition polymerisations and the resulting polymers called addition polymers.

- **Mechanism for the polymerisation of ethene**

Initiation: (homolytic fission of organic peroxide)

Propagation: (chain building)

then:

Termination:

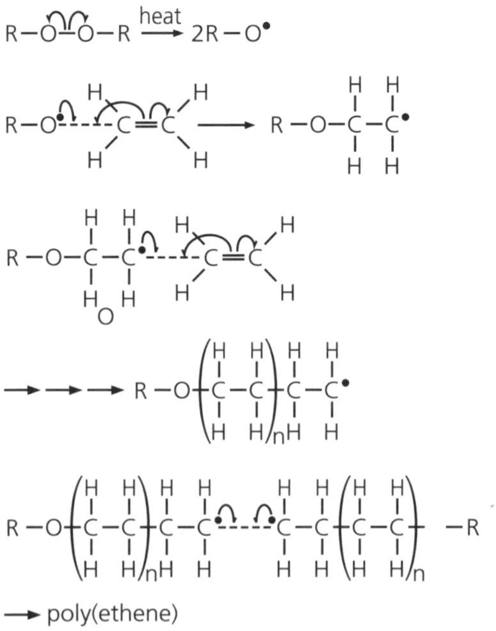

3.8 With acidified or alkaline potassium manganate(VII) solution

This reaction converts the alkene into a diol (having two hydroxyl groups).

For example:

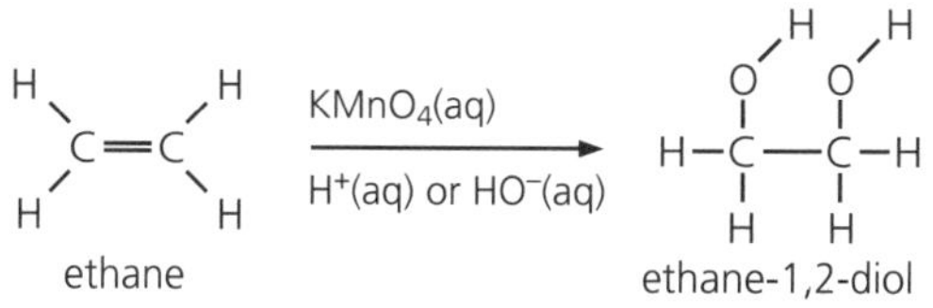

C Benzene chemistry

1 What is benzene?

Benzene is an unsaturated cyclic hydrocarbon of molecular formula, C_6H_6.

The molecule has a perfect planar hexagonal structure. It consists of a planar σ bonded framework in which the H$\hat{C}$H angles are all 120° together with a delocalised π system above and below the plane of atoms (Figure 15.2).

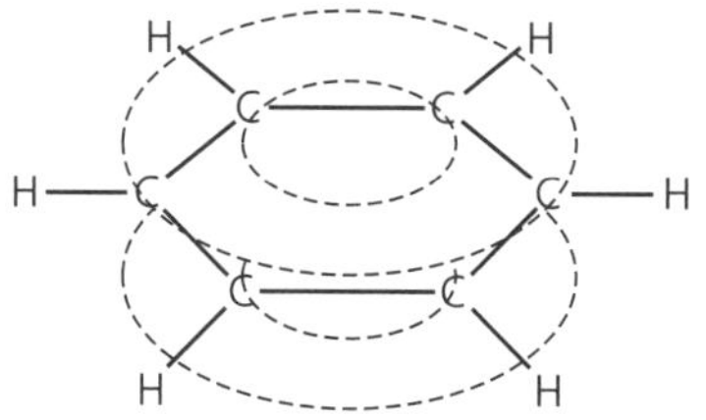

Figure 15.2 The benzene ring showing the delocalised π electrons

The carbon–carbon bonds in benzene are intermediate in length between a formal single and double bond (C–C = 0.154 nm, C=C = 0.134 nm and for benzene C⩦C 0.139 nm).

Although benzene is drawn as shown, there are six hydrogen atoms that are bonded to the ring that are often not shown.

The benzene ring (sometimes called an aromatic ring) is best represented as:

although it is sometimes convenient to consider the Kekule form:

Kekule form
of benzene

Notice that the hydrogen atoms are not normally indicated in these structures.

The reaction of benzene and the hypothetical compound, cyclohexa-1,3,5-triene, with hydrogen can be used in an energy cycle to deduce the relative stability of benzene and therefore the energy lowering due to the delocalised electrons.

Molecules of benzene are attracted to each other by van der Waals forces acting between the molecules. Benzene is a non-polar molecule and, as a liquid, is a good solvent for other non-polar solutes like alkanes and alkenes. Benzene is extremely poisonous as well as powerfully carcinogenic.

The thermodynamic stability of benzene is well known. This stability is due to the delocalised ring system. In order to quantify this thermodynamic stability, the energy cycle (Figure 15.3) involving **hydrogenation processes** is used. The relative stability of real benzene (with its delocalisation) and its other hypothetical form that involves no electron delocalisation (cyclohexa-1,3,5-triene) is quantified.

Using Hess's Law:

$$\Delta H = -208.4 - (-119.6 \times 3)$$
$$= +150.4 \, kJ \, mol^{-1}$$

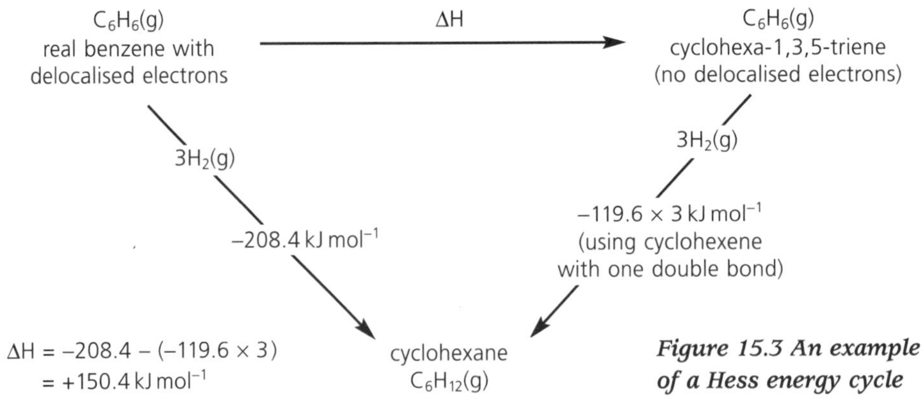

Figure 15.3 An example of a Hess energy cycle

Real benzene is therefore more thermodynamically stable than 'theoretical benzene' (without any electron delocalisation) by a significant **150.4 kJ mol⁻¹**.

2 | *The chemical reactions of benzene*

The reactions of benzene are called **electrophilic substitution processes** and, in these reactions, the benzene structure substitutes one or more of its hydrogen atoms for another group.

2.1 NITRATION

*Conditions: concentrated nitric(V) and concentrated sulphuric(VI) acid and a maximum temperature of 50 °C.

benzene + HNO₃ → nitrobenzene + H₂O catalyst: conc. H₂SO₄

- **The electrophilc substitution reaction of benzene with conc. HNO₃ and conc. H₂SO₄**

$$HNO_3 + H_2SO_4 \rightleftharpoons H_2NO_3^+ + HSO_4^-$$
$$H_2NO_3^+ \longrightarrow H_2O + NO_2^+$$

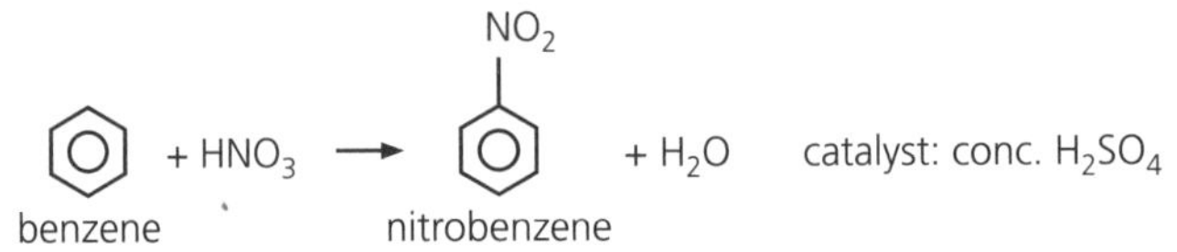

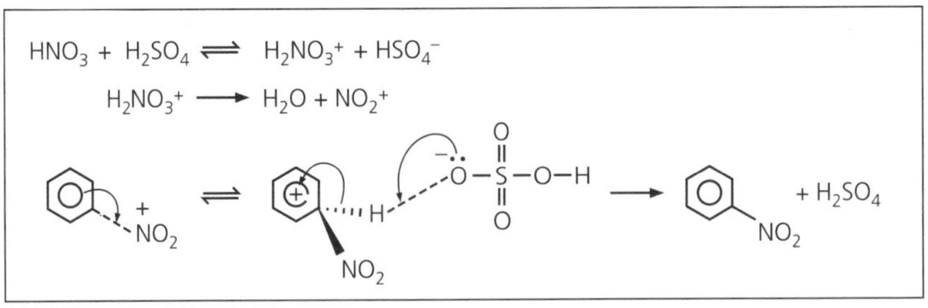

It is important to control the temperature of this reaction since further substitutions on the ring are possible. The resulting molecule could contain more than one nitro group at higher temperatures and these molecules can be very unstable and may even explode.

2.2 REDUCTION OF THE AROMATIC NITRO GROUP

The reduction of the aromatic nitro compound is achieved on refluxing with tin in concentrated hydrochloric acid and this yields the corresponding aromatic amine.

In the nitration of benzene, concentrated nitric and concentrated sulphuric acids are needed and a maximum temperature of 50 °C (to prevent further substitutions taking place).

This mechanism is very important. Notice how the benzene ring temporarily has its delocalised electron system disrupted; it is then restored by losing a proton to the hydrogen sulphate(VI) ion.

Nitration of a molecule containing a benzene ring is often used in the manufacture of explosives.

$$NO_2 \quad\quad\quad NH_2$$

nitrobenzene + $4H^+$ + $4e^-$ ⟶ phenylamine + $2H_2O$

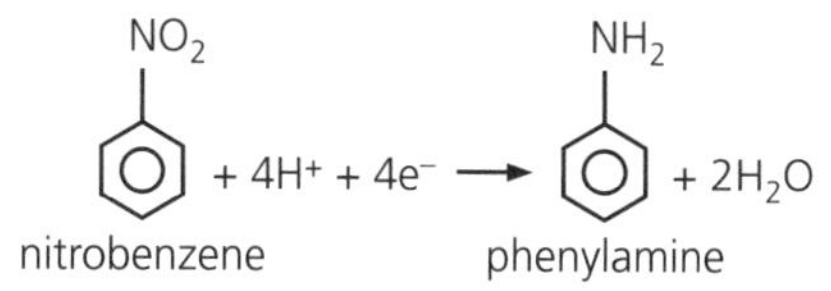

This is an important reaction to remember, particularly for organic synthesis.

2.3 SULPHONATION ~ REACTION WITH SULPHUR TRIOXIDE, SO₃

*Conditions: fuming sulphuric(VI) acid, reflux.

An electrophilic substitution reaction occurs in which a proton on the ring is substituted for an $-SO_3$ group. The electron-withdrawing effect of the three electronegative oxygen atoms on the central sulphur atom in SO_3 gives the sulphur atom a slight positive charge. The π electron system then donates a pair of electrons into the sulphur as the first stage in the mechanism.

benzene + SO_3 ⟶ benzene sulphonic acid

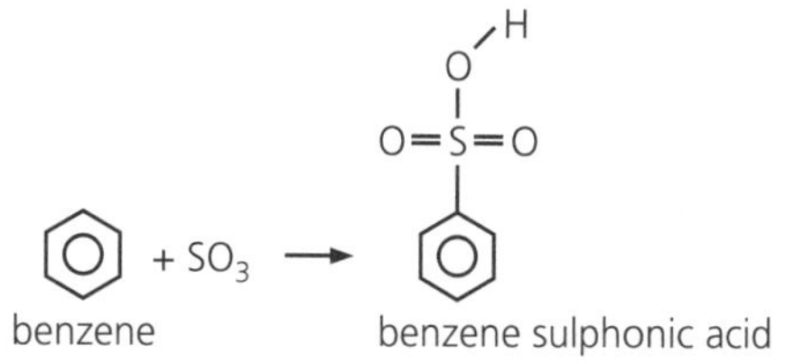

This product is reacted with sodium hydroxide solution when making cationic sulphonate detergents.

● The electrophilic substitution reaction of benzene SO_3

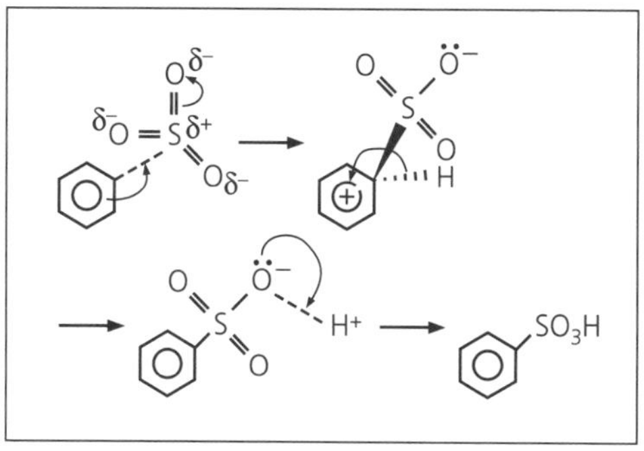

This is called an electrophilic substitution process

2.4 ALKYLATION OR ACYLATION ~ FRIEDEL~CRAFTS REACTION

Conditions: halogenoalkane, RX or acid chloride, ROCl and anhydrous aluminium chloride catalyst, reflux.

● The electrophilic substitution reaction of benzene with chloroethane and $AlCl_3$

$$AlCl_3 + C_2H_5Cl \longrightarrow [AlCl_4]^-[\,C_2H_5]^+$$

$$C_2H_5^+ \quad\quad C_2H_5 \quad\quad C_2H_5 + H^+$$

$$\left(\text{then } ([AlCl_4]^- + H^+ \longrightarrow \begin{array}{l} AlCl_3 + HCl \\ \text{catalyst} \\ \text{regenerated} \end{array}\right)$$

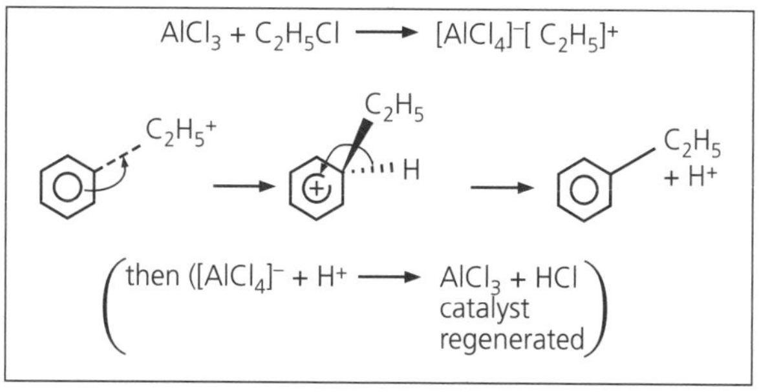

If 1-chloropropane is used, the primary carbo-cation $CH_3CH_2C^+H_2$ is formed. This may undergo a skeletal rearrangement to form the more stable secondary carbocation $CH_3C^+HCH_3$. This carbocation then substitutes onto the benzene ring.

In alkylations of the benzene ring, further substitutions on the ring can take place. To avoid this problem, an acylation is often carried out. The influence of the carbonyl group withdraws electron density from the ring, making it less likely to undergo more substitutions with electrophiles.

Note that many substitutions are possible with the carbocation, but the carbonyl group of the acyl chloride, when attached, deactivates the benzene ring towards further electrophilic attack. Acyl chlorides, for this reason, are of great use when forming long chain alkyl benzene molecules (prior to being sulphonated with SO_3 when making detergents) in which only **one** substitution is required.

2.5 WITH ETHENE

*Conditions: $HCl(g)$, $AlCl_3$ (catalyst).

This reaction is important for producing ethylbenzene as a precursor to the preparation of styrene (which is then polymerised to form polystyrene).

$$\text{benzene} + CH_2 = CH_2(g) \longrightarrow \text{ethylbenzene} \; (-C_2H_5)$$

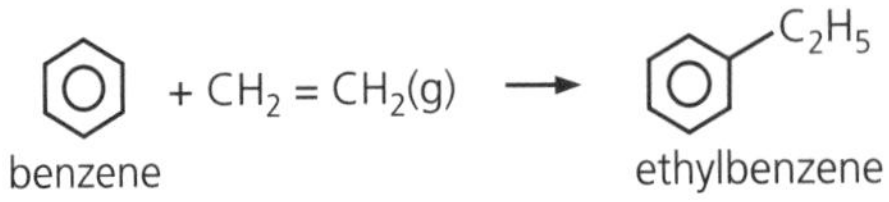

2.6 REACTION OF ALKYL BENZENES WITH ALKALINE POTASSIUM MANGANATE(VII)

This reaction can be used in converting an alkyl side chain to a synthetically more useful carboxylic acid group. Whatever the length of the alkyl group, the group remaining on the ring is –COOH.

$$\text{alkyl benzene (R)} \xrightarrow[\text{filter, then acidify}]{MnO_4^-(aq)/OH^-(aq)} \text{benzoic acid (COOH)}$$

If there is more than one alkyl group, the same process takes place to produce a dicarboxylic acid.

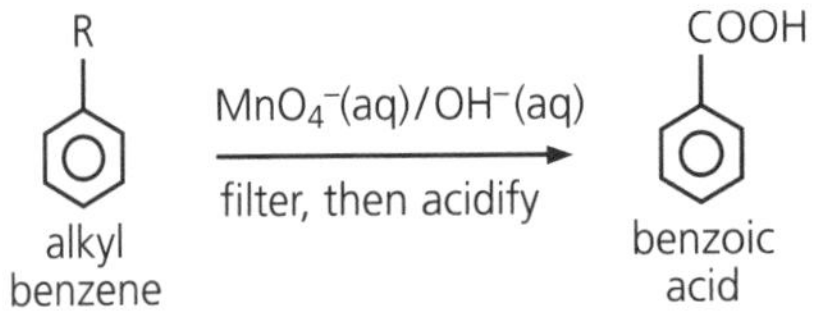

UNIT 16 The halogenoalkanes, alcohols, ketones and aldehydes

A The halogenoalkanes

1 What are halogenoalkanes?

Halogenoalkanes are alkanes that have had one or more of the hydrogen atoms substituted by halogen atoms.

- Examples of halogenoalkanes:

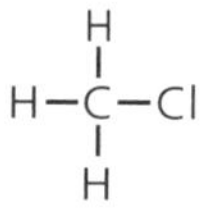
chloromethane

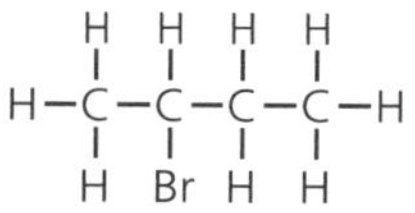
2-bromobutane

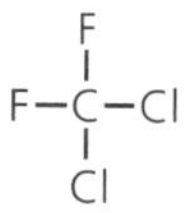
dichlorodifluoromethane

Note: 2-bromobutane is an example of an optically active molecule.

Halogenoalkanes are of importance in organic synthesis since the halide ion is a very good leaving group and may readily be substituted.

The carbon–halogen bond is polarised in such a way that the carbon atom is slightly positively charged and the halogen atom, X, slightly negatively charged: $\mathbf{C^{\delta+}–X^{\delta-}}$

The polarity of the bond increases in the order C–F > C–Cl > C–Br > C–I because the electronegativity difference between carbon and the halogen atom is increasing as Group VII is descended.

Halogenoalkanes are classed as either primary, secondary or tertiary depending on the number of carbon–carbon bonds on the carbon atom bonded directly to the halogen atom.

Primary halogenoalkane:

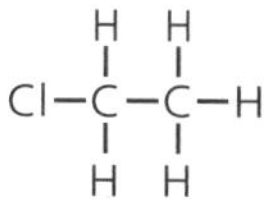
chloroethane

Secondary halogenoalkane:

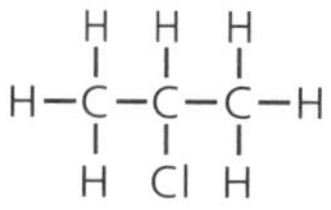
2-chloropropane

Tertiary halogenoalkane:

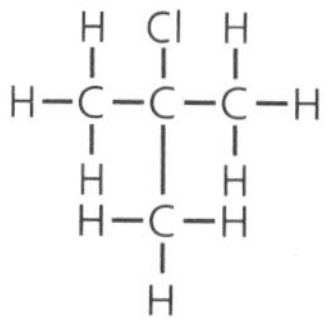
2-chloro-2-methylpropane

The reactivity of halogenoalkanes is determined by the strength of the C–X bond and not the bond polarity.

The carbon–halogen bond becomes weaker as Group VII is descended. This is an important factor in determining the reactivity halogenoalkanes. In substitution reactions, in which the halogen atom is removed and substituted, the order of reactivity is:

iodoalkanes > bromoalkanes > chloroalkanes ≫ fluoroalkanes

CFCs are halogenoalkanes containing chlorine, fluorine and carbon (and possibly hydrogen). Since the carbon–fluorine and carbon–chlorine covalent bonds are strong bonds, the CFC molecules are resistant to attack by nucleophiles like water molecules, and can remain in the environment for considerable time. When the CFC molecules reach the stratosphere, they undergo homolytic fission in the presence of ultraviolet light and form chlorine radicals, $Cl^{\bullet}$. These chlorine radicals may then react with an ozone molecule:

$O_3 + Cl^{\bullet} \rightarrow OCl^{\bullet} + O_2$
then $OCl^{\bullet} + O_3 \rightarrow 2O_2 + Cl^{\bullet}$, so one $Cl^{\bullet}$ can decompose many ozone molecules.

The effect is that volatile halogenoalkanes containing chlorine may form chlorine radicals when they reach the ozone layer. They may then decompose the ozone, increasing the intensity of ultraviolet light reaching the surface of the Earth.

2 Physical properties of halogenoalkanes

Halogenoalkanes exist as simple molecules. Between these molecules, van der Waals forces as well as dipole–dipole attractions (resulting from the polar C–X bond) operate. The existence of the dipole–dipole attractions explains why halogenoalkanes have slightly higher melting and boiling points compared with the corresponding alkane.

3 Chemical reactions of halogenoalkanes

Typical reactions of halogenoalkanes are **nucleophilic substitution** or **elimination processes**. Details of the conditions and mechanisms of the more important reactions are given below.

3.1 With the aqueous hydroxide ion

*Conditions: sodium hydroxide solution, reflux.
Mechanism type: nucleophilic substitution.

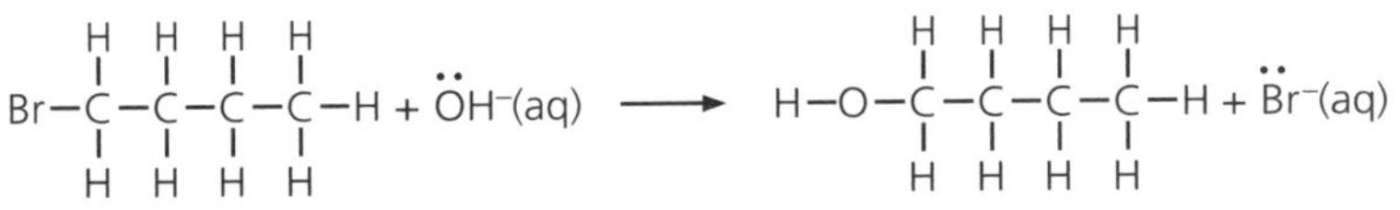

1-bromobutane   hydroxide ion   butan-1-ol

The halide ion leaves the molecule and is called a leaving group.

In this reaction, the hydroxide ion is behaving as a nucleophile (a lone pair of electrons donor). The hydroxide ion substitutes the halogen atom; the halide ion is the **leaving group** in this process.

- **Mechanism for the reaction between 2-bromobutane and $\ddot{O}H^-$**

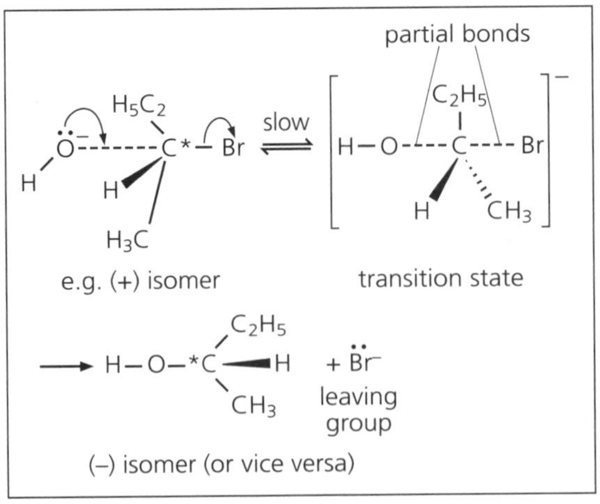

This is a nucleophilic substitution process

3.2 With the cyanide ion

*Conditions: potassium cyanide, KCN, in ethanol and water (and a trace of alkali), reflux.
Mechanism type: nucleophilic substitution.

In this reaction, the cyanide ion, ^-CN, substitutes the halogen atom for a cyanide group:

$$Br-CH_2-CH_2-CH_2-CH_3 + \ ^{..}_{}CN^- \longrightarrow N\equiv C-CH_2-CH_2-CH_2-CH_3 + \ \ddot{B}r^-$$

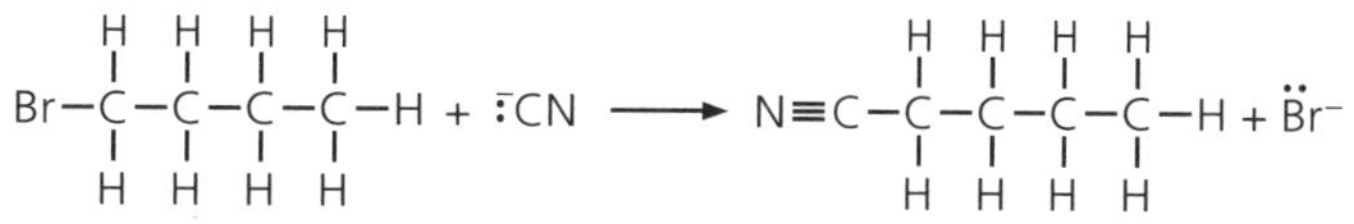

1-bromobutane pentanenitrile

The cyanide ion substitutes the halogen atom; the halide ion is the leaving group in this process.

3.3 WITH CONCENTRATED AMMONIA SOLUTION

*Conditions: concentrated ammonia or 0.88 ammonia solution at 100 °C and high pressure (where using ammonia gas).
Mechanism type: nucleophilic substitution.

Ammonia molecules donate their lone pair of electrons towards the electron deficient carbon atom in the halogenoalkane. The ammonia molecule substitutes the halogen atom; the halide ion is the leaving group in this process. When the first amine is formed, since it possesses a lone pair of electrons, this may behave as another nucleophile towards more 1-bromobutane (if this is in excess). The concentration of products depends on the relative concentrations of the reactants used.

Further substitutions take place on the amine when the halogeno-alkane is in excess.

For example:

$2NH_3(g) + CH_3CH_2Cl(l) \qquad \rightarrow CH_3CH_2NH_2(l) + NH_4Cl(s)$
ammonia + chloroethane $\qquad\qquad \rightarrow$ ethylamine (a primary amine)
$CH_3CH_2NH_2(l) + CH_3CH_2Cl(l) \quad \rightarrow (CH_3CH_2)_2NH(l) + HCl(g)$
$\qquad\qquad\qquad\qquad\qquad\qquad$ diethylamine (a secondary amine)
$(CH_3CH_2)_2NH(l) + CH_3CH_2Cl(l) \rightarrow (CH_3CH_2)_3N(l) + HCl(g)$
$\qquad\qquad\qquad\qquad\qquad\qquad$ triethylamine (a tertiary amine)
$(CH_3CH_2)_3N(l) + CH_3CH_2Cl(l) \rightarrow (CH_3CH_2)_4N^+Cl^-(l)$
$\qquad\qquad\qquad\qquad\qquad\qquad$ ethylammoniumchloride (a quaternary alkyl ammonium salt – used for making cationic detergents)

- **Mechanism for the reaction between chloroethane and NH$_3$**

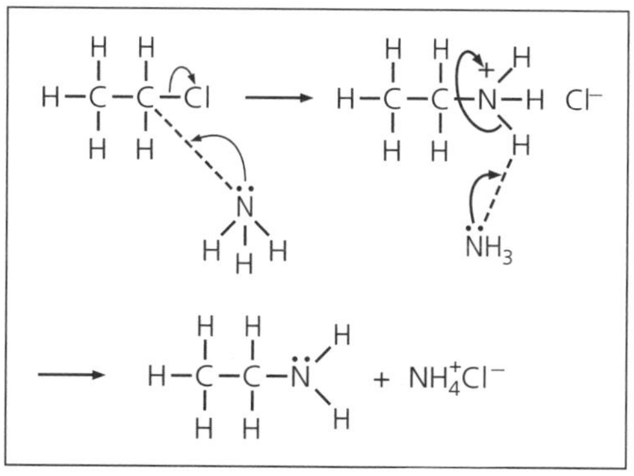

This is a nucleophilic substitution process

3.4 WITH ETHANOLIC HYDROXIDE IONS

*Conditions: potassium hydroxide in ethanol, heat.
Mechanism type: elimination.

In this reaction, an elimination process, the hydroxide ion behaves as a base and not a nucleophile.

$CH_3CH_2CH_2Br(l) + OH^-(ethanol) \rightarrow CH_3CH=CH_2(g) + H_2O(l) + Br^-(in\ ethanol)$

• **Mechanism for the reaction between 1-bromopropane and ethanolic OH⁻**

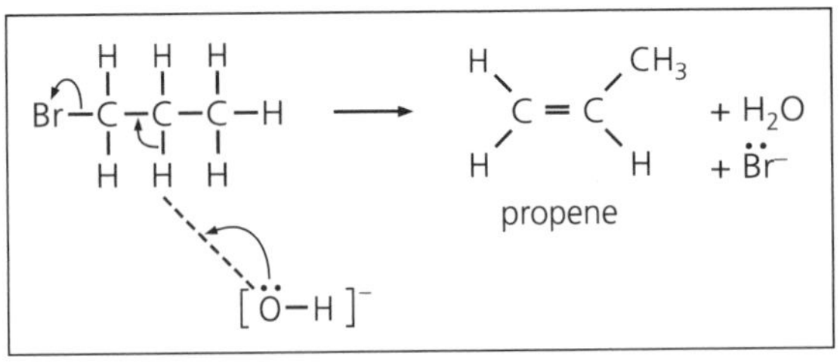

This is an elimination process

In this reaction, when more than one possible alkene product could form, the most substituted product tends to form (the alkene that forms bonds to most alkyl groups). It should also be understood that halogenoalkanes and hydroxide ions tend to result in either nucleophilic substitution processes (forming an alcohol) or elimination processes (forming an alkene); they will always be competing at the same time. However, in order to enhance one reaction process over the other, a fairly non-polar solvent, e.g. ethanol, is used in order to promote elimination, and aqueous solutions are used to promote nucleophilic substitutions. Primary halogenoalkanes also tend to favour substitution, whereas tertiary favour elimination processes.

Nucleophilic substitution processes are always in competition with elimination processes. The structures of the halogenoalkane and the solvent play very important parts in determining which of the processes pre-dominates.

B The alcohols

1 *What are alcohols?*

Alcohols are alkylated water, ROH: one hydrogen atom in the water molecule is replaced by an alkyl group.

Alcohols are classified in a similar way to halogenoalkanes. The number of alkyl groups attached to the carbon atom with the hydroxyl group, –OH, determines the classification.

Alcohols may be either primary, secondary or tertiary in their structure. Each class has different chemical properties.

Primary:
one alkyl group

$H_3C\!-\!CH_2\!-\!OH$
ethanol

Secondary:
two alkyl groups

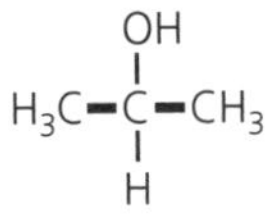

$H_3C\!-\!\underset{H}{\overset{OH}{C}}\!-\!CH_3$
propan-2-ol

Tertiary:
three alkyl groups

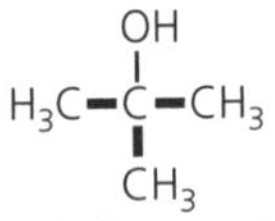

$H_3C\!-\!\underset{CH_3}{\overset{OH}{C}}\!-\!CH_3$
2-methylpropan-2-ol

Alcohols have significantly higher boiling points compared with the corresponding alkanes and halogenoalkanes due to the occurrence of extensive hydrogen bonding between molecules.

• **H-bonding between molecules of methanol**

hydrogen bond

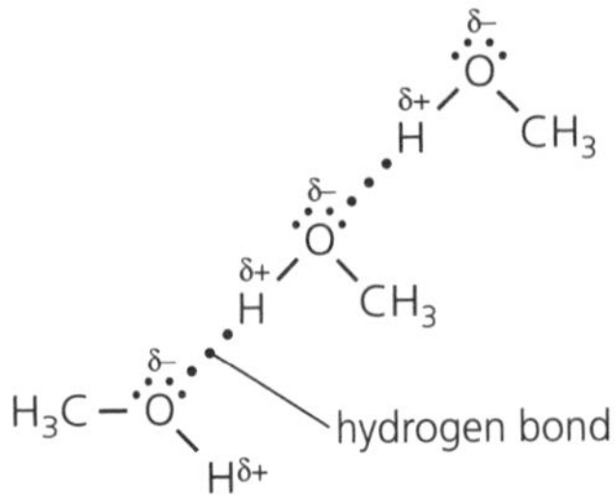

Due to the extensive hydrogen bonding properties of the alcohols, they are more soluble in water than the corresponding alkanes and halogenoalkanes. The alcohols of lower relative molecular mass are more soluble in water (ethanol is soluble in water in all proportions) than those alcohols of higher relative molecular mass.

The alcohols are less polar than water. This is reflected in their ability to dissolve non-polar substances better than water, and ionic and polar substances less effectively than water.

The hydroxyl group in alcohols, −OH, is slightly acidic as there is a very slight tendency for the O−H bond to break and hydrogen ions to form (although the equilibrium position is largely on the left-hand side). Water ($K_w = 10^{-14}\,mol^2\,dm^{-6}$) is more acidic than all alcohols.

> Alcohols are weaker acids than water due to the influence of the inductive effect of the alkyl group on the strengthening of the O–H bond in the alcohol. This makes it less likely to dissociate to form hydrogen ions.

2 Chemical reactions of the alcohols

2.1 WITH SODIUM METAL
Alcohols display acidic behaviour (willingness to donate a proton) with sodium metal.

Reactive metals like sodium react at room temperature with alcohols to form a solution of the sodium alkoxide and hydrogen gas. The metal alkoxide is a white ionic solid with a fairly high melting point (as predicted by its ionic bonding). The resulting alkoxide anion is more nucleophilic (has a greater tendency to donate an electron pair) compared to the corresponding alcohol.

For example:

$$2H-\underset{\underset{H}{|}}{\overset{\overset{H}{|}}{C}}-\underset{\underset{H}{|}}{\overset{\overset{H}{|}}{C}}-O-H + 2Na(s) \longrightarrow 2H-\underset{\underset{H}{|}}{\overset{\overset{H}{|}}{C}}-\underset{\underset{H}{|}}{\overset{\overset{H}{|}}{C}}-O^-Na^+ + H_2(g)$$

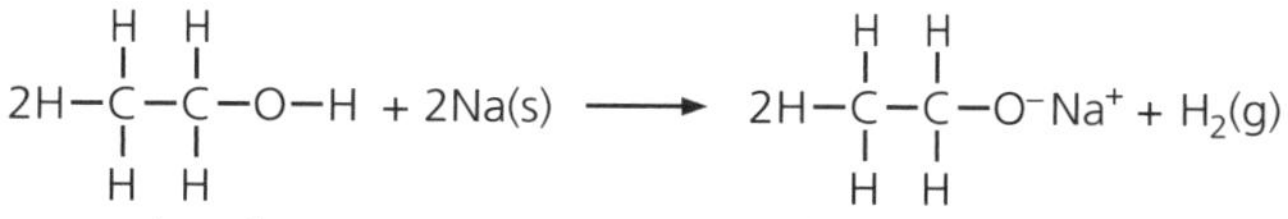

ethanol sodium ethoxide

Methanol reacts more quickly than ethanol which reacts faster than does propan-1-ol and this order is also the order of their power as acids (methanol being the more acidic).

2.2 COMBUSTION
In plenty of oxygen, carbon dioxide and water are formed when an alcohol is burned, whereas in limited oxygen, carbon monoxide and water are formed.

All alcohols are flammable, although the vapour pressures above the surface of the alcohols reflect the strengths of the intermolecular interactions taking place. Methanol is the most flammable, with ethanol next, and so on. For example, the complete combustion of propan-1-ol:

$$2C_3H_7OH(l) + 9O_2(g) \rightarrow 6CO_2(g) + 8H_2O(l)$$

2.3 OXIDATION WITH ACIDIFIED DICHROMATE(VI)
Conditions:
- complete oxidation: increase the proportion of oxidising agent, concentrated sulphuric(VI) acid, reflux
- partial oxidation: minimise the proportion of oxidising agent, dilute sulphuruc(VI) acid, distil

The acidified dichromate(VI) acts according to the half equation:

$$Cr_2O_7^{2-}(aq) + 14H^+(aq) + 6e^- \rightleftharpoons 2Cr^{3+}(aq) + 7H_2O(l)$$

When the alcohol is oxidised, the **orange dichromate(VI) solution turns green**, $Cr^{3+}(aq)$ (and then maybe blue, $Cr^{2+}(aq)$). Although acidified sodium or potassium dichromate(VI) solutions are ideal for the required oxidation, bacteria within the air are also able to slowly oxidise the alcohols. Ethanol will oxidise naturally in the air to form ethanal and then ethanoic acid; this process is of great use in the manufacture of the various types of vinegar.

Oxidation processes normally use acidified potassium dichromate(VI) – do not forget about the acid.

- **Primary alcohols**

  Partial oxidation:

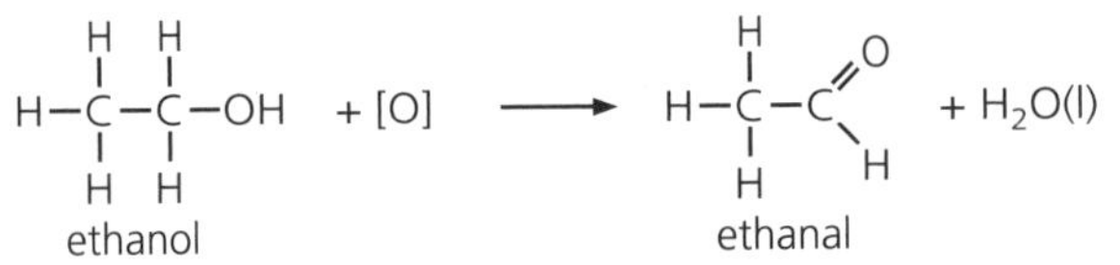
H H
H–C–C–OH
H H
ethanol
+ [O]
H
H–C–C
O
H
H
ethanal
+ $H_2O(l)$

A primary alcohol forms an **aldehyde** when partially oxidised.

Complete oxidation:

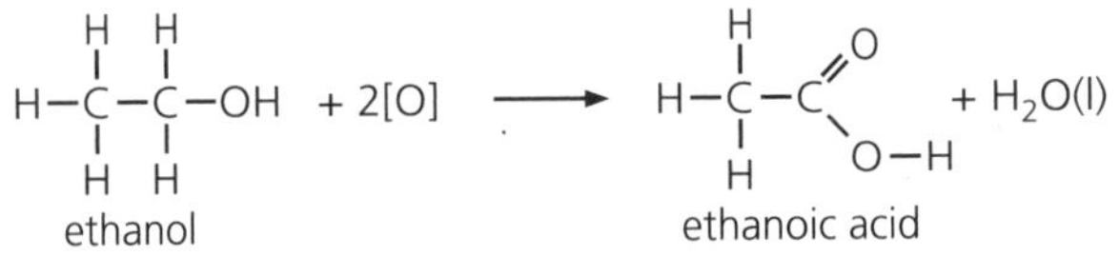
H H
H–C–C–OH
H H
ethanol
+ 2[O]
H
H–C–C
O
O–H
H
ethanoic acid
+ $H_2O(l)$

A primary alcohol forms a **carboxylic acid**, via an aldehyde, when completely oxidised.

Oxidising primary alcohols gives aldehydes and then carboxylic acids. Oxidising secondary alcohols gives ketones. Oxidising tertiary alcohols is not possible using the reagents mentioned.

- **Secondary alcohols**

  Only one organic product is possible when oxidising a secondary alcohol: a ketone.

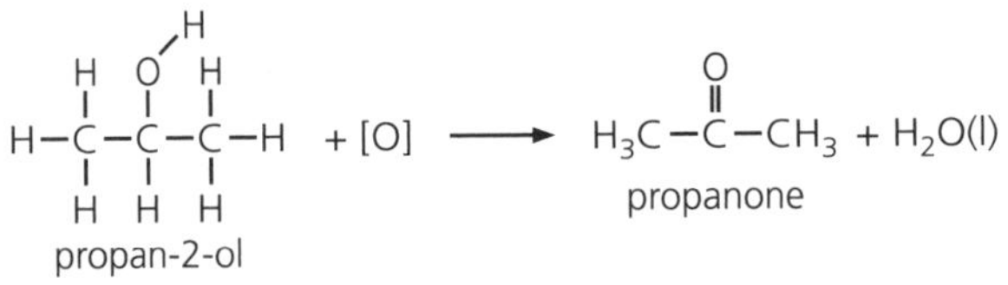
H
H O H
H–C–C–C–H
H H H
propan-2-ol
+ [O]
O
H_3C–C–CH_3
propanone
+ $H_2O(l)$

- **Tertiary alcohols**

  Tertiary alcohols are not oxidised using acidified dichromate(VI) solutions since, in order to do so, a strong carbon–carbon bond would need to be broken.

2.4 Dehydration

When an alcohol is heated under special conditions, the atoms which make water are lost from the molecule and an alkene is formed. This reaction is an **elimination process**. The conditions under which each class is dehydrated vary: primary alcohols tend to require hotter temperatures than secondary alcohols or tertiary alcohols (lower still).

There are many ways of achieving the dehydration of an alcohol:

- aluminium oxide (catalyst) at 300 °C
- concentrated phosphoric(V) acid (catalyst)/heat
- concentrated sulphuric(VI) acid (catalyst)/heat

For example:

$$H-\overset{\displaystyle H}{\underset{\displaystyle H}{C}}-\overset{\displaystyle H}{\underset{\displaystyle H}{C}}-OH \longrightarrow \overset{\displaystyle H}{\underset{\displaystyle H}{C}}=\overset{\displaystyle H}{\underset{\displaystyle H}{C} } + H_2O(l)$$

ethanol ethene

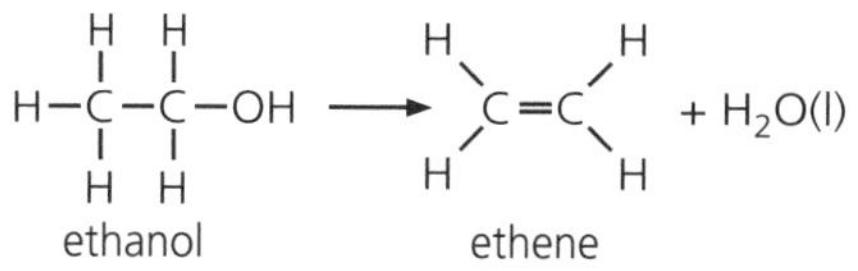

- **Mechanism for dehydration involving concentrated H_2SO_4 on ethanol**

This is an elimination process

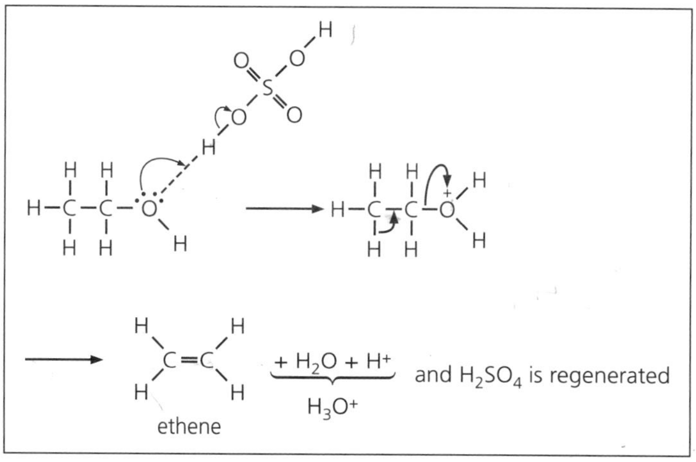

The hydroxyl group, −OH, is a very poor leaving group, so it is first protonated to form $-OH_2{}^+$ and this then will be eliminated, as water, with the generation of a double bond within the molecule.

2.5 ESTERIFICATION

*Conditions: alcohol, carboxylic acid, concentrated sulphuric(VI) acid (catalyst), reflux.

All classes of alcohol react **reversibly** with carboxylic acids, under acidic conditions, to form an **ester** and water.

ethanol ethanoic acid ethyl ethanoate (an ester)

Esters are sweet-smelling organic liquids that have many uses in the perfumery and food industries.

2.6 HALOGENATION

The process of removing the hydroxyl group and replacing with a halogen atom can be achieved in many ways, e.g.

- phosphorus(V) chloride, $PCl_5(s)$
- dichlorosulphur(IV) oxide, $SOCl_2(l)$
- the hydrogen halide: $HCl(g)$, $HBr(g)$, $HI(g)$

ethanol bromoethane

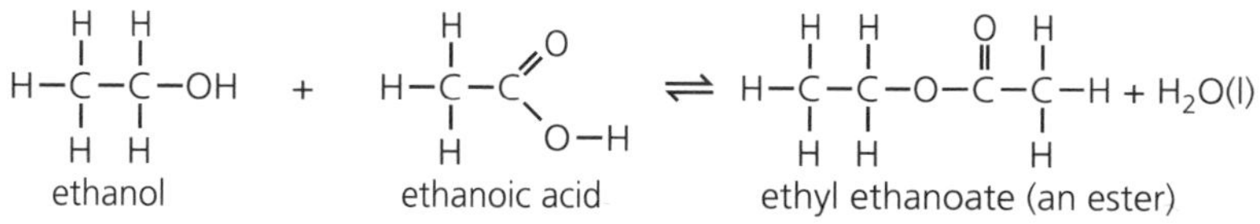

A test for a hydroxyl group is to add phosphorus(V) chloride, PCl_5. If an O–H group is present, hydrogen chloride gas is produced and this in turn produces dense white fumes with concentrated ammonia solution. Carboxylic acids perform the same test, but phenol does not perform this reaction which means it can be used to distinguish between an aliphatic and aromatic alcohol.

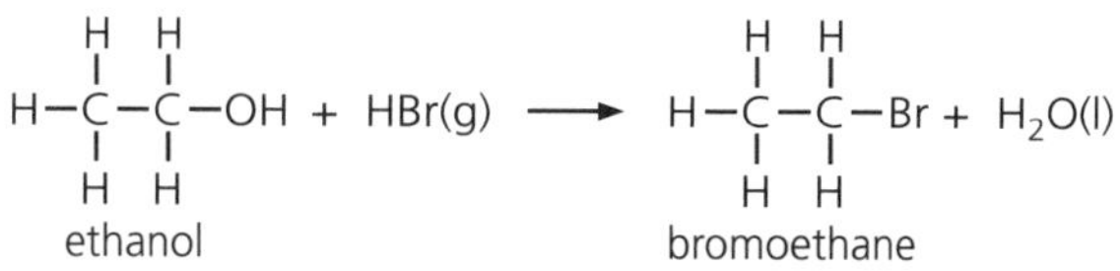

- **Mechanism for the halogenation of ethanol using HBr**

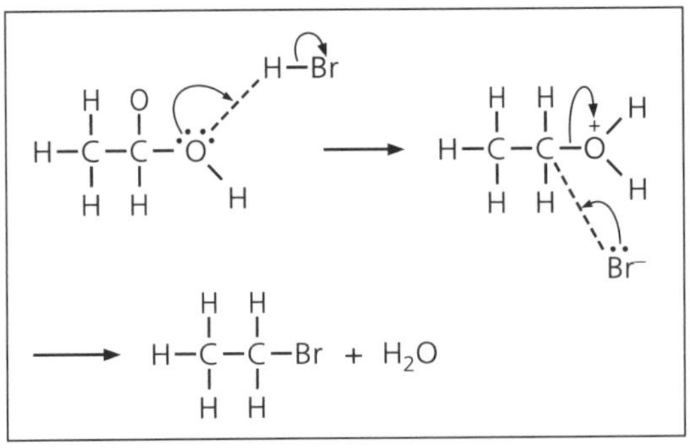

This is a nucleophilic substitution process

2.7 Fermentation

Alcohols are made naturally by an anaerobic (without oxygen) enzymic process in which sugars and other carbohydrates are converted to ethanol. This process is called **fermentation**. Ethanol, which has been assessed as a potential fuel for the future, can be made relatively cheaply using this process (followed by a fractional distillation).

For example, the fermentation of glucose to form ethanol and carbon dioxide:

$$C_6H_{12}O_6 \xrightarrow{\text{zymase}} 2CH_3CH_2OH + 2CO_2$$

3 Phenol, C_6H_5OH

Although phenol, an aromatic alcohol, can be considered as an ordinary alcohol, its chemistry is remarkably different from that of aliphatic alcohols. Figure 16.1 shows the delocalisation of the oxygen lone pairs of electrons into the π-system of the benzene ring.

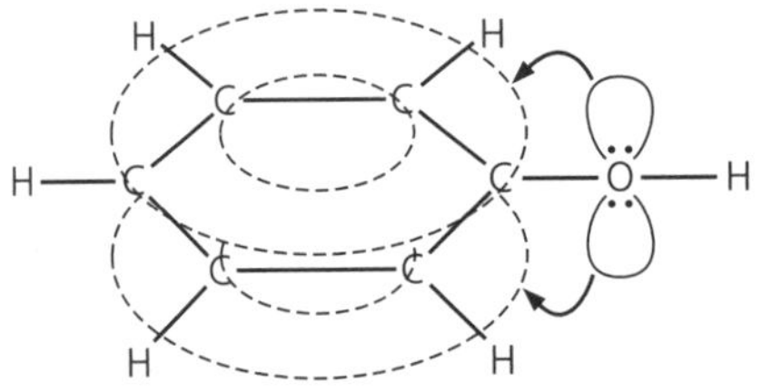

Figure 16.1

The overlap of the lone pairs of electrons on the oxygen atom with the π-system on the benzene ring brings about the following changes:

- It increases the strength of the C–O bond, thus making the bond stronger and shorter and less likely to break. Therefore, phenol does not normally undergo nucleophilic substitution reactions, e.g. reacting with hydrogen halides to form aromatic halogenalkanes.
- It reduces the availability of the lone pairs of electrons on the oxygen atom, making it less basic and nucleophilic in its reactions than with an ordinary aliphatic alcohol.
- It reduces the O–H bond strength, increasing the tendency for the O–H bond to break. This makes phenol more acidic than an ordinary aliphatic alcohol. K_a for phenol is $1.3 \times 10^{-10}\,\text{mol dm}^{-3}$, whereas for methanol K_a has a value of $10^{-16}\,\text{mol dm}^{-3}$.

Phenol is a stronger acid that an ordinary aliphatic alcohol due to the lone pairs of electrons in phenol being delocalised in the π-system of the ring. This process weakens the O–H bond, making dissociation more likely.

- It increases the electron density on the benzene ring, particularly at the 2, 4 and 6 positions. Phenol therefore reacts faster than benzene with electrophiles, e.g. NO_2^+ and Br_2.

3.1 Reactions of phenol

3.1a With sodium metal and sodium hydroxide solution

$$2C_6H_5OH(aq) + 2Na(s) \rightarrow 2C_6H_5O^-Na^+(s) + H_2(g)$$

or

$$C_6H_5OH(aq) + NaOH(aq) \rightarrow C_6H_5O^-Na^+(aq) + H_2O(l)$$

Phenol undergoes electrophilic substitution processes more rapidly than benzene due to the increased electron density in the benzene ring in phenol. This makes phenol more nucleophilic.

3.1b Bromination and nitration

An electrophilic substitution process:

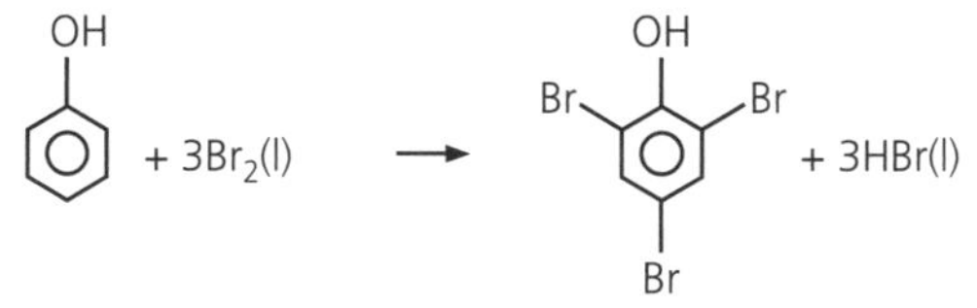

phenol 2,4,6-tribromophenol

Only dilute nitric(V) acid is required in this reaction. Compare this with the nitration of benzene in which concentrated nitric(V) and concentrated sulphuric(VI) acids are required together with elevated temperatures to effect any change.

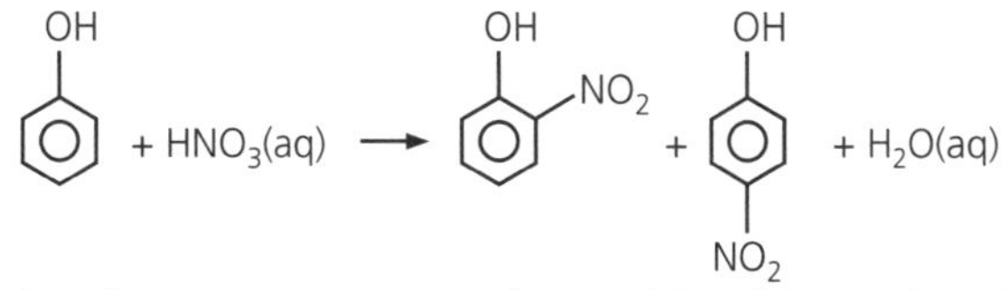

phenol a mixture of 2-and 4-nitrophenol

3.1c With acid chlorides (in sodium hydroxide solution)

$C_6H_5–OH + NaOH \rightarrow C_6H_5–O^-Na^+ + H_2O$ and then:

$C_6H_5–O^-Na^+ + C_6H_5–COCl \rightarrow C_6H_5–O–CO–C_6H_5 + NaCl$

benzoyl chloride phenyl benzoate (an ester)

The test for the phenolic group is to add neutral iron(III) chloride solution. A blue precipitate should form.

C Carbonyl compounds: aldehydes and ketones

1 *What are aldehydes and ketones?*

The **carbonyl group** is the C=O group and it is polarised as $C^{\delta+}=O^{\delta-}$. Carbonyl compounds contain this group. These include aldehydes and ketones.

Aldehydes are compounds containing the functional group 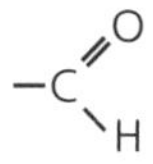 which is written as –CHO.

That is, they contain a carbonyl group with an alkyl group or benzene ring on one side of the carbon atom of the carbonyl group and a hydrogen atom on the other. The general formula for an aldehyde is RCHO.

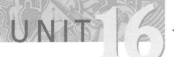

Ketones are organic compounds that follow the general formula 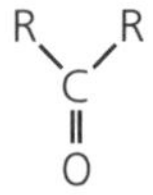 which may be written as RCOR or R_2CO.

The R groups are alkyl groups and not a hydrogen atom (as in an aldehyde).

The molecules of both aldehydes and ketones are polar since the presence of the electronegative oxygen atom creates a significant dipole moment in the carbonyl, C = O, bond. As a result, ketones and aldehydes tend to be soluble in polar solvents as well as non-polar solvents.

Aldehydes and ketones exist as simple molecules that are attracted to each other mainly by dipole–dipole attractions, although van der Waals forces also act.

- **The intermolecular forces acting between molecules of propanone**

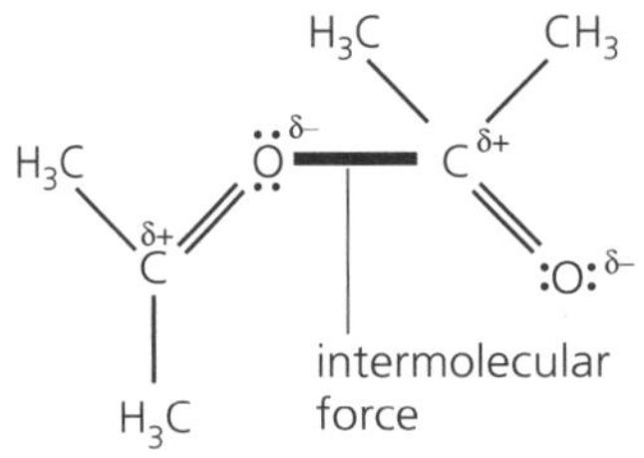

2 Molecular structures for aldehydes and ketones

The carbonyl group is represented by C=O and it is polarised as $C^{\delta+}=O^{\delta}$.

2.1 Aldehydes

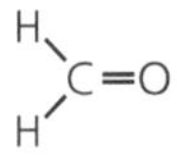
methanal

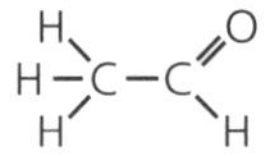
ethanal

2.2 Ketones

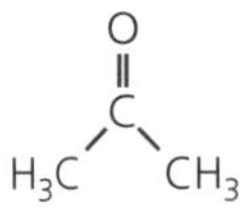
propanone

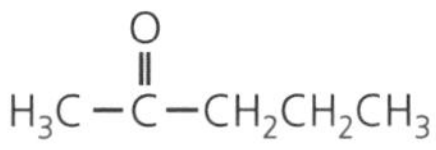
pentan-2-one

3 Chemical reactions of aldehydes and ketones

Aldehydes are synthesised by the use of mild oxidising conditions on primary alcohols.

Ketones are synthesised similarly by the effect of oxidising agents on secondary alcohols.

The reactions of **aldehydes** tend to be either:

- **redox reactions** in which they behave as reducing agents and are oxidised themselves to carboxylic acids, or
- **nucleophilic addition reactions** in which a nucleophile donates a lone pair of electrons towards the carbonyl carbon atom, pushing the π electrons of the carbonyl bond onto the oxygen atom.

Ketones **cannot** be oxidised further using standard oxidising agents since a strong carbon–carbon covalent bond would need to be broken.

3.1 REACTIONS IN WHICH THE ALDEHYDE IS OXIDISED

3.1a With acidified solutions of dichromates(VI) of either sodium or potassium

Aldehydes are easily oxidised by these reagents to form carboxylic acids. The chromium in the chromate(VI) ion is reduced from the orange Cr(VI) state to the green Cr(III) state.

For example, the oxidation of propanal to propanoic acid:

$$CH_3CH_2-C\overset{O}{\underset{H}{\big<}} + [O] \longrightarrow CH_3CH_2-C\overset{O}{\underset{O-H}{\big<}}$$

As mentioned above, ketones do not undergo any oxidation with acidified dichromates(VI), so this reaction can be used to distinguish aldehydes from ketones.

Distinguishing an aldehyde from a ketone: add 1 cm^3 of orange dichromate(VI) solution to a similar quantity of the carbonyl compound. Acidify and warm gently in a water bath. The aldehyde solution will turn from orange to green, whereas the ketone solution will remain orange.

3.1b With Fehling's solution

Fehling's solution contains a copper(II) tartrate complex and the copper(II) ion is reduced to the orange–red precipitate copper(I) oxide in this process. The aldehyde again forms the carboxylic acid.

$$CH_3-C\overset{O}{\underset{H}{\big<}} + 2H_2O(l) + 2Cu^{2+}(aq) \longrightarrow Cu_2O(s) + CH_3-C\overset{O}{\underset{O-H}{\big<}} + 4H^+$$

ethanal orange–red precipitate ethanoic acid

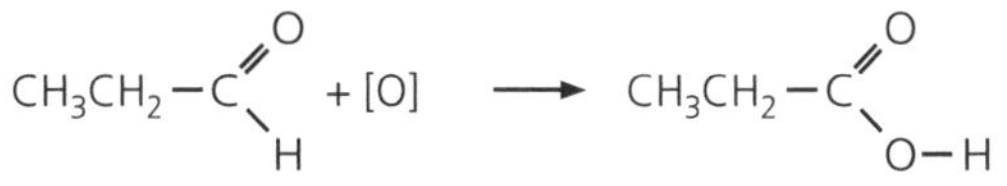

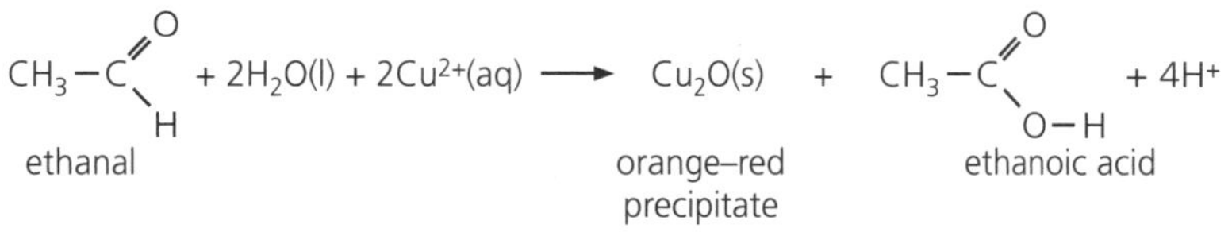

This reaction may also be used to detect reducing sugars like glucose that have free aldehyde groups, as well as other aldehydes, but ketones do not undergo this particular reaction.

3.1c With Tollen's reagent: the silver mirror test

Tollen's reagent is formed by adding ammonia solution to a solution containing the silver(I) ion. A brown precipitate is observed of silver(I) oxide and then this complexes with further ammonia to form the linear diamminesilver(I) ion, $[Ag(NH_3)_2]^+$.

The chemistry in this reaction is very similar to the one involving Fehling's solution in which the metal ion is reduced.

$$CH_3-C\overset{O}{\underset{H}{\big<}} + 2Ag^+(aq) + H_2O(l) \longrightarrow CH_3-C\overset{O}{\underset{O-H}{\big<}} + 2Ag(s) + 2H^+(aq)$$

ethanal ethanoic acid

When Tollen's reagent is warmed with an aldehyde, the solution darkens and metallic silver is deposited on the glass to form a silver mirror. This reaction can be used as a **distinguishing test between an aldehyde and a ketone**, since the ketone will not undergo this reaction so a colourless solution will remain.

Remember when describing a chemical test to give the names of all reagents used. Briefly describe how to carry out the test and what you would see in both cases (including negative results).

Distinguishing between an aldehyde and a ketone: (i) Tollen's reagent forms a silver mirror with an aldehyde only; (ii) Fehling's solution turns from a blue solution to form an orange–red precipitate with an aldehyde; (iii) warming with acidified potassium dichromate(VI) produces a green solution with the aldehyde (the solution stays orange with the ketone).

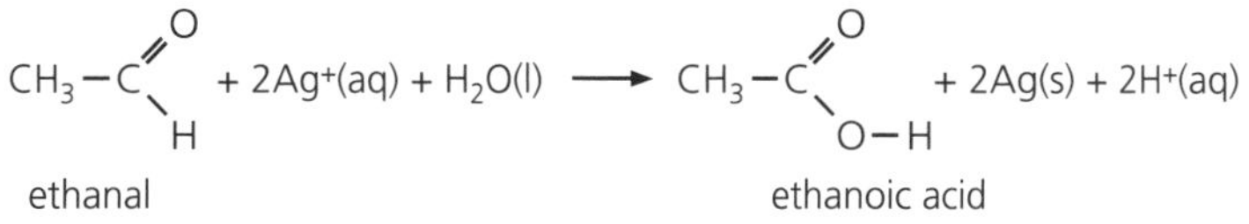

Some examination boards do not consider Tollen's reagent to be a reagent (despite its name). A reagent can sometimes be defined as a substance that you could find on a shelf in the laboratory.

3.2 Reactions in which the aldehyde or ketone undergoes nucleophilic addition

3.2a With potassium cyanide

*Conditions: ethanol/water, reflux.

The cyanide ion, [:C≡N]⁻, attacks the carbonyl carbon in this process to form a molecule called a hydroxynitrile.

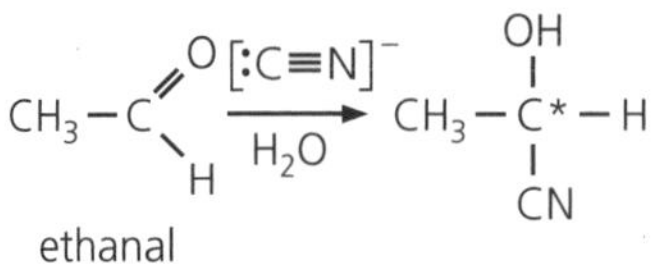

ethanal

(Notice that this molecule possesses a chiral carbon atom)

- **Mechanism for the reaction between ethanal and $^{-}$:CN/H_2O**

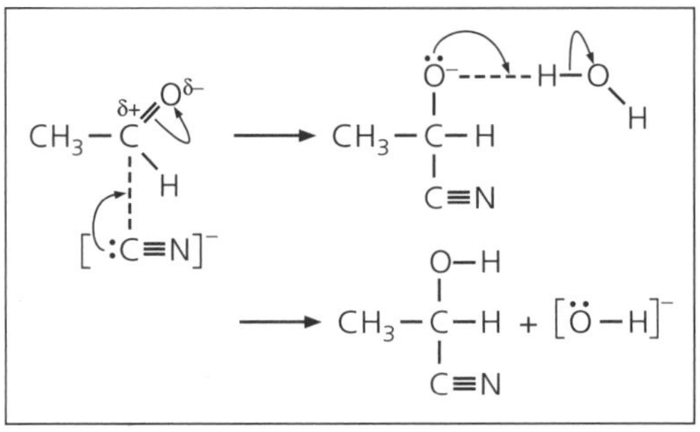

This is a nucleophilic addition reaction

The intermediate in this process is tetrahedral in configuration and the water will protonate the negative charge on the oxygen atom to form the final product. The starting ketone or aldehyde is based on the trigonal planar molecule and the nucleophile can approach from either above or below the plane of the organic molecule. The effect of this is to produce a racemic mixture of both optical isomers.

3.2b With the reducing agents sodium borohydride(III) (sodium tetrahydridoborate(III): $NaBH_4$) or lithium aluminium hydride (lithium tetrahydridoaluminate(III): $LiAlH_4$)

Sodium borohydride(III) and lithium aluminium hydride are both powerful reducing agents. Sodium borohydride(III) works in aqueous solution, whereas lithium aluminium hydride operates in ether solvents. Both reducing agents give rise to the formal hydride ion (H⁻).

A useful interconversion is for an aldehyde or a ketone to be reduced to the original alcohol; this is accomplished using either:

- sodium borohydride, $NaBH_4$, in an aqueous solution, or
- lithium aluminium hydride, $LiAlH_4$ in a non-aqueous solution, e.g. in **dry** ether.

These reagents work by apparently donating the hydride ion, H⁻, as a nucleophile and then reacting according to a nucleophilic addition process. In these reactions, either boron or aluminium organic complexes are formed and the organic alcohol is freed by adding water and boiling.

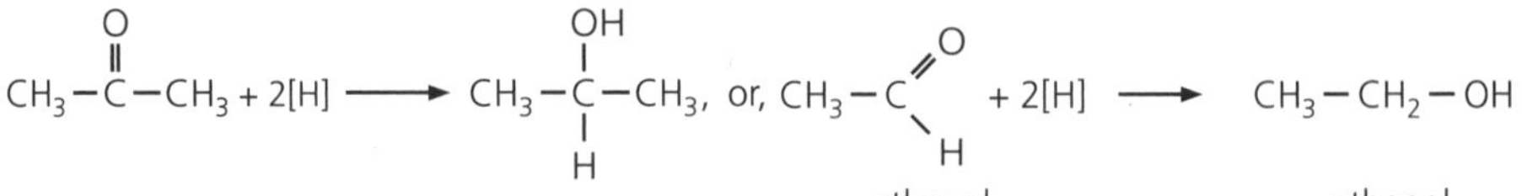

propanone propan-2-ol ethanal ethanol

3.2c With amines

Amines react with aldehydes and ketones to form enamines. The reaction is best described as a **nucleophilic addition process** followed by an **elimination** of water. Sometimes these processes are described as condensation reactions.

$$CH_3-C\overset{O}{\underset{H}{\big\langle}} + CH_3-\ddot{N}H_2 \longrightarrow \overset{H}{\underset{H_3C}{\big\rangle}}C=N\overset{\frown}{\underset{CH_3}{}} + H_2O$$

ethanal

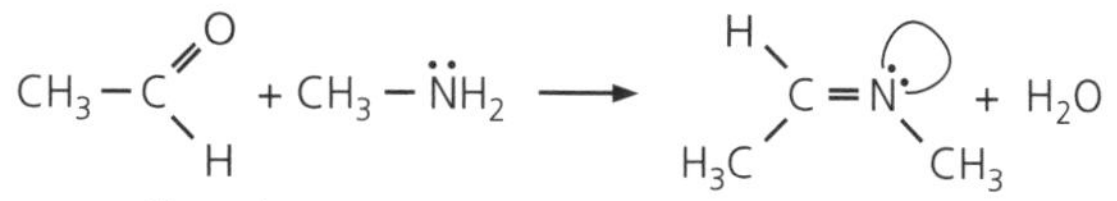

- **Mechanism between ethanal and methyl amine**

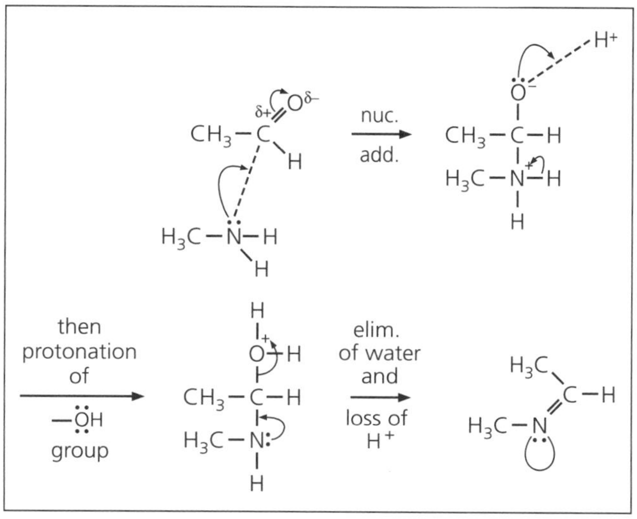

This is a nucleo-philic addition elimination process

The resulting enamine may exist in geometrical forms since no rotation occurs about the C = N bond and the lone pair of electrons can be considered as an ordinary group in this case.

3.2d With 2,4-dinitrophenylhydrazine (2,4-DNP, Brady's reagent)

This is a variation on the previous reaction.

2,4-DNP cannot be used to distinguish between a ketone and an aldehyde; it can only be used to tell us when a ketone or aldehyde is present. It is not a distinguishing test.

The reaction with 2,4-DNP is very suitable for indicating that either a ketone or an aldehyde functional group is present. It will not distinguish between a ketone or an aldehyde (warming with acidified potassium dichromate(VI) would accomplish this).

2,4-dinitrophenylhydrazine has the following molecular structure:

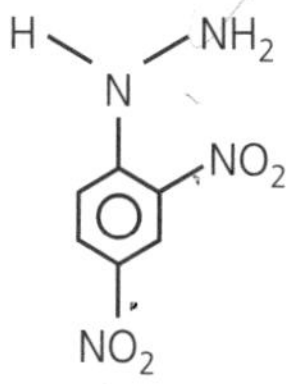

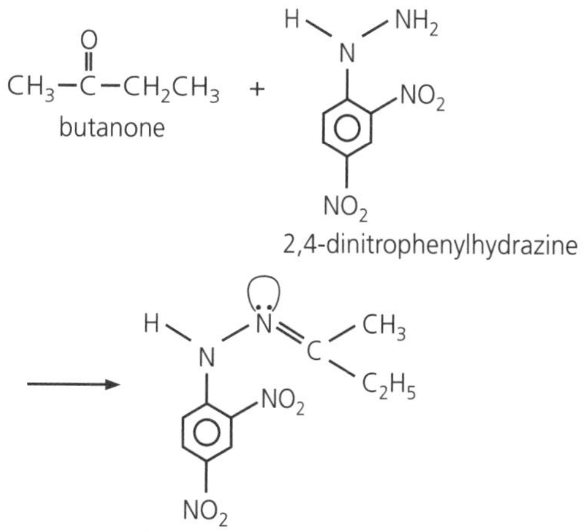

Derivatives of 2,4-DNP are called hydrazones. They have characteristic melting points that can be used to identify the original ketone or aldehyde.

2,4-dinitrophenylhydrazine is normally provided in the form of an orange solution and, when a few drops of the solution are added to the ketone or aldehyde, an orange precipitate forms of the corresponding 2,4-dinitrophenyl-hydrazone.

2,4-dinitrophenylhydrazine

butanone-2,4-dinitrophenylhydrazone

This reaction is described as a nucleophilic addition–elimination process.

The product hydrazones can be recrystallised from ethanol and then the melting points determined to deduce the nature of the original ketone or aldehyde.

3.3 THE IODOFORM REACTION

This classic reaction involves warming a compound with sodium hydroxide solution in which has been placed a small amount of solid iodine. A pale yellow solid called iodoform, $CHI_3(s)$, may form if the original organic molecule contains one of the following groups of atoms:

The structures in their entirety must be present (not just an alcohol or ketone).

$$
\begin{array}{c}
\text{H} \quad \text{O} \\
| \quad \ \ || \\
\text{H}-\text{C}-\text{C}- \\
| \\
\text{H}
\end{array}
\qquad \text{or} \qquad
\begin{array}{c}
\text{H} \quad \text{O}-\text{H} \\
| \quad \ \ | \\
\text{H}-\text{C}-\text{C}- \\
| \quad \ \ | \\
\text{H} \quad \text{H}
\end{array}
$$

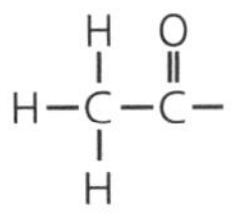

e.g. ethanal, propanone
butan-2-one, pentan-2-one

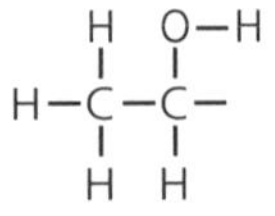

e.g. ethanol, propan-2-ol
butan-2-ol

UNIT 17 The amines

A What are amines?

Amines can be considered as alkylated ammonia in which one or more hydrogen atoms are replaced by an alkyl group.

Amines may be viewed as alkylated ammonia, i.e. a hydrogen atom(s) in ammonia which is substituted with one or more alkyl group.

Amine molecules, like ammonia, are **pyramidal** in the spatial arrangement of covalent bonds around the nitrogen atom:

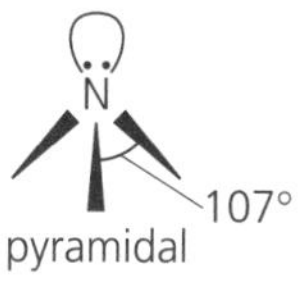

Amines are classified according to the number of alkyl groups (or C–N) bonds surrounding the central nitrogen atom.

Primary amines: one attached alkyl group, e.g. ethylamine

$CH_3-CH_2-\ddot{N}H_2$

Secondary amines: two attached alkyl groups, e.g. dimethyl amine

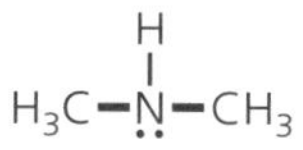

Tertiary amines: three attached alkyl groups, e.g. triphenylamine

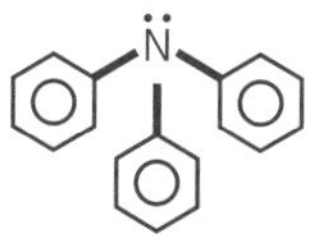

Note that quaternary ammonium ions of the form (H.R.R′.R″)N$^+$ may exhibit optical isomerism since they can form tetrahedral enantiomers.

Quaternary amines: four attached alkyl groups, e.g. methylammonium chloride

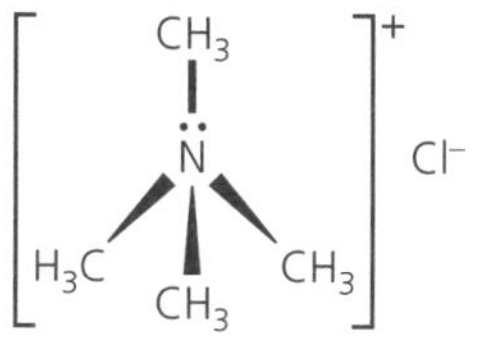

1 *Phenylamine ($C_6H_5NH_2$)*

Aromatic amines, e.g. phenylamine, may be prepared from the corresponding nitro compound, e.g. nitrobenzene, by refluxing with tin metal in concentrated hydrochloric acid, e.g. $C_6H_5NO_2 + 6[H] \rightarrow C_6H_5NH_2 + 2H_2O$.

Phenylamine consists of an amino group (–NH_2) attached directly to a benzene ring.

The nitrogen lone pair may overlap with the π-system on the ring and, as a result, the electron lone pair on the nitrogen atom is delocalised into the π-system on the ring. This process also occurs in phenol (C_6H_5OH) and it affects the properties of the phenylamine molecule in some important ways.

Phenylamine is a weaker base than ammonia since the nitrogen lone pair is delocalised into the π-system on the ring and therefore less available for protonation on the nitrogen atom. The basic order for bases, including phenylamine, is expected to be:

tertiary > secondary > primary > ammonia ≫ phenylamine.

So, aromatic amines are much weaker bases than aliphatic amines.

When discussing the basic strength of amines, it is also important to consider the stabilisation of the resulting cation by hydrogen bonding with water molecules.

For example:

trimethylamine	$K_b = 6.3 \times 10^{-5}\,mol\,dm^{-3}$
dimethylamine	$K_b = 5.9 \times 10^{-4}\,mol\,dm^{-3}$
methylamine	$K_b = 4.4 \times 10^{-4}\,mol\,dm^{-3}$
ammonia	$K_b = 1.8 \times 10^{-5}\,mol\,dm^{-3}$
phenylamine	$K_b = 4.2 \times 10^{-10}\,mol\,dm^{-3}$

Also, K_b for the amine $C_6H_5CH_2–NH_2$ is $2.2 \times 10^{-5}\,mol\,dm^{-3}$; the increase in the value for K_b compared to phenylamine reflects the lack of delocalisation of the nitrogen lone pair into the π-system in the ring, making it more likely to be protonated (a stronger base).

The C–N bond in phenylamine is stronger and shorter than in aliphatic amines (so is less susceptible to breaking). The $–NH_2$ group is very unlikely to be substituted by another group in a reaction.

Electrophilic substitutions on the ring have a lower activation energy than in benzene and are therefore faster. The benzene π-system has an increased electron density in phenylamine and, as a result, makes the ring more nucleophilic in its reactions with species accepting lone pairs of electrons (electrophiles).

2 Chemical reactions of amines

2.1 With water

Amines, like ammonia, partially dissociate in water to form alkaline solutions. They do this by using their lone pair of electrons on the nitrogen atom to form a dative bond to a proton from a water molecule.

$$CH_3\ddot{N}H_2 + H_2O(l) \rightleftharpoons CH_3NH_3^+(aq) + OH^-(aq)$$

methylamine

2.2 With mineral acids

For example, hydrochloric acid or sulphuric(VI) acid.

The amine lone pair of electrons is protonated to form the alkyl ammonium salt and water in a neutralisation process.

$$CH_3\ddot{N}H_2 + HCl(aq) \longrightarrow CH_3\overset{+}{N}H_3Cl^-$$

methylamine

2.3 With transition metal ions

The availability of the nitrogen lone pair makes it suitable for acting as a **ligand** with an acceptor ion, like a transition metal ion in a ligand substitution process. When a solution of the amine is added to an aqueous solution of copper(II) ions, a pale blue precipitate of copper(II) hydroxide, $Cu(OH)_2(s)$, is formed and this then dissolves in excess amine to form the corresponding copper–amine complex.

$$[Cu(H_2O)_6]^{2+}(aq) + 4CH_3\ddot{N}H_2 \rightleftharpoons [Cu(methylamine)_4 (H_2O)_2]^{2+}(aq) + 4H_2O(l)$$

methylamine

This is a nucleophilic substitution process.

2.4 WITH HALOGENOALKANES

Halogenoalkanes contain the polar C–halogen bond and this is attacked by amine molecules displacing the halogen atom as the halide leaving group.

CH₃I + CH₃CH₂N̈H₂ ⟶ H₃C–N(H)–C₂H₅ + HI(g)

methyl iodide ethylmethylamine
(primary amine) (secondary amine)

If sufficient halogenoalkane is available, further reactions on the halogenoalkane, by the now secondary amine, are possible. This process may continue until the quaternary amine is formed.

H₃C–N(H)–C₂H₅ + CH₃I ⟶ H₃C–N̈(–CH₃)(C₂H₅) + HI(g)

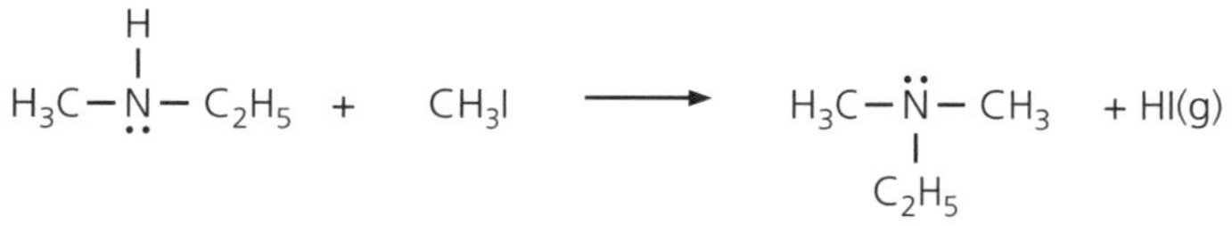

ethylmethylamine methyl iodide ethyldimethylamine
(secondary amine) (tertiary amine)

and then

H₃C–N̈(–CH₃)(C₂H₅) + CH₃I ⟶ [N(CH₃)₃ (C₂H₅)]⁺I⁻

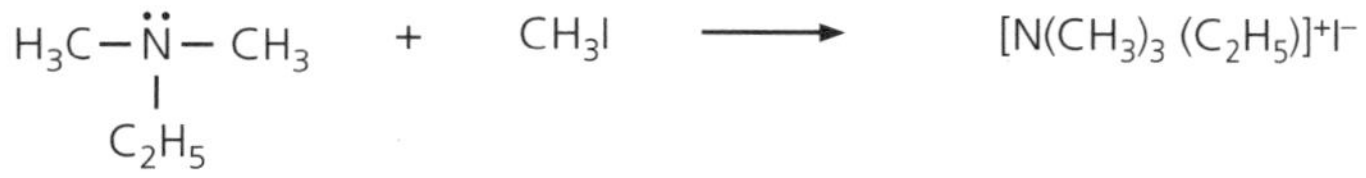

ethyldimethylamine methyl iodide ethyltrimethylammonium iodide
(tertiary amine) (quaternary amine)

This is a nucleophilic addition–elimination process.

2.5 WITH ACYL CHLORIDES

Primary and seconday amines react with acyl chlorides at room temperature to form the corresponding amides. Tertiary amines react to form a salt, but no hydrogen chloride gas is formed in this case.

CH₃–C(=O)Cl + CH₃N̈H₂ ⟶ CH₃–C(=O)–N(H)–CH₃ + HCl(g)

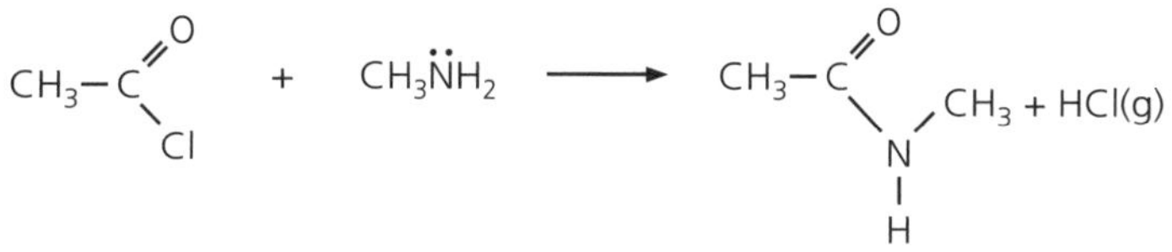

ethanoyl chloride methylamine amide product
 (primary amine)

Alternatively, the reaction between ethanoyl chloride and methylamine may be represented as:
$CH_3COCl(l) + 2CH_3NH_2(l) \rightarrow CH_3CONHCH_3(s) + CH_3NH_3^+Cl^-(s).$

2.6 WITH CARBOXYLIC ACIDS

Carboxylic acids will react with amines in a neutralisation process.

CH₃N̈H₂ + HCOOH ⟶ CH₃N̈H₃.⁻OOCH + H₂O

methylamine methanoic acid methylammonium
 methanoate

When this salt is heated, it may decompose to form an amide and water.

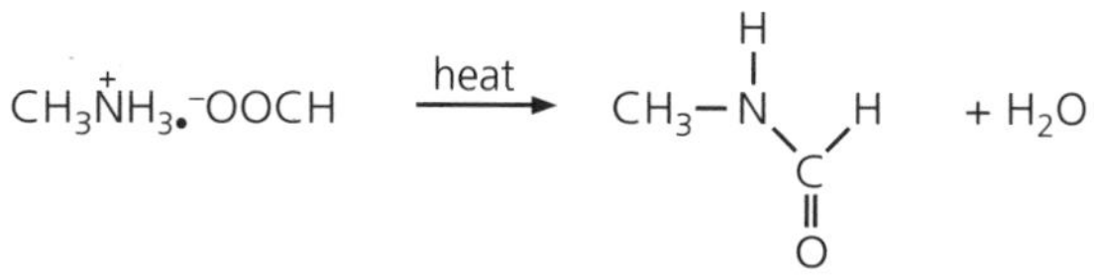

CH₃N̈H₃.⁻OOCH —heat→ CH₃–N(H)–C(=O)H + H₂O

methylammonium N-methylmethanamide
methanoate

UNIT 18 Carboxylic acids and their derivatives

A Carboxylic acids

1 What are carboxylic acids?

Carboxylic acids are molecules containing the –COOH group which has the structure:

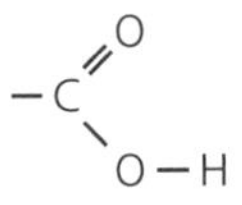

They have the general formula RCOOH. If R is a benzene ring, the acid is called benzoic acid.

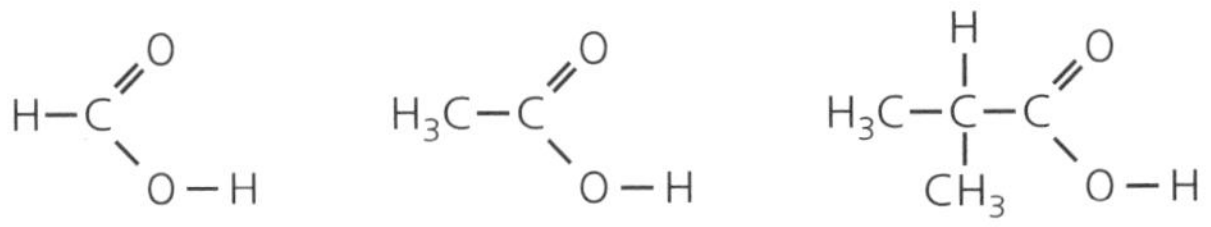

methanoic acid   ethanoic acid   methylpropanoic acid

The carbonyl group, C=O, withdraws electrons from the hydroxyl group, O–H, making the bond weaker and therefore inducing dissociation to form the carboxylate anion and a hydrated proton. For example:

$$CH_3COOH(aq) + H_2O(l) \rightleftharpoons CH_3COO^-(aq) + H_3O^+(aq)$$

Methanoic acid is the stronger carboxylic acid and, as the length of the hydrocarbon chain increases, the acids become weaker.

Carboxylic acids are weak acids since they only dissociate partially in solution. Methanoic acid is the stronger acid, but as the length of the hydrocarbon chain increases, the acids become weaker. The hydrocarbon chain pushes electrons (an inductive effect) towards the carboxylic acid group, therefore strengthening the hydroxyl group. This effect makes the acid weaker, increases the value of the acid dissociation constant, K_a, and decreases the value for pK_a.

2 Chemical reactions of carboxylic acids

Be aware of the typical reactions of acids. Many students are aware of salts forming, but is it water that forms? Is it hydrogen gas? Is it carbon dioxide gas? Is water and the salt the only product? If you are unsure, check the section on writing chemical equations in Unit 1.

2.1 With bases

Since carboxylic acids are acids, they react predictably in the same way as other acids:

- with reactive metals (with a $E^\ominus < 0$) to form a carboxylate salt and hydrogen:
  $2Na(s) + 2CH_3COOH(aq) \rightarrow 2CH_3COO^-Na^+(aq) + H_2(g)$
  or ionically as $2Na(s) + 2H^+(aq) \rightarrow 2Na^+(aq) + H_2(g)$
- with metal oxides to form a salt and water:
  $CuO(s) + 2CH_3COOH(aq) \rightarrow (CH_3COO^-)_2Cu(s) + H_2O(l)$
- with metal hydroxides to form a salt and water:
  $NaOH(aq) + CH_3COOH(aq) \rightarrow CH_3COO^-Na^+(aq) + H_2O(l)$
- with metal carbonates to form a salt, water and carbon dioxide gas:
  $K_2CO_3(s) + 2CH_3COOH(aq) \rightarrow 2CH_3COO^-K^+(aq) + H_2O(l) + CO_2(g)$

In the salt formed from a carboxylic acid, the anion is the corresponding carboxylate anion. For example, the anion of ethanoic acid is ethanoate. In the carboxalate ion, the bond lengths of the C–O bonds are identical. This is due to delocalisation within the anion:

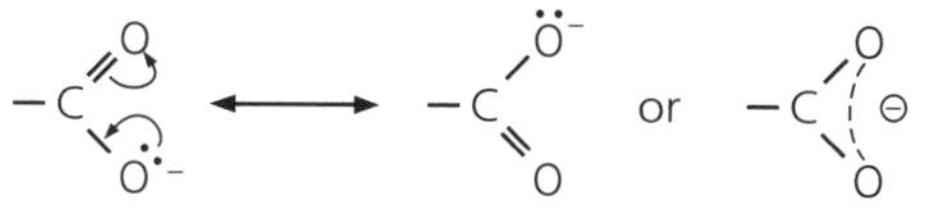

2.2 With ammonia and amines

Ammonia and amines are both Brønsted–Lowry bases since they are able to use their lone pair of electrons on the nitrogen atom to accept a proton. They will react with carboxylic acids in neutralisation reactions:

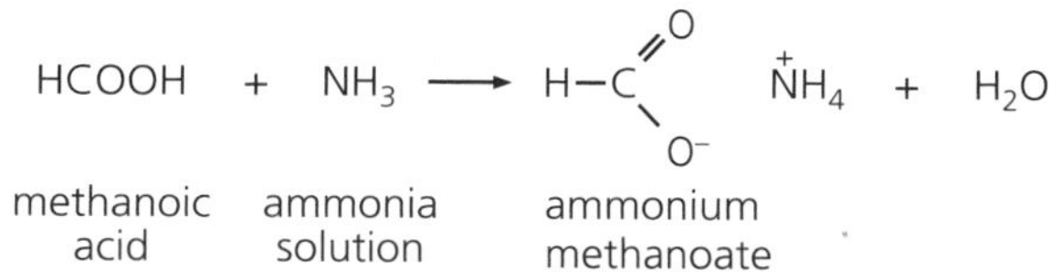

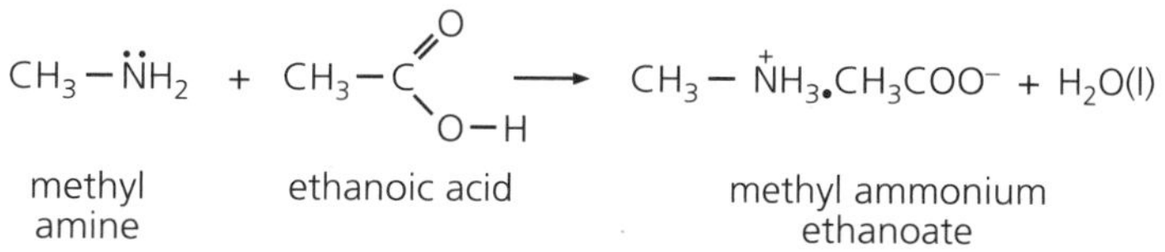

On heating ammonium and amine salts of carboxylic acids, the salts will decompose to form **amides** and water.

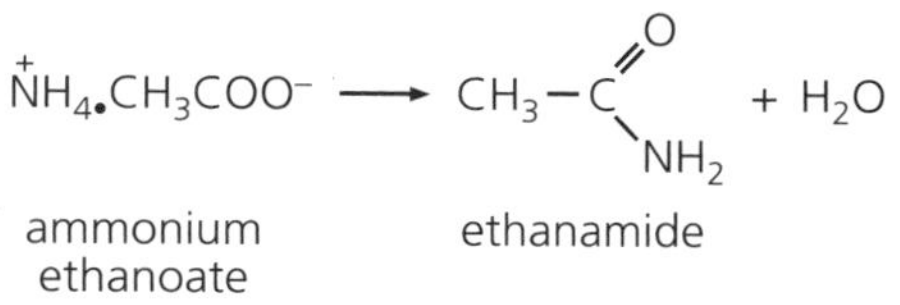

2.3 With alcohols

*Conditions: concentrated sulphuric(VI) acid catalyst, reflux.

As mentioned in Unit 16, all carboxylic acids react with alcohols to form an equilibrium mixture in which the reaction products are an **ester** and water.

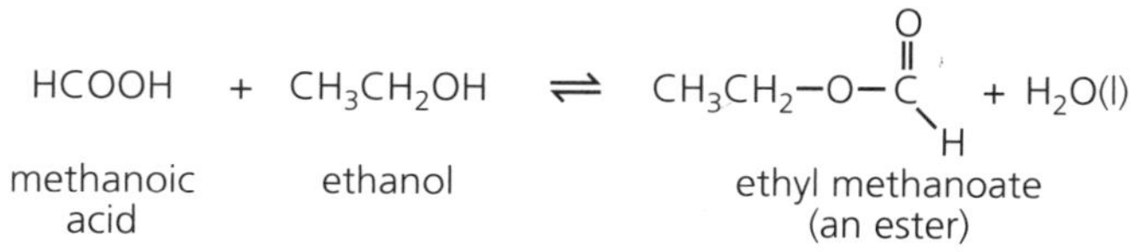

Esters are used in the food and perfumery industries as well as being good solvents and plasticisers. Organic molecules containing more than one carboxylic acid functional group may react with alcohols containing more than one hydroxyl group and the resulting ester will be a polymer called a **polyester**.

2.4 With chlorinating agents

For example: phosphorus(V) chloride, PCl_5, or $SOCl_2$.

The ability of amine groups to bond with carboxylic acid functional groups, forming a peptide linkage, is the basis behind the formation of proteins from amino acids.

One test for carboxylic acids is to add ethanol and a few drops of concentrated sulphuric(VI) acid. On warming in a water bath a sweet-smelling substance is formed; this is an ester. Alternatively, adding aqueous sodium carbonate produces carbon dioxide gas with a carboxylic acid, and this gas turns limewater milky.

Carboxylic acids, like alcohols, have a hydroxyl group that can be replaced with a chlorine atom. Reagents such as phosphorus(V) chloride, PCl_5, or $SOCl_2$, react in this way to yield organic molecules called acyl chlorides.

> The reaction with PCl_5 may be used to detect a free hydroxyl group, O–H. HCl(g) is produced and forms dense white fumes with ammonia.

$$CH_3COOH \ + \ PCl_5(s) \ \longrightarrow \ CH_3-C\begin{smallmatrix}O\\Cl\end{smallmatrix} \ + \ POCl_3(s) \ + \ HCl(g)$$

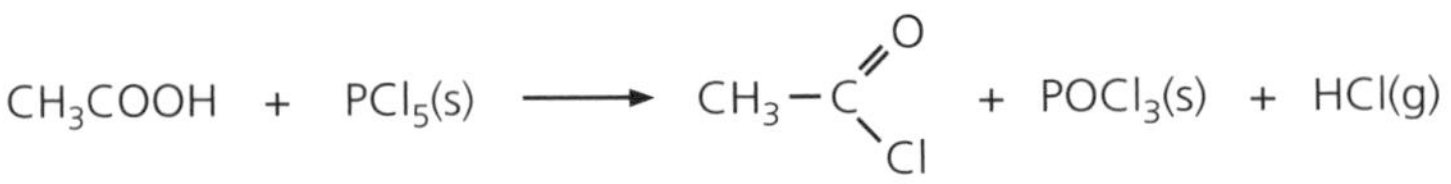

ethanoic
acid

The product molecules are synthetically useful since they react faster, and often with higher yields, than the corresponding carboxylic acid. This is an advantage to the pharmaceutical industry.

2.5 WITH REDUCING AGENTS

For example: lithium aluminium hydride ($LiAlH_4$) in ether.

The reduction of a carboxylic acid is very difficult to achieve using sodium borohydride or hydrogen over a Raney nickel catalyst. However, $LiAlH_4$ will achieve the reduction to the corresponding primary alcohol.

$$\underset{}{\bigcirc}{-}COOH \ + \ 4[H] \ \longrightarrow \ \underset{}{\bigcirc}{-}CH_2OH \ + \ H_2O(l)$$

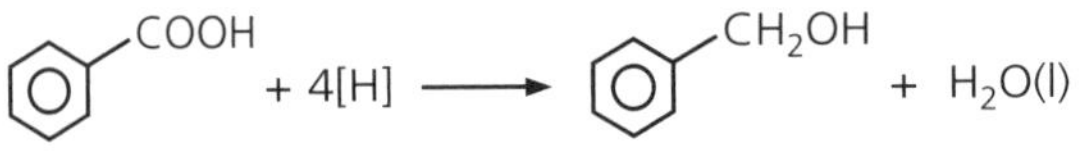

2.6 WITH A DEHYDRATING AGENT

For example: phosphorus(V) oxide, P_4O_{10}.

Carboxylic acids can be dehydrated by phosphorus(V) oxide, P_4O_{10}, to form acid anhydrides. Acid anhydrides are also of use in organic synthesis (e.g. the synthesis of aspirin) since they, like acyl chlorides, are more reactive than carboxylic acids.

> In terms of reactivity, acid anhydrides are more reactive than carboxylic acids; they will therefore react faster and will often produce higher yields in their reactions.

$$2 \ CH_3-C\begin{smallmatrix}O\\O-H\end{smallmatrix} \ \longrightarrow \ \begin{matrix}CH_3-C\\CH_3-C\end{matrix}\begin{smallmatrix}O\\O\\O\end{smallmatrix} \ + \ H_2O$$

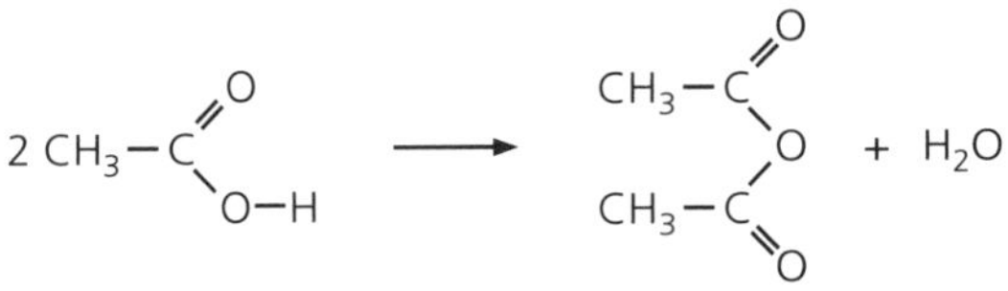

ethanoic acid ethanoic anhydride

3 *The synthesis of carboxylic acids*

- The oxidation of a primary alcohol with acidified potassium dichromate(VI) ions and refluxing yields the aldehyde and then the carboxylic acid.
- Ethanol will be slowly oxidised in solution in the presence of certain enzymes to form ethanoic acid solution; this process is of particular importance when making vinegar in the food industry.
- When manufacturing pure ethanoic acid industrially, a catalytic process involving methanol and carbon monoxide over a rhodium–iodine catalyst is used. This process gives a yield of over 99% and there is only one organic product using this method.

$$CH_3OH + CO \ \xrightarrow[\text{30 atm/450 K}]{Rh/I_2} \ CH_3COOH$$

B Carboxylic acid derivatives

The main carboxylic acid derivatives are:

- esters
- acyl chlorides
- acid anhydrides
- amides
- nitriles

1 *Esters*

Esters follow the general structure:

$$R-C\overset{O}{\underset{O-R'}{\diagup}}$$

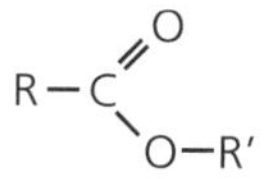

This is written as RCOOR'.

- **Examples of esters**

$$H_3C-\overset{O}{\overset{\|}{C}}-O-CH_3 \qquad H_3C-\overset{O}{\overset{\|}{C}}-O-C_2H_5 \qquad H_3C-\overset{O}{\overset{\|}{C}}-O-C_3H_7$$

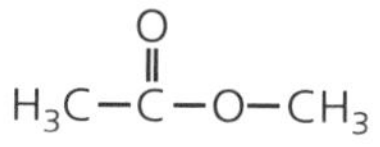

methyl ethanoate　　　　ethyl ethanoate　　　　propyl ethanoate

When naming esters, the **alkyl** group which has come from the alcohol is named first, followed by the carboxylate part. This part is derived from the corresponding carboxylic acid and is written second, e.g. methanoate, ethanoate, propanoate, etc.

- **The reaction mode of esters:**

The functional group tends to be attacked by **nucleophiles**.

The lone pair of electrons from the nucleophile is donated into the carbon atom of the carbonyl group in the ester.

The lone pair is shifted onto the carbonyl oxygen atom to produce a negatively charged oxygen.

This then shifts back to reform the carbonyl group and then moves to break the C–O bond.

1.1 REACTIONS OF ESTERS

1.1a With sodium hydroxide solution – hydrolysis reactions

*Conditions: reflux under heat or dilute acidic solutions/reflux under heat.

In these reactions the base and the acid are catalysts, so the actual processes are called **acid or base catalysed hydrolysis reactions**. It is important to note that in basic conditions, esters undergo complete hydrolysis to yield the corresponding alcohol and sodium salt of the carboxylic acid, whereas acids do not completely hydrolyse the ester. In the latter case, an equilibrium mixture is formed in which some of the ester is still present.

Many students find drawing unsymmetrical esters difficult. For example, ethyl propanoate is: CH₃CH₂O–CO.CH₂CH₃ and not CH₃CO.O– CH₂CH₂CH₃; the latter molecule is propyl ethanoate.

Esters are hydrolysed to form the corresponding alcohol and carboxylic acid. However, the reaction is very slow and the rate of reaction may be increased either by using aqueous base or acid. In the latter case, the reaction forms an equilibrium mixture; in the former case, the reaction goes to completion.

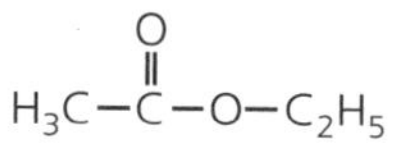

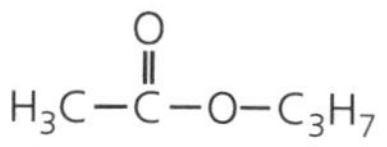

The process of breaking down esters is called saponification and it is of use in the manufacture of soap.

- **In basic conditions:**

$$CH_3CH_2-O-\overset{\overset{\displaystyle O}{\|}}{C}-CH_2CH_3 \ + \ OH^-(aq) \ \longrightarrow \ CH_3CH_2-C\overset{\displaystyle O}{\underset{\displaystyle O^-}{\diagup}} \ + \ CH_3CH_2OH$$

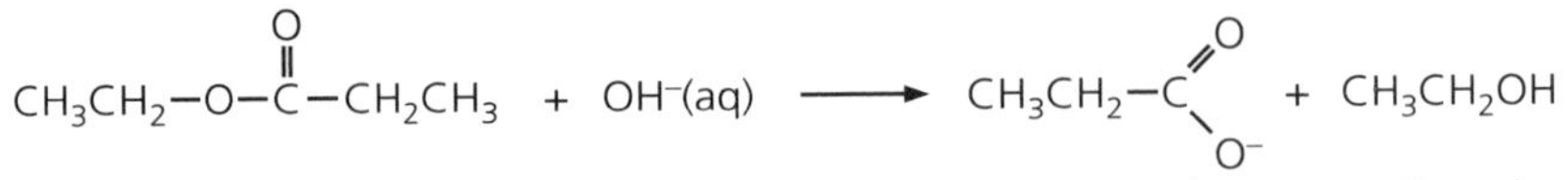

ethyl propanoate hydroxide ions propanoate ions ethanol

Note that the carboxylate anion reacts partially with water to reform the hydroxide ion catalyst.

- **In acidic conditions:**

$$CH_3CH_2-O-\overset{\overset{\displaystyle O}{\|}}{C}-CH_2CH_3 \ + \ H_2O \ \overset{H_3O^+(aq) \text{ catalyst}}{\rightleftharpoons} \ CH_3CH_2COOH \ + \ CH_3CH_2OH$$

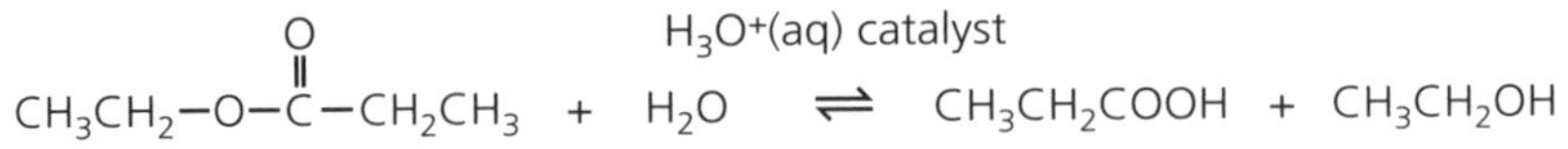

ethyl propanoate water propanoic acid ethanol

Naturally occurring fats and oils are themselves esters of propane-1,2,3-triol and fatty acids (a long chain saturated or unsaturated carboxylic acid). If fats or oils are heated in concentrated sodium hydroxide solution, the ester is hydrolysed to form the corresponding alcohol (propane-1,2,3-triol – used in the food and cosmetics industries) and the sodium salt of the fatty acid (used in making soap).

- **A fat being hydrolysed in basic conditions to form a soap**

$$
\begin{array}{l}
CH_2-O-\overset{\overset{\displaystyle O}{\|}}{C}-C_{17}H_{35} \\[4pt]
CH_2-O-\overset{\overset{\displaystyle O}{\|}}{C}-C_{17}H_{35} \quad + \ 3\ NaOH \\[4pt]
CH_2-O-\overset{\overset{\displaystyle O}{\|}}{C}-C_{17}H_{35}
\end{array}
\longrightarrow
\begin{array}{l}
CH_2-OH \\[4pt]
CH_2-OH \quad + \ 3\ C_{17}H_{35}COO^-Na^+ \\[4pt]
CH_2-OH
\end{array}
$$

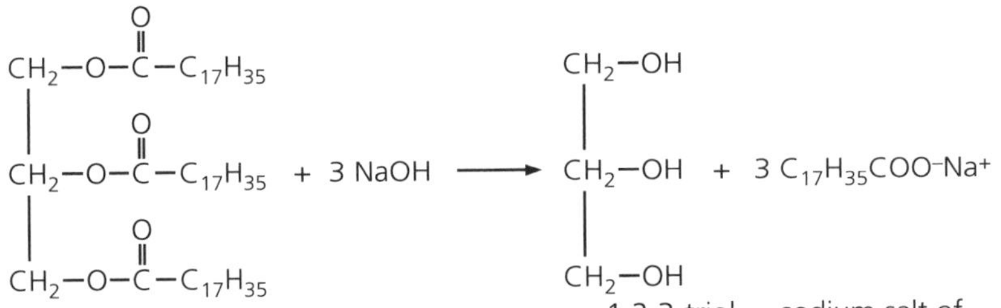

propane-1,2,3-triol sodium salt of a fatty acid

If the reaction is carried out using concentrated sulphuric(VI) acid, a soapless detergent is formed.

1.1b With reducing agents

For example: lithium aluminium hydride, $LiAlH_4$(ether), or sodium borohydride, $NaBH_4$(aq).

The polar ester will be attacked by the hydride ion to yield a mixture of alcohols.

$$CH_3CH_2-O-C\overset{\displaystyle O}{\underset{\displaystyle H}{\diagup}} \ \overset{LiAlH_4(\text{ether})}{\longrightarrow} \ CH_3CH_2OH \ + \ CH_3OH$$

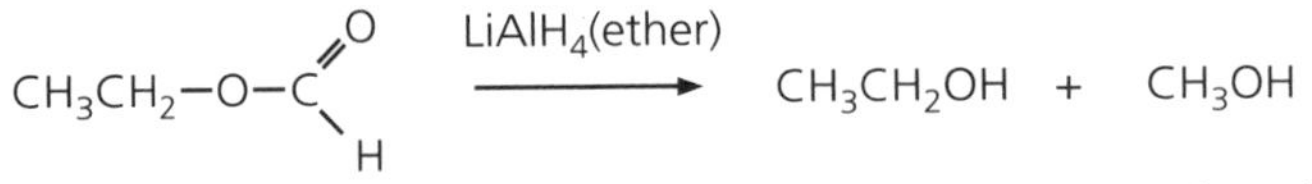

ethyl methanoate ethanol methanol

1.1c With ammonia solution and amines

On heating the ester with either ammonia or the amine, the ester is attacked to form the alcohol and the amide.

$$CH_3CH_2-O-\overset{\overset{\displaystyle O}{\|}}{C}-CH_2CH_3 \ \overset{NH_3}{\longrightarrow} \ CH_3CH_2OH \ + \ CH_3CH_2-C\overset{\displaystyle O}{\underset{\displaystyle NH_2}{\diagup}}$$

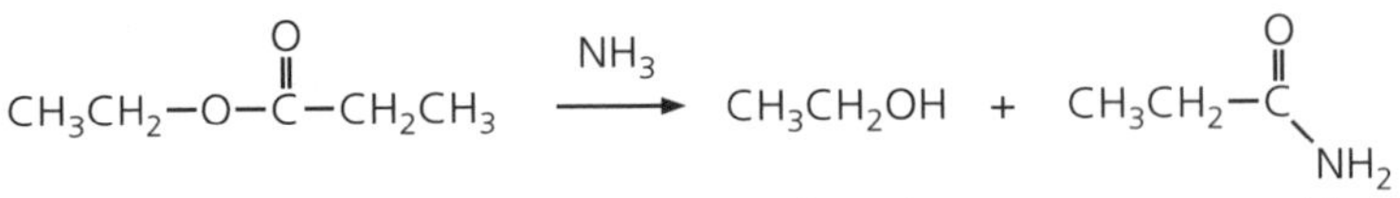

ethyl propanoate ethanol propanamide

Acid chlorides are extremely reactive organic molecules. This is due to the electron-withdrawing effect of the oxygen and chlorine atoms, present within the molecule, on the electron density around the carbon atom. This makes the carbon atom very electrophilic or susceptible to attack by nucleophiles.

Acyl chlorides react very quickly and energetically. On reaction, they often produce hydrogen chloride gas and this is extremely corrosive. For this reason, acyl chlorides may often be replaced with a safer alternative reagent, e.g. ethanoic anhydride.

2 Acyl chlorides

Acyl chlorides follow the general formula RCOCl and contain the functional group:

$$-C\overset{\displaystyle O}{\underset{\displaystyle Cl}{<}}$$

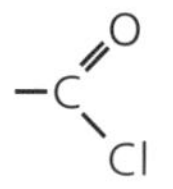

The acyl chlorides are reactive organic molecules. They react, often rapidly, with nucleophiles. Since the chlorine atom and the oxygen atom are both extremely electronegative atoms, the carbon is made very δ^+ charged by the electron movement away from the carbon atom and to the chlorine and oxygen:

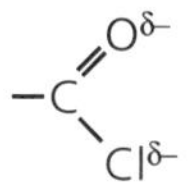

$$-C\overset{\displaystyle O^{\delta-}}{\underset{\displaystyle Cl^{\delta-}}{<}}$$

The mechanism for reaction is similar to ester processes but with the chloride ion acting as leaving group (instead of $R\ddot{O}^-$).

- **Reaction scheme for acyl chlorides**

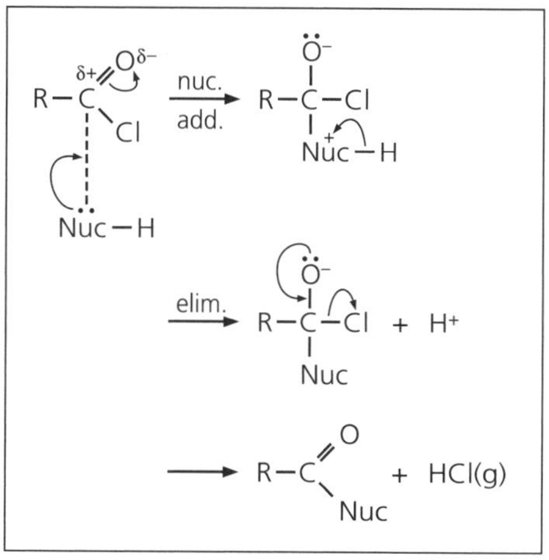

The mechanism by which acyl chlorides react can be described as nucleophilic addition followed by elimination.

2.1 CHEMICAL REACTIONS OF ACYL CHLORIDES

2.1a With water

Acyl chlorides react with the water by the water molecule donating a lone pair of electrons to the carbon atom of the acyl group. The resulting molecules formed are the carboxylic acid and hydrogen chloride gas.

$$CH_3-C\overset{\displaystyle O}{\underset{\displaystyle Cl}{<}} \quad + \quad H_2O \quad \longrightarrow \quad CH_3-C\overset{\displaystyle O}{\underset{\displaystyle O-H}{<}} \quad + \quad HCl(g)$$

ethanoyl chloride ethanoic acid

2.1b With ammonia and amines

Ammonia and amines react with the ethanoyl chloride to form the corresponding amide and hydrogen chloride gas. The lone pair of electrons on the nitrogen atom are donated to form a new carbon–nitrogen bond.

$$CH_3-C\overset{\displaystyle O}{\underset{\displaystyle Cl}{<}} \quad + \quad NH_3(aq) \quad \longrightarrow \quad CH_3-C\overset{\displaystyle O}{\underset{\displaystyle NH_2}{<}} \quad + \quad HCl(g)$$

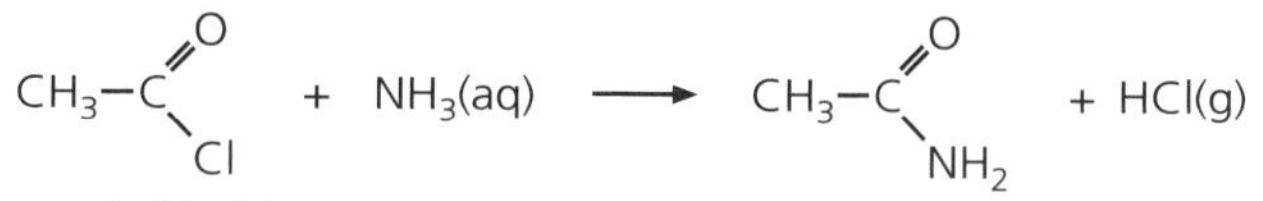

ethanoyl chloride ethanamide

Diamines react with diacyl chlorides to form a polyamide. This is one example of condensation polymerisation. Nylon is an example of a polymer formed in this way:

$$H_2\ddot{N}-(CH_2)_6-\ddot{N}H_2 \quad + \quad \overset{O}{\underset{Cl}{\underset{\|}{C}}}-(CH_2)_4-\overset{O}{\underset{Cl}{\underset{\|}{C}}} \quad \longrightarrow$$

hexane-1,6-diamine a diacyl chloride

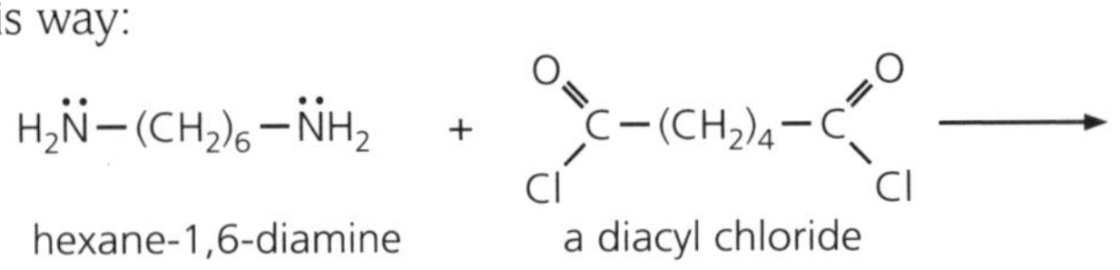

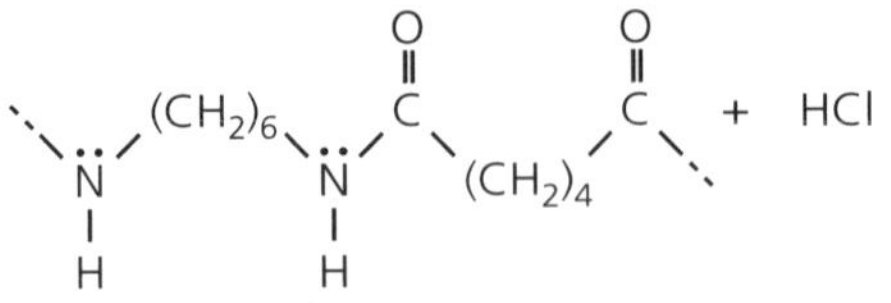

section of a strand of nylon

2.1c With alcohols (or the corresponding sodium salt (the alkoxide))

Alcohols will react with acyl chlorides but, on deprotonating the alcohol with sodium metal, the more nucleophilic alkoxide ion, $R-\ddot{O}^-$, is formed. The resulting nucleophile reacts with the acyl chloride to form the corresponding ester and hydrogen chloride gas.

$$CH_3C\overset{O}{\underset{Cl}{\big<}} \quad + \quad CH_3CH_2OH \quad \longrightarrow \quad CH_3CH_2O-\overset{O}{\underset{\|}{C}}-CH_3 + HCl(g)$$

ethanoyl chloride ethanol ethyl ethanoate

or

$$CH_3-C\overset{O}{\underset{Cl}{\big<}} \quad + \quad CH_3CH_2O\text{-}Na^+ \quad \longrightarrow \quad CH_3CH_2O-\overset{O}{\underset{\|}{C}}-CH_3 \quad + \quad NaCl(s)$$

ethanoyl chloride sodium ethoxide ethyl ethanoate sodium chloride

2.1d With carboxylic acids (or the corresponding salt)

To make the carboxylic acid more nucleophilic in its reactions, sodium hydroxide may be added. This removes the proton from the acid to reveal the more nucleophilic carboxylate anion. This will react with acyl chlorides to form an acid anhydride and hydrogen chloride gas.

$$CH_3-C\overset{O}{\underset{Cl}{\big<}} \quad + \quad CH_3-C\overset{O}{\underset{O^-Na^+}{\big<}} \quad \longrightarrow \quad \overset{\displaystyle CH_3-C\overset{O}{\big<}}{\underset{\displaystyle CH_3-C\overset{}{\big<}_O}{O}} \quad + \quad Na^+(aq) + Cl^-(aq)$$

ethanoyl chloride sodium ethanoate ethanoic anhydride

3 *Acid anhydrides*

Acid anhydrides follow the general formula RCOOCOR' and contain the functional group:

$$\begin{array}{c} -C\overset{O}{\big<} \\ \quad O \\ -C\overset{}{\big<}_O \end{array}$$

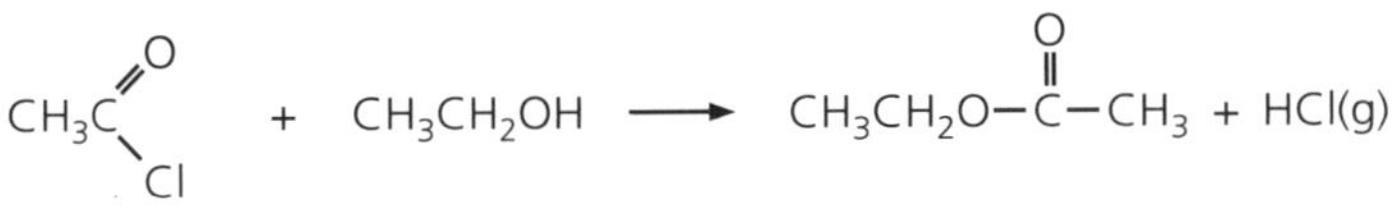

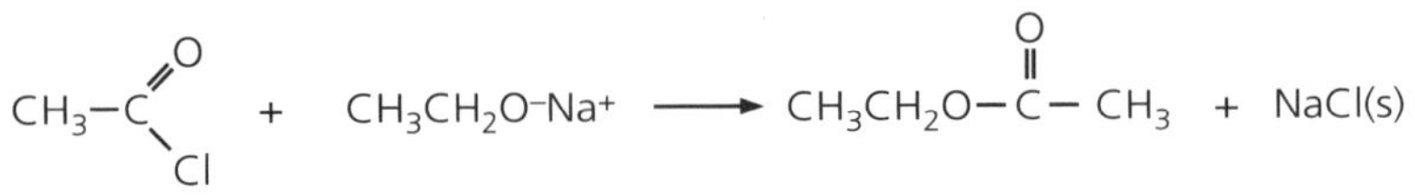

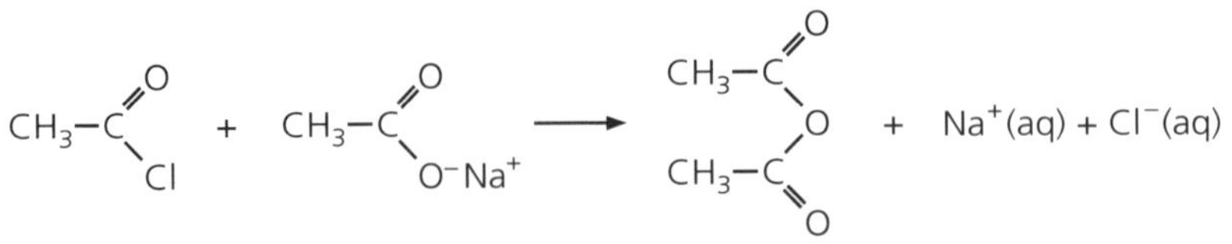

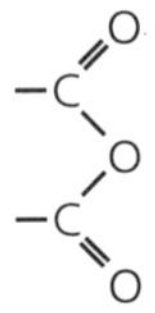

They are not as reactive as acyl chlorides but they are still of use in synthesis since they are safer.

Reaction products are identical to those produced with acyl chlorides. The only difference is that the carboxylate anion acts as the leaving group instead of the chloride ion, but the organic molecule produced is the same. Using the same reactions as with acyl chlorides above, we will use the molecule ethanoic anhydride to illustrate the reactions of acid anhydrides.

The reactions of acid anhydrides will produce the same products as with acyl chlorides, but the ethanoate ion is the leaving group rather than the chloride ion (as with acyl chlorides).

- **With water**

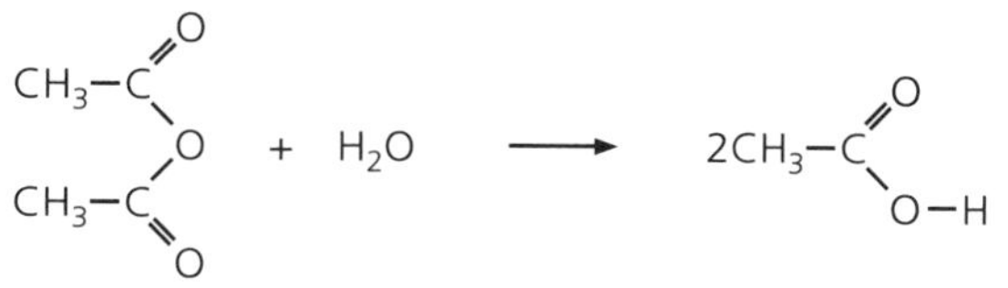

ethanoic anhydride — ethanoic acid

- **With ammonia and amines**

ethanoic anhydride — ethanamide

- **With alcohols**

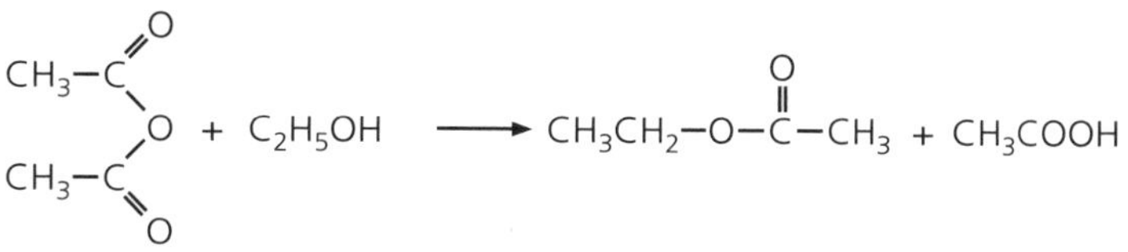

ethanoic anhydride — ethyl ethanoate

4 Amides

Amides follow the general formula RCONHR′, with the simplest amide being ethanamide, where R is a hydrogen atom, CH_2CONH_2. They contain the group:

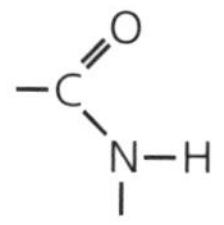

Amides tend to be more soluble in water and have higher melting points than some other functional groups because the lone pair of electrons on the nitrogen atom is delocalised into the carbonyl group to yield an ionic form:

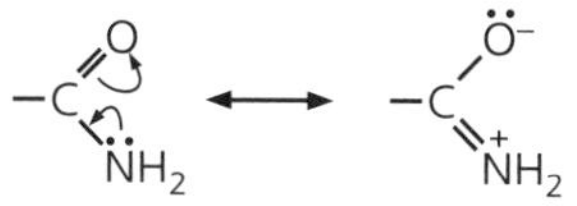

Amides are very weak bases because the nitrogen lone pair, as in phenylamine, is delocalised into another part of the molecule, thus decreasing its basic power.

Propanamide is used below to illustrate the typical reactions of amides.

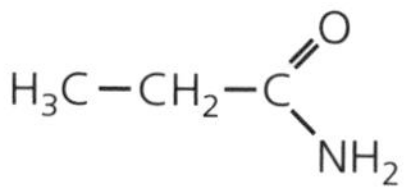

propanamide

4.1 CHEMICAL REACTIONS OF AMIDES

4.1a With dehydrating agents

For example: phosphorus(V) oxide, P_4O_{10}.

$$CH_3-CH_2-C\overset{O}{\underset{NH_2}{\big<}} \xrightarrow{P_4O_{10}(s)} CH_3CH_2-C\equiv N \ + \ H_2O(l)$$

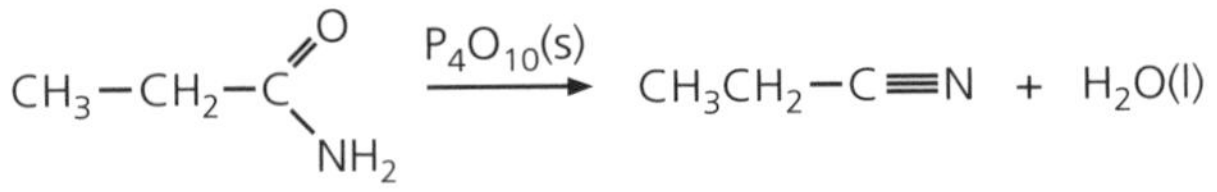

propanamide propanenitrile

4.1b With water

This reaction tends to be very slow, so base or acid is added to catalyse this hydrolysis.

- Base catalysed hydrolysis:

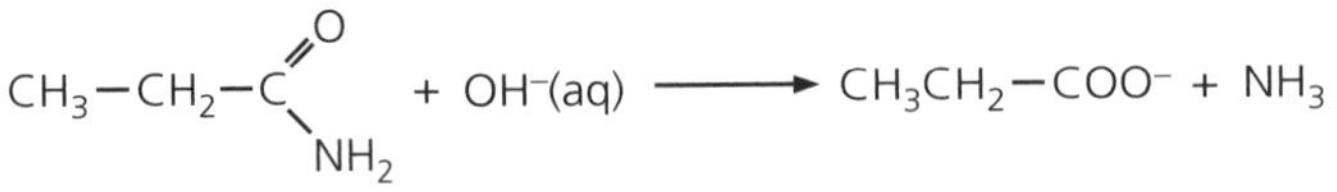

$$CH_3-CH_2-C\overset{O}{\underset{NH_2}{\big<}} + \ OH^-(aq) \longrightarrow CH_3CH_2-COO^- + NH_3$$

propanamide

The ammonia molecule formed may interact with water molecules to regenerate the hydroxide ion.

- Acid catalysis:

$$CH_3CH_2-C\overset{O}{\underset{NH_2}{\big<}} + \ H_3O^+(aq) \longrightarrow CH_3CH_2COOH \ + \ NH_4^+(aq)$$

propanamide

The ammonium ion formed may interact with water molecules to regenerate the acid catalyst.

4.1c With reducing agents

For example, lithium aluminium hydride, $LiAlH_4$(ether), or sodium borohydride, $NaBH_4$(aq).

$$CH_3CH_2-C\overset{O}{\underset{NH_2}{\big<}} + \ 4[H] \longrightarrow CH_3CH_2CH_2-\overset{..}{N}H_2 \ + \ H_2O(l)$$

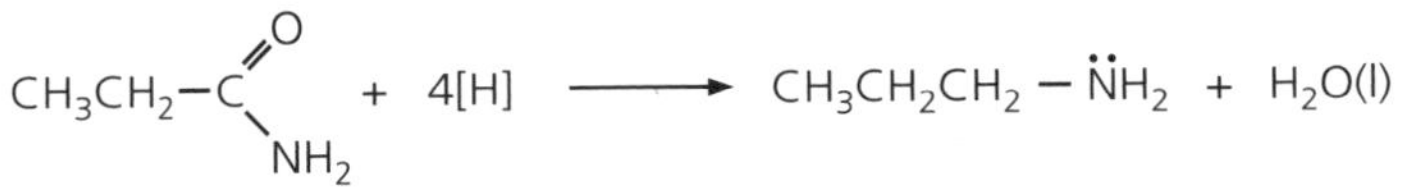

propanamide propylamine

4.1d The Hoffmann Degradation process

*Conditions: refluxing with bromine in potassium hydroxide solution.

This synthetically useful process allows conversion from an amide to an amine with one less carbon atom.

$$CH_3CH_2-C\overset{O}{\underset{NH_2}{\big<}} \longrightarrow CH_3CH_2\overset{..}{N}H_2$$

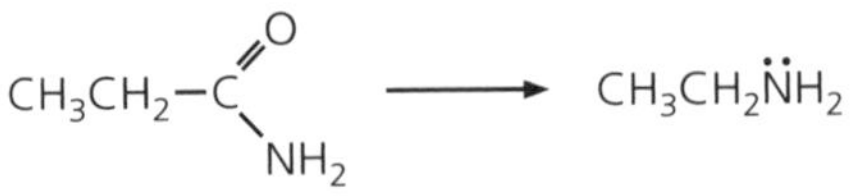

propanamide ethylamine

5 | Nitriles

Nitriles contain the functional group $-C\equiv N$ and they have the general formula RCN.

Phosphorus(V) oxide, P_4O_{10}, is a good dehydrating agent since it combines with the water from the organic molecule to form phosphoric(V) acid; $P_4O_{10}(s) + 6H_2O(l) \rightarrow 4H_3PO_4(aq)$.

Many examination boards allow the use of [H] to represent the reducing agent in an equation, but make sure that the equation balances. The use of [O] to represent an oxidising agent is also allowed.

5.1 Chemical reactions of nitriles

5.1a With water

Base and acid catalysed hydrolysis.

- Base catalysed hydrolysis:

$$CH_3CH_2{-}C{\equiv}N \xrightarrow[H_2O(l)]{^-OH(aq)} CH_3CH_2{-}C(=O)O^- + NH_3(aq)$$

propanenitrile → propanoate ion

- Acid catalysis:

$$CH_3CH_2{-}C{\equiv}N \xrightarrow[H_2O(l)]{H_3O^+(aq)} CH_3CH_2COOH + NH_4^+(aq)$$

propanenitrile → propanoic acid

5.1b With reducing agents

For example: lithium aluminium hydride, $LiAlH_4$(ether) or sodium borohydride, $NaBH_4$(aq).

This process produces a primary amine from a nitrile.

$$CH_3CH_2{-}C{\equiv}N + 4[H] \longrightarrow CH_3CH_2CH_2 - \ddot{N}H_2$$

propanenitrile → propylamine

UNIT 19 Spectroscopic techniques

A What is spectroscopy?

There are many modern analytical techniques of use in determining the structures of molecules. Some of the major techniques include:

- mass spectroscopy
- infrared spectroscopy (ir)
- nuclear magnetic resonance spectroscopy (nmr)
- visible and ultraviolet spectroscopy

All of the techniques are often used to provide as much analytical evidence as possible.

Visible and ultraviolet spectroscopy are now mentioned in all syllabuses as a new addition, so make sure that you are aware of their existence.

1 *The fundamentals of spectroscopy*

The energy of electrons in molecules and atoms, vibrating atoms within molecules, rotating molecules and nuclear spin (amongst others) cannot possess any value. We say that the energy is **quantised**. It follows that there must be energy levels and energy gaps between these levels. When a particle is on its lowest level we say it is in its **ground state**. When the particle gains energy equivalent to $E_2–E_1$ (the exact energy difference between energy levels), it is **promoted** to a higher energy level and creates an **excited state**. The spectroscopic processes associated with various regions of the electromagnetic spectrum are shown in Table 19.1.

Table 19.1

Wavelength/m			
10^{-8}	10^{-6}	10^{-4}	10^{-2}
Ultraviolet/visible Atomic and molecular electronic changes	Infrared Molecular vibrations	Microwave Molecular rotations	Radiowave Nuclear magnetic energy levels

B Infrared spectroscopy (ir)

Atoms in covalent bonds are vibrating about a fixed position. The frequency of the vibration varies according to the nature of the atoms in the bond: the greater the mass of the atoms in the bond, the slower are the vibrations taking place. The frequency of such a vibration can be quoted in Hz or normally as the reciprocal of the wavelength in cm (called the wave number or the number of waves in 1 cm). The greater the wave number, the greater is the frequency of the oscillations. One particular bond will vibrate at a certain set frequency and the vibrational frequencies of some covalent bonds are given in Table 19.2.

In infrared spectroscopy, bond vibrations are exposed to infrared radiation. If the frequency of the radiation coincides exactly with the bond-vibrating frequency, then absorption occurs; this is known as resonance.

Infrared radiation has a frequency that coincides with the natural frequency of vibrating covalent bonds. Radiation of the same frequency as a vibrating bond

Generally, the lower the mass of the atoms in the bond and the stronger the bond, the faster are the vibrations and the greater the wave number.

Infrared absorptions between 1680 and 1750 cm^{-1} are due to the carbonyl (C=O) stretch; broad absorptions between 3230 and 3550 cm^{-1} are due to hydrogen bonded O–H groups in alcohols or in carboxylic acids.

Table 19.2

Bond	Vibrational frequency in wave numbers/cm^{-1}
C–H in alkanes	2850–2960
C–C	750–1100
C–O	1000–1300
C=O	1680–1750
O–H in hydrogen-bonded alcohols	3230–3550 (broad absorption)
C–Cl	600–800
C–Br	500–600
C–I	500

will be absorbed (a resonance effect) and the energy of the vibration will move up to the next available vibrational energy state. If a molecule is exposed to infrared radiation of variable frequency and the intensity of radiation passing through the sample is monitored, a spectrum should be obtained. A typical infrared spectrum for ethyl ethanoate, $CH_3CO_2C_2H_5$, is shown in Figure 19.1. Note how the frequency at which an absorption occurs can be used to identify the bond giving rise to the absorption. Also, the numerous complex absorptions that are associated, for example, with a benzene ring can be used to identify this particular group; this is called a fingerprint region. The presence of groups capable of hydrogen bonding, e.g. O–H and N–H, is indicated as very broad absorptions over a wide range of wave numbers (this effect is even more pronounced in the strongly bonded carboxylic acids).

Analysis of an infrared spectrum will indicate the type of bonds present in a molecule. There may also be a complex part of the spectrum that is called a fingerprint region (less than 1500 cm^{-1}); this may be used to identify certain characteristic features associated with the molecule.

Figure 19.1 Infrared spectrum of ethyl ethanoate

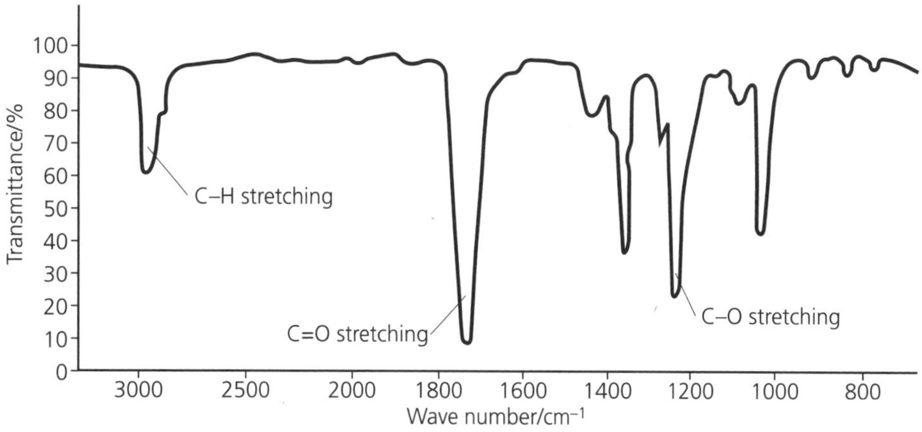

C Visible and ultraviolet spectroscopy

In visible and ultraviolet spectroscopy, electronic transitions take place within atomic orbitals as well as in molecular orbitals.

Ultraviolet spectroscopy relies on the electronic excitation of **electrons** in covalent bonds as well as in atoms. Electrons in molecular orbitals can only possess certain energies and are said to be quantised (as in atoms). If radiation of a certain frequency is incident upon a molecule and this energy is the same as the energy required for an electronic transition, then a resonance situation has been satisfied and an absorption of energy will take place. This type of absorption will occur in the visible or the higher energy ultraviolet region of the electromagnetic spectrum. For example, a molecule of propanone will absorb at 280 nm and 188 nm and these absorptions are characteristic of the carbonyl group C=O (although a variation of between 275–295 nm is often seen, depending on the aldehyde or ketone used).

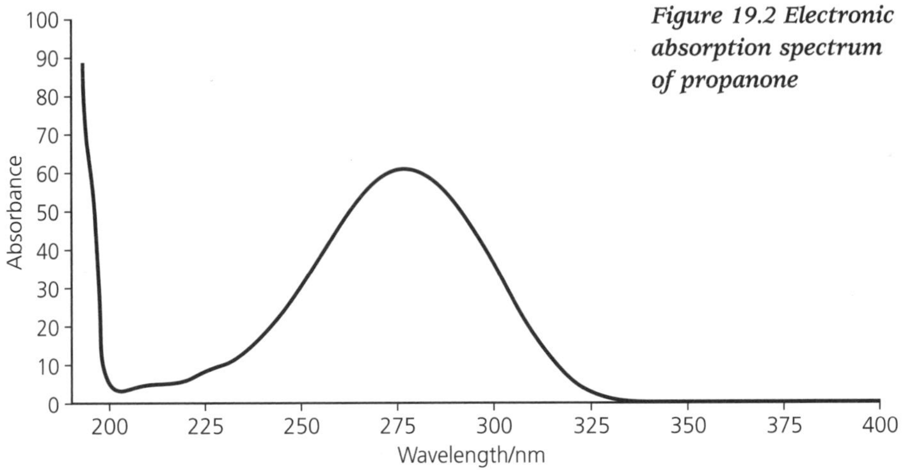

Figure 19.2 Electronic absorption spectrum of propanone

The transitions taking place are normally due to electrons in sigma (σ) or pi (π) molecular orbitals of double bonds, or lone pairs of electrons, being promoted to unoccupied anti-bonding orbitals (molecular orbitals that concentrated the electron density away from the inter-nuclear region, resulting in bond weakening or 'anti-bonding').

It is also known that if the electrons being excited are part of a delocalised or conjugated system (where double bonds are concerned), the wavelength increases or the energy required for absorption decreases. For example, for propanone, the two absorptions taking place are at 188 nm and 279 nm, whereas with butenone the absorption is 219 nm and 324 nm respectively. The increase in wavelength for molecules can therefore be used to detect conjugated systems in molecules.

- **Structure of butenone showing arrow pushing for delocalisation**

Remember that colour relies on incomplete d sub-shells in transition metal ions. However, other ions like MnO_4^- may also absorb in the visible region, despite appearing not to have any d electrons. This is a molecular orbital transition rather than an electronic transition within an atom or ion.

1 Visible spectroscopy

Transition metal complexes are coloured as electrons are being promoted to a higher energy state within the metal complex. The colour of the complex is dictated by the energy of the visible light absorbed, since the remainder is transmitted. Figure 19.3 shows the visible absorption spectrum for the hydrated titanium(III) ion, $[Ti(H_2O)_6]^{3+}$. There is one electron remaining in this ion, d^1, and it is promoted to a higher energy state at 20 100 cm^{-1}. This corresponds to the green part of the visible spectrum. The colour that we see (that is transmitted) is therefore the remaining part of the visible spectrum: red and blue (so we see purple).

The colour of the ion is the 'remainder' of the colour that is absorbed on promoting the electron from the lower to higher energy states. The rest is transmitted; this is the colour that we see.

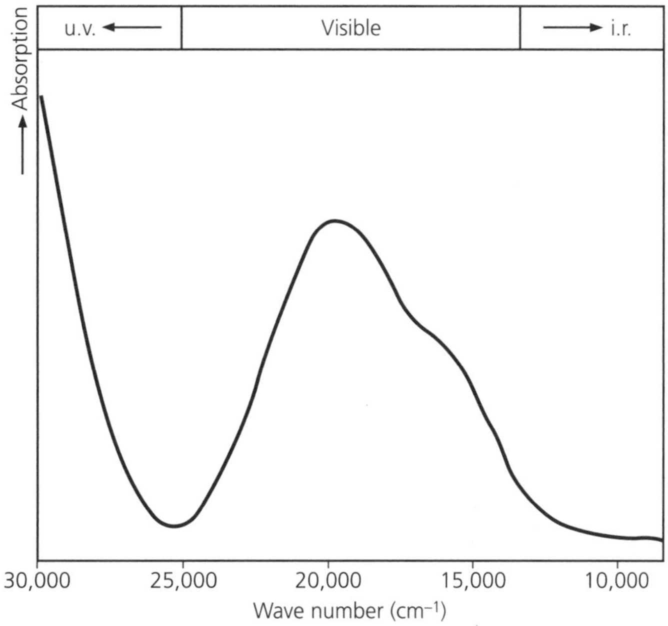

Figure 19.3 Visible spectrum of $[Ti(H_2O)_6]^{3+}$

However, the complex $[TiF_6]^{3-}$ absorbs at 17500 cm^{-1} which corresponds to the red end of the spectrum. We therefore see everything apart from red. A blue/green colour is therefore seen.

D Nuclear magnetic resonance spectroscopy (nmr)

nmr spectroscopy is usually employed for detecting protons within organic compounds, although it may be used to detect ^{13}C atoms (these also possess nuclear spin).

Nuclei that either have an odd number of protons or an odd number of neutrons (or both) have the property of nuclear spin. Some nuclei possess nuclear spin, e.g. ^{1}H, ^{13}C, ^{19}F, but not ^{12}C and ^{16}O. These nuclei, when spinning, generate their own magnetic field. Relative to a strong external magnetic field, the direction of the magnetic field of the nucleus may be either aligned in the same direction as the magnetic field or opposed to it (see Figure 19.4).

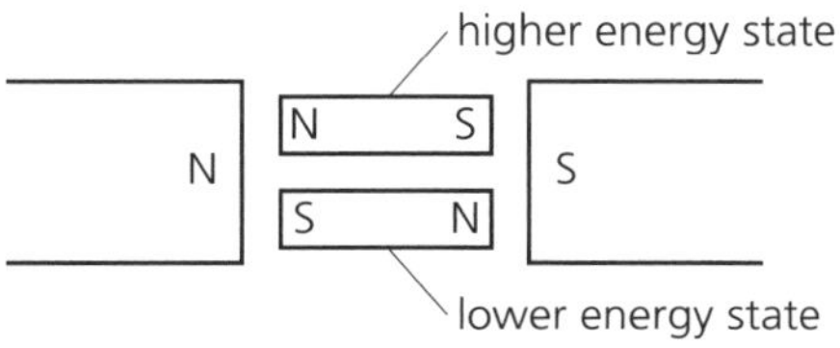

Figure 19.4 The arrangements of nuclei in a magnetic field

The energies of these two states are not equivalent and there will be a slight energy difference between them.

When a spinning nucleus is exposed to radiation of a certain frequency that coincides exactly with the energy difference between the two states, a resonance situation is established (an absorption takes place). We call this **nuclear magnetic resonance, nmr**. This absorption takes place in the radiowave region of the spectrum. In practice, a very high magnetic field strength of about 2.3 tesla is used and, at this field strength, resonance occurs at 100 MHz.

In practice, the difference between the magnetic fields that protons experience in different chemical environments is only parts per million (ppm):

delta (δ) = $\Delta B/B_o \times 10^6$

where delta is called the chemical shift and $\Delta B = B_{standard} - B_{sample}$

TMS is used as a reference and all other resonances are compared with the strong signal from this compound.

The reference sample used in nmr is called tetramethylsilane (TMS), $Si(CH_3)_4$. The important features of this substance that make it ideal for its purpose as a standard are:

- it has 12 protons per molecule so it gives a strong signal
- it is chemically inert so reaction with the test sample is very unlikely
- it is volatile so it can easily be removed by evaporation (to leave the sample)

In a typical nmr spectrum, delta (the chemical shift) is measured on the x-axis (where delta increases from right to left) and absorption of energy is on the y-axis.

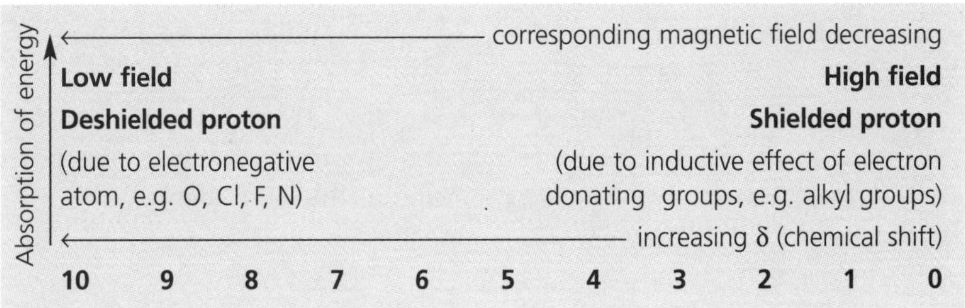

Figure 19.5 shows a typical low resolution nmr spectrum for ethanol.

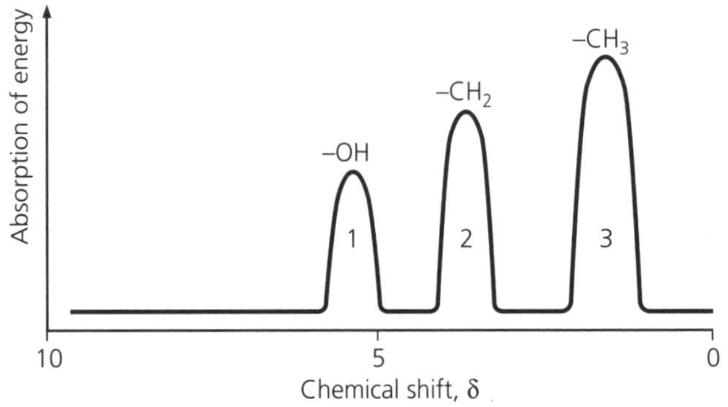

Figure 19.5 nmr spectrum for CH_3CH_2OH

Points to note about this spectrum:

- There are **three** general peaks, so there are **three** different proton environments in the molecule.
- The CH_3 protons resonate at a higher field than both the CH_2 protons and the OH proton (the latter being shifted downfield).
- The hydrogen attached to the oxygen atom is shifted to a lower field since it is being **deshielded** by the electronegative oxygen atom.
- The areas under each absorption area are proportional to the number of protons giving rise to that absorption. Area under peaks: 1 : 2 : 3, i.e. OH, CH_2, CH_3.

The area under a peak is proportional to the number of protons giving rise to that absorption.

This spectroscopic technique is very powerful since it enables the calculation of:

- the number of proton environments in a molecule
- the ratio of protons giving rise to each absorption in each peak

The delta value tells us (by looking up in correlation tables) the likely chemical nature of each of the proton environments (see Table 19.3).

Table 19.3

Type of proton	Chemical shift/δ/ppm
CH_3–C–	0.9
CH_3–C=C	1.6
C–CH_2–C	1.4
CH_2=C	4.7
H–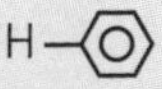	7.3
CH_3–	2.2
CH_3–C=O	2.1
CH_3–O–	3.3
CH_3–O–CO	3.7
–C–CH_2–Br	3.5

The more electronegative the neighbouring atom, the lower will be the required field to induce resonance and the greater will be the chemical shift from the standard TMS.

1 Spin–spin coupling (high resolution spectra)

The magnetic field at which protons in one chemical environment resonate is affected by the presence of **non-equivalent** neighbouring protons in another environment. In a molecule of ethoxyethane, $CH_3CH_2OCH_2CH_3$, there are two general proton environments: the CH_3 protons and the CH_2 protons (the molecule is symmetrical, so both CH_3 and CH_2 protons are equivalent). The low resolution spectrum will look similar to that in Figure 19.6.

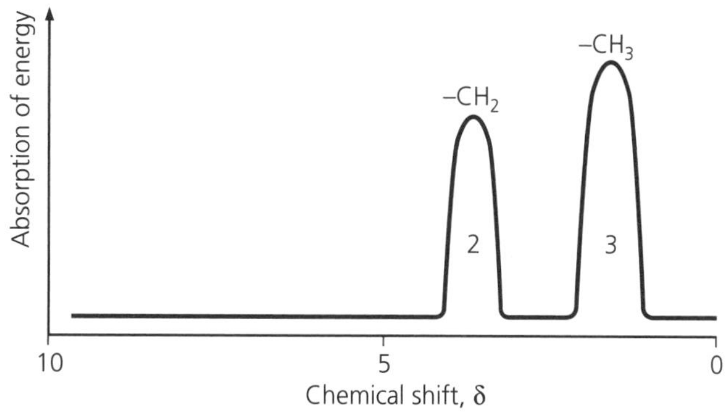

Figure 19.6* *Low resolution spectrum for ethoxyethane

Consider the CH_3 protons in this molecule. The CH_2 protons are in close proximity to these CH_3 protons and the possible spins of these two protons will affect the 'single' peak observed due to the CH_3 protons in the low resolution spectrum for this compound. How may the two protons in the CH_2 group be arranged relative to the external field?

- **Both up:** ↑↑
- **One up and one down (two ways of doing this):** ↑↓ or ↓↑
- **Both down:** ↓↓

The original single peak will be **split** into a triplet (of the same original area) but represented as a 1 : 2 : 1 grouping.

As far as the CH_2 protons are concerned, these will have their peak split into a quartet of heights 1 : 3 : 3 : 1 as:

three up: ↑↑↑

two up and one down: ↑↑↓ ↑↓↑ ↓↑↑

one up and two down: ↑↓↓ ↓↑↓ ↓↓↑

three down: ↓↓↓

The overall spectrum will therefore consist of two general absorptions of total areas ratio 2 : 3 but these peaks will be split into a quartet (1 : 3 : 3 : 1) and a triplet (1 : 2 : 1) respectively (see Figure 19.7).

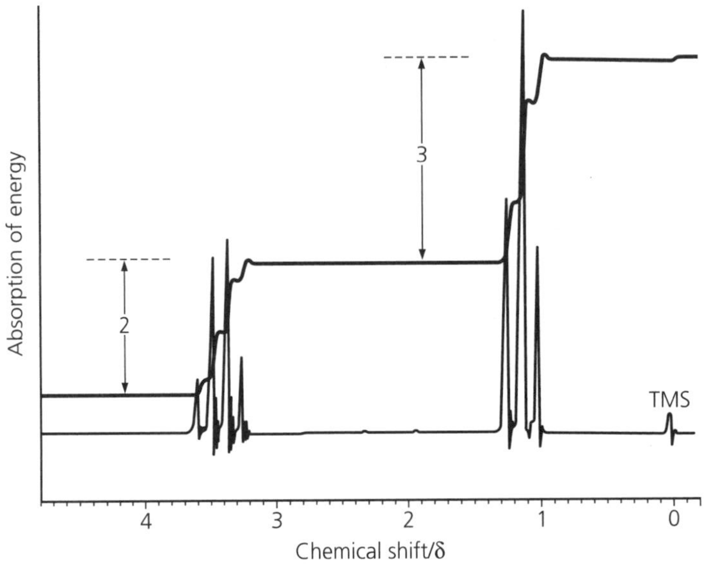

Figure 19.7 The high resolution spectrum for ethoxyethane

Protons are split by unequivalent protons only. They are split into the number of adjacent protons plus one. Pascal's triangle is then used to determine the splitting pattern.

Remember Pascal's triangle from GCSE mathematics; it is of use in nmr spectroscopy when determining the splitting pattern.

1.1 General rules to follow with splitting

Number of protons causing splitting:	Splitting pattern (relative intensities)
1	1 1
2	1 2 1
3	1 3 3 1
4	1 4 6 4 1
5	1 5 10 10 5 1

The pyramid of numbers above is known as Pascal's triangle where each pair of numbers in each row, when added, creates the next number in the line below.

The number of splits that takes place is always equal to the number of protons in the adjacent group + 1.

Splitting does **not** occur over more than one carbon–carbon bond (normally).

By looking at the number of splits, the number of hydrogen atoms giving rise to that split will be the number of splits – 1.

Splitting can only occur with non-equivalent protons.

Specification (syllabus) summary

The following table relates the contents of these Exam Revision Notes to the specifications published by the major examining boards. It is not meant as a substitute for a specification – you must be aware of the details that are appropriate as far as your own specification is concerned. 'Option' refers to a part of the course that is not in the compulsory components of the examination. It is to be found in an optional paper – check to see which optional papers you may be sitting (if any).

	BOARD	**OCR**	**AQA**	**EDEXCEL**
	Specification code for AS	**AS 3882**	**AS 5421**	**AS 8080**
	Specification code for A2	**A2 7882**	**A2 6421**	**A2 9080**
Unit 1	**Writing chemical equations**			
	A Which products form in a reaction?	AS	AS	AS
	B Symbols and formulae	AS	AS	AS
	1 Elements	AS	AS	AS
	1.1 Metallic elements	AS	AS	AS
	1.2 Non-metallic elements	AS	AS	AS
	2 Compounds	AS	AS	AS
	2.1 Using ions to help	AS	AS	AS
	2.2 Elements as ions	AS	AS	AS
	2.3 Examples of formulae	AS	AS	AS
	C Writing overall balanced chemical equations for reactions	AS	AS	AS
	D Ionic equations	AS	AS	AS
	1 Examples of ionic equations	AS	AS	AS
Unit 2	**Atomic structure**			
	A The structure of atoms	AS	AS	AS
	1 The structure of ions	AS	AS	AS
	2 Isotopes	AS	AS	AS
	B The relative atomic mass scale	AS	AS	AS
	1 Isotopic considerations	AS	AS	AS
	C The mass spectrometer	AS	AS	AS
	D Electronic structure of atoms	AS	AS	AS
	1 Electron shells	AS	AS	AS
	2 Order of filling sub-shells	AS	AS	AS
	3 Relationship between the Periodic Table and the electronic configuration	AS	AS	AS
	4 Orbital box diagrams	AS	AS	AS
	5 Trends and patterns in ionisation enthalpies	AS/**A2**	AS/**A2**	AS/**A2**
Unit 3	**Calculations**			
	A The mole	AS	AS	AS
	1 Elements	AS	AS	AS
	2 Compounds	AS	AS	AS
	B The mole and chemical equations	AS	AS	AS
	1 Mass relationships	AS	AS	AS
	1.1 Example calculations	AS	AS	AS
	C Calculations involving solutions	AS	AS	AS
	1 Solutions and equations	AS	AS	AS

	OCR	AQA	EDEXCEL
D Calculations involving gases	AS	AS	AS
1 Equations involving gases	AS	AS	AS
2 The ideal gas equation	Option	AS	-
E Calculation of empirical and molecular formulae	AS	AS	AS
Unit 4 Structure and bonding			
A Bonding	AS	AS	AS
1 Ionic bonding and giant ionic structures	AS	AS	AS
1.1 Elements forming ionic bonds: metal with non-metal	AS	AS	AS
2 Covalent bonding and structures consisting of covalent bonds	AS	AS	AS
2.1 Elements forming covalent bonds: non-metal with non-metal	AS	AS	AS
2.2 Simple molecular structures	AS	AS	AS
2.3 Giant covalent or macromolecular	AS	AS	AS
2.4 Sigma (σ) and pi (π) bonds	AS	AS	AS
2.5 The dative bond	AS	AS	AS
3 Deviations from pure ionic and from pure covalent bonding	AS	AS	AS
3.1 Polarising power	AS	AS	AS
3.2 Electronegativity differences	AS	AS	AS
4 Intermolecular forces	AS	AS	AS
4.1 Dipole–dipole attractions	AS	AS	AS
4.2 Hydrogen bonding	AS	AS	AS
4.3 Van der Waals Forces	AS	AS	AS
4.4 Ion–dipole attractions	AS	AS	AS
B Shapes of molecules	AS	AS	AS
C Metallic structures	AS	AS	AS
Unit 5 Thermodynamics			
A The concept of enthalpy change	AS	AS	AS
1 The sign of ΔH	AS	AS	AS
B Calculating the enthalpy change using Hess's Law	AS	AS	AS
1 Cycle 1: calculating $\Delta H^{\ominus}$ for a reaction using enthalpy of formation data	AS	AS	AS
2 Cycle 2: calculating an enthalpy change from combustion data	AS	AS	AS
3 Cycle 3: enthalpy changes from atomisation and bond enthalpy data	AS	AS	AS
3.1 Using bond dissociation enthalpies to calculate $\Delta H^{\ominus}$ for a reaction	AS	AS	AS
4 Cycle 4: the Born–Haber cycle	**A2**	**A2**	**A2**
4.1 Uses of the lattice enthalpy	**A2**	**A2**	**A2**
4.2 Common mistakes made in using Born–Haber cycles	**A2**	**A2**	**A2**
5 Cycle 5: the relationship between enthalpy of solution, ΔH_{sol}, lattice enthalpy, ΔH_{latt}, and hydration enthalpy, ΔH_{hyd}	**A2**	**A2**	**A2**
C The Gibb's free energy change, ΔG	-	**A2**	-
Unit 6 Kinetics			
A What is kinetics?	AS	AS	AS
B Following the rate of a chemical reaction	AS	AS	AS
C Factors affecting the rate of reaction	AS	AS	AS
1 Concentration	AS	AS	AS

	OCR	AQA	EDEXCEL
1.1 Instantaneous rate	AS	AS	AS
1.2 Average rate	AS	AS	AS
1.3 How does concentration affect the rate of a chemical reaction?	AS	AS	AS
1.4 Determining the order of reaction with respect to a reactant	**A2**	**A2**	**A2**
1.5 Concentration versus time graphs	**A2**	**A2**	**A2**
1.6 Rate versus concentration graphs	**A2**	**A2**	**A2**
1.7 Deducing rate equations using initial rates	**A2**	**A2**	**A2**
1.8 The rate-determining step	**A2**	**A2**	-
2 Temperature	AS	AS	AS
3 The effect of pressure on gas phase reactions	AS	AS	AS
4 Catalysis	AS	AS	AS
4.1 Homogeneous catalysis	**A2**	**A2**	**A2**
4.2 Heterogeneous catalysis	**A2**	**A2**	**A2**

Unit 7 Chemical equilibria

A Reversible reactions	AS	AS	AS
B Factors affecting chemical equilibrium	AS	AS	AS
C The Equilibrium Law	**A2**	**A2**	**A2**
1 Example reactions and equilibrium constant, K_c, expressions	**A2**	**A2**	**A2**
1.1 Homogeneous equilibria	**A2**	**A2**	**A2**
1.2 Heterogeneous equilibria	**A2**	**A2**	**A2**
2 Calculations involving the equilibrium constant, K_c	**A2**	**A2**	**A2**
2.1 Calculating K_c from equilibrium concentrations	**A2**	**A2**	**A2**
2.2 Deducing whether a reaction is at equilibrium or not	**A2**	**A2**	**A2**
2.3 Calculating K_c given the number of moles of one of the substances at equilibrium	**A2**	**A2**	**A2**
2.4 Calculating equilibrium concentrations using K_c when no equilibrium concentrations are known	**A2**	**A2**	**A2**
3 The equilibrium constant, K_p	**A2**	**A2**	**A2**
3.1 Writing expressions for K_p	**A2**	**A2**	**A2**
3.2 Calculations involving K_p	**A2**	**A2**	**A2**
D The quantification of the effect of temperature on the equilibrium constant	**A2**	**A2**	**A2**

Unit 8 Acid–base equilibria

A The Brønsted–Lowry definitions of acids and bases	AS/**A2**	AS/**A2**	AS/**A2**
1 Conjugate acid–base processes	AS/**A2**	AS/**A2**	AS/**A2**
2 Examples of acid–base reactions	AS/**A2**	AS/**A2**	AS/**A2**
B Strong and weak acids and bases	AS/**A2**	AS/**A2**	AS/**A2**
C The quantities pH and pOH	**A2**	**A2**	**A2**
D The ionic product of water, K_w	**A2**	**A2**	**A2**
1 Calculating the pH of solutions containing strong acids or bases	**A2**	**A2**	**A2**
E The weak acid dissociation constant, K_a	**A2**	**A2**	**A2**
1 Calculating the pH for solutions of weak acids	**A2**	**A2**	**A2**
F The weak base dissociation constant, K_b	-	**A2**	-
1 Examples of calculations involving weak bases in solution	-	**A2**	-
G Salt hydrolysis	**A2**	**A2**	**A2**
H pH titration curves	**A2**	**A2**	**A2**

		OCR	AQA	EDEXCEL
	I Indicators	**A2**	**A2**	**A2**
	1 Choice of indicator for a titration	**A2**	**A2**	**A2**
	J Buffers	**A2**	**A2**	**A2**
	1 How does a buffer work?	**A2**	**A2**	**A2**
	2 Quantitative buffer considerations	**A2**	**A2**	**A2**
Unit 9	**Redox reactions**			
	A What are redox reactions?	AS	AS	AS
	B The oxidation number concept	AS	AS	AS
	1 Working out oxidation numbers from chemical formulae	AS	AS	AS
	2 Naming compounds and ions using oxidation numbers	AS	AS	AS
	C Writing half equations for redox reactions	AS	AS	AS
	1 Writing overall balanced equations by combining half equations	AS	AS	AS
	D The electrode potential, $E^{\ominus}$	Option	**A2**	**A2**
	1 How do we measure the standard electrode potential of a substance?	Option	**A2**	**A2**
	2 Cell diagrams	Option	**A2**	**A2**
	3 Calculating overall electrode potentials of cells using individual cell potentials	Option	**A2**	**A2**
Unit 10	**Periodicity**			
	A The idea of periodicity	AS	AS	AS
	B Periodicity in element structure	AS	AS	AS
	1 Metals	AS	AS	AS
	2 Semi-metals (metalloids)	AS	AS	AS
	3 Non-metals	AS	AS	AS
	C The melting points of the elements	AS	AS	AS
	D First ionisation enthalpy	AS	AS	AS
	E Atomic and ionic radius	AS	AS	AS
	1 Atomic radius	AS	AS	AS
	2 Ionic radius	AS	AS	AS
	F Electronegativities of the elements	AS	AS	AS
	1 Trends in electronegativity	AS	AS	AS
	G Electrical conductivity of the elements	AS	AS	AS
	H The chlorides and oxides of Period 3 elements	**A2**	**A2**	**A2**
	1 Reactions of the chlorides with water	**A2**	**A2**	**A2**
	2 Reactions of the oxides with water	**A2**	**A2**	**A2**
	3 Structure and bonding of the oxides and chlorides	**A2**	**A2**	**A2**
Unit 11	**Extraction of metals**			
	A Aluminium	-	AS	AS
	1 The purification of bauxite	-	AS	AS
	2 The electrolysis	-	AS	AS
	B Iron	-	AS	-
	1 The blast furnace	-	AS	-
	2 Manufacture of steel	-	AS	-
	C Chromium	-	-	-
	D Sodium and the chlor–alkali industry	-	-	AS
	1 The Downs Cell	-	-	-
	2 The diaphragm cell	-	-	AS
	3 The production of sodium chlorate(I)	-	AS	AS
	E Titanium	-	AS	-

	OCR	AQA	EDEXCEL
Unit 12 Inorganic group chemistry			
A Group I: the alkali metals	-	-	AS
B Group II: the alkaline earth metals	AS	AS	AS
C Group III: aluminium	-	-	-
D Group VII: the halogens	AS	AS	AS
Unit 13 Transition metals			
A Properties of the transition metals	**A2**	**A2**	**A2**
B What is a transition metal?	**A2**	**A2**	**A2**
1 Electronic configuration of transition metal atoms	**A2**	**A2**	**A2**
2 Electronic configuration of transition metal ions	**A2**	**A2**	**A2**
3 Electronic configurations for ions of transition metals	**A2**	**A2**	**A2**
C Colour of transition metal compounds	**A2**	**A2**	**A2**
D Complex formation	**A2**	**A2**	**A2**
1 Structural, geometrical and optical isomers of transition metal complexes	Option	-	-
2 Reactions of hydrated transition metal ions	**A2**	**A2**	**A2**
2.1 Transition metal ions in the +2 oxidation state	**A2**	**A2**	**A2**
2.2 Transition metal ions in the +3 oxidation state	**A2**	**A2**	**A2**
E Variable oxidation state	**A2**	**A2**	**A2**
1 Electrode potential considerations	Option	**A2**	**A2**
2 Ligand stabilisation of oxidation states	Option	-	-
3 Redox processes involving transition metal ions	Option	**A2**	**A2**
3.1 Chromium, Cr	Option	-	**A2**
3.2 Vanadium, V	Option	-	-
3.3 Manganese, Mn	-	-	-
3.4 Iron, Fe	-	-	**A2**
F Catalytic behaviour	**A2**	**A2**	**A2**
1 Heterogeneous catalysis	**A2**	**A2**	**A2**
2 Homogeneous catalysis	**A2**	**A2**	**A2**
Unit 14 Functional groups and isomerism in organic chemistry			
A Recognising functional groups	AS	AS	AS
B Isomerism	AS	AS	AS
1 Structural isomerism	AS	AS	AS
2 Stereoisomerism	AS/**A2**	AS/**A2**	AS/**A2**
2.1 Geometric isomerism	AS	AS	AS
2.2 Optical isomerism	**A2**	**A2**	**A2**
Unit 15 The alkanes, alkenes and benzene			
A The alkanes	AS	AS	AS
1 What are alkanes?	AS	AS	AS
2 Molecular structures for alkanes	AS	AS	AS
3 Physical properties of alkanes	AS	AS	AS
4 Chemical reactions of alkanes	AS	AS	AS
4.1 Combustion	AS	AS	AS
4.2 With a halogen	AS	AS	AS
4.3 Cracking to form alkenes and shorter chain alkanes	AS	AS	AS
B The alkenes	AS	AS	AS
1 What are alkenes?	AS	AS	AS
1.1 Molecular structures of alkenes	AS	AS	AS
2 Geometrical isomerism in alkenes	AS	AS	AS

	OCR	AQA	EDEXCEL
3 Chemical reactions of alkenes	AS	AS	AS
3.1 With halogen	AS	AS	AS
3.2 With hydrogen gas	AS	AS	AS
3.3 With hydrogen halides	AS	AS	AS
3.4 With concentrated sulphuric(VI) acid	-	AS	-
3.5 With steam	AS	AS	-
3.6 With oxygen	AS	AS	AS
3.7 With another alkene	AS	AS	AS
3.8 With acidified or alkaline potassium manganate(VII) solution	-	-	AS
C Benzene chemistry	**A2**	**A2**	**A2**
1 What is benzene?	**A2**	**A2**	**A2**
2 The chemical reactions of benzene	**A2**	**A2**	**A2**
2.1 Nitration	**A2**	**A2**	**A2**
2.2 Reduction of the aromatic nitro group	**A2**	**A2**	**A2**
2.3 Sulphonation – reaction with sulphur trioxide, SO_3	-	-	-
2.4 Alkylation or acylation – Friedel–Crafts reaction	**A2**	**A2**	**A2**
2.5 With ethene	**A2**	**A2**	**A2**
2.6 Reaction of alkyl benzenes with alkaline potassium manganate(VII)	-	-	**A2**

Unit 16 The halogenoalkanes, alcohols, ketones and aldehydes

A The halogenoalkanes	AS	AS	AS
1 What are the halogenoalkanes?	AS	AS	AS
2 Physical properties of the halogenoalkanes	AS	AS	AS
3 Chemical reactions of halogenoalkanes	AS	AS	AS
3.1 With the aqueous hydroxide ion	AS	AS	AS
3.2 With the cyanide ion	AS	AS	AS
3.3 With concentrated ammonia solution	AS	AS	AS
3.4 With ethanolic hydroxide ions	AS	AS	AS
B The alcohols	AS	AS	AS
1 What are alcohols?	AS	AS	AS
2 Chemical reactions of the alcohols	AS	AS	AS
2.1 With sodium metal	AS	-	-
2.2 Combustion	AS	AS	AS
2.3 Oxidation with acidified dichromate(VI)	AS	AS	AS
2.4 Dehydration	AS	AS	AS
2.5 Esterification	AS	AS	AS
2.6 Halogenation	AS	AS	AS
2.7 Fermentation	AS	AS	AS
3 Phenol, C_6H_5OH	**A2**	-	-
3.1 Reactions of phenol	**A2**	-	-
C Carbonyl compounds: aldehydes and ketones	AS	AS	AS
1 What are aldehydes and ketones?	AS	AS	AS
2 Molecular structures for aldehydes and ketones	AS	AS	AS
2.1 Aldehydes	AS	AS	AS
2.2 Ketones	AS	AS	AS
3 Chemical reactions of aldehydes and ketones	AS/**A2**	AS/**A2**	AS/**A2**
3.1 Reactions in which the aldehyde is oxidised	AS/**A2**	AS/**A2**	AS/**A2**
3.2 Reactions in which the aldehyde or ketone undergoes nucleophilic addition	AS/**A2**	AS/**A2**	AS/**A2**
3.3 The iodoform reaction	-	-	**A2**

Unit 17 The amines

	OCR	AQA	EDEXCEL
A What are amines?	**A2**	**A2**	**A2**
1 Phenylamine ($C_6H_5NH_2$)	**A2**	**A2**	**A2**
2 Chemical reactions of amines	**A2**	**A2**	**A2**
2.1 With water	**A2**	**A2**	**A2**
2.2 With mineral acids	**A2**	**A2**	**A2**
2.3 With transition metal ions	-	-	-
2.4 With halogenoalkanes	**A2**	**A2**	**A2**
2.5 With acyl chlorides	**A2**	**A2**	**A2**
2.6 With carboxylic acids	**A2**	**A2**	**A2**

Unit 18 Carboxylic acids and their derivatives

A Carboxylic acids	AS/**A2**	AS/**A2**	AS/**A2**
1 What are carboxylic acids?	AS/**A2**	AS/**A2**	AS/**A2**
2 Chemical reactions of carboxylic acids	AS/**A2**	AS/**A2**	AS/**A2**
2.1 With bases	AS	AS	AS/**A2**
2.2 With ammonia and amines	**A2**	**A2**	**A2**
2.3 With alcohols	AS	AS	**A2**
2.4 With chlorinating agents	-	-	**A2**
2.5 With reducing agents	**A2**	**A2**	**A2**
2.6 With a dehydrating agent	-	-	-
3 The synthesis of carboxylic acids	AS/**A2**	AS/**A2**	AS/**A2**
B Carboxylic acid derivatives	AS/**A2**	AS/**A2**	AS/**A2**
1 Esters	AS/**A2**	AS/**A2**	AS/**A2**
1.1 Reactions of esters	**A2**	**A2**	**A2**
2 Acyl chlorides	**A2**	**A2**	**A2**
2.1 Chemical reactions of acyl chlorides	-	**A2**	**A2**
3 Acid anhydrides	-	**A2**	-
4 Amides	**A2**	**A2**	**A2**
4.1 Chemical reactions of amides	-	-	**A2**
5 Nitriles	**A2**	**A2**	**A2**
5.1 Chemical reactions of nitriles	**A2**	**A2**	**A2**

Unit 19 Spectroscopic techniques

A What is spectroscopy?	AS	AS	AS
1 The fundamentals of spectroscopy	AS	AS	AS
B Infrared spectroscopy (ir)	AS	AS	AS
C Visible and ultraviolet spectroscopy	**A2**	**A2**	**A2**
1 Visible spectroscopy	Option	**A2**	**A2**
D Nuclear magnetic resonance spectroscopy (nmr)	**A2**	**A2**	**A2**
1 Spin–spin coupling (high resolution spectra)	**A2**	**A2**	-
1.1 General rules to follow with splitting	**A2**	**A2**	-